ELEMENTARY IRRIGATION ENGINEERING

ELEMENTARY IRRIGATION ENGINEERING

G L ASAWA

Professor and Dean (Admin)
GLA University, Mathura (UP)
(Ex. Prof. and Head, Department of Civil Engineering
Indian Institute of Technology
Roorkee, India)

Publishing Globally

NEW AGE INTERNATIONAL (P) LIMITED, PUBLISHERS

New Delhi • Bangalore • Chennai • Cochin • Guwahati • Hyderabad
Jalandhar • Kolkata • Lucknow • Mumbai • Ranchi
Visit us at **www.newagepublishers.com**

Published by New Age International (P) Ltd., Publishers
First Edition: 1999
Reprint: 2014

BRANCHES

- **Bangalore** 37/10, 8th Cross (Near Hanuman Temple), Azad Nagar, Chamarajpet, Bangalore-560 018, Tel.: (080) 26756823, Telefax: 26756820 **E-mail: bangalore@newagepublishers.com**
- **Chennai** 26, Damodaran Street, T. Nagar, Chennai-600 017 Tel.: (044) 24353401, Telefax: 24351463, **E-mail: chennai@newagepublishers.com**
- **Cochin** CC-39/1016, Carrier Station Road, Ernakulam South, Cochin-682 016 Tel.: (0484) 2377004, Telefax: 4051303, **E-mail: cochin@newagepublishers.com**
- **Guwahati** Hemsen Complex, Mohd. Shah Road, Paltan Bazar, Near Starline Hotel, Guwahati-781 008 Tel.: (0361) 2513881, Telefax: 2543669, **E-mail: guwahati@newagepublishers.com**
- **Hyderabad** 105, 1st Floor, Madhiray Kaveri Tower, 3-2-19, Azam Jahi Road, Near Kumar Theater Nimboliadda, Kachiguda, Hyderabad-500 027, Tel.: (040) 24652456, Telefax: 24652457 **E-mail: hyderabad@newagepublishers.com**
- **Kolkata** RDB Chambers (Formerly Lotus Cinema) 106A, 1st Floor, S N Banerjee Road, Kolkata-700 014 Tel.: (033) 22273773, Telefax: 22275247 **E-mail: kolkata@newagepublishers.com**
- **Lucknow** 16-A, Jopling Road, Lucknow-226 001, Tel.: (0522) 2209578, 4045297 Telefax: 2204098, **E-mail:lucknow@newagepublishers.com**
- **Mumbai** 142C, Victor House, Ground Floor, N.M. Joshi Marg, Lower Parel Mumbai-400 013, Tel.: (022) 24927869, Telefax: 24915415 **E-mail: mumbai@newagepublishers.com**
- **New Delhi** 22, Golden House, Daryaganj, New Delhi-110 002 Tel.: (011) 23262368, 23262370, Telefax: 43551305 **E-mail: sales@newagepublishers.com**

ISBN: 978-81-224-1202-4

₹ 175.00

C-14-02-7380

Printed in India at Kanishik Printing Press, New Delhi.

PUBLISHING GLOBALLY
NEW AGE INTERNATIONAL (P) LIMITED, PUBLISHERS
7/30 A, Daryaganj, New Delhi - 110002
Visit us at **www.newagepublishers.com**

Dedicated
to
my grandparents

(Late) Shri Radha Kishan Asawa
and
(Late) Smt. Kesar Devi Asawa

Preface

Following the suggestion of the publishers of this book, who are also the publishers of the author's another book *"Irrigation Engineering"* for the students of the degree course in civil engineering, the writing of this book was attempted keeping in view the requirements and technical background of the students of the diploma course in civil engineering.

This book primarily deals with the basic hydraulic engineering aspects of irrigation engineering. Other relevant aspects of irrigation have also been dealt with briefly. Major part of the contents of this book is similar (at times, even verbatim) to those of the author's above-mentioned book — the writing of which required the author to consult several publications. The bibliography relevant to this book has been given at the end of this book.

I should appreciate receiving suggestions from the readers of this book to make it still more useful for the students of the diploma course in civil engineering.

The forbearance of my wife Savi during the period I was busy preparing the manuscript of this book is heartily appreciated. The staff of the publishers of the book deserve all praise for their nice jobs of editing, printing and publishing.

G. L. ASAWA

Contents

Chapter 1

Introduction

1.1 IRRIGATION

Soil, seed and water are the basic requirements of any agricultural production. In addition, fertilisers, insecticides, sunshine, suitable climate and human labour are also needed. Water is essential for plant growth as it performs the following functions :

i) It provides moisture for germination of seeds, and chemical and bacterial processes during plant growth.
ii) It cools the soil and makes the environment more favourable for plant growth.
iii) It washes out completely or dilutes salts in the soil.
iv) It helps in tillage operations.
v) It enables application of fertilisers.
vi) It reduces the adverse effects of frost action on plant growth.

In several parts of the world, the moisture available in the root-zone soil may not be sufficient to meet the requirements of the plant life. To make up this deficiency, water needs to be added to the root-zone soil. This artificial application of water to land for supplementing the naturally available moisture in the root-zone soil for the purpose of agricultural production is termed *irrigation.*

Irrigation water delivered into the soil is usually more than the crop requirement. Sometimes, soil has more water, naturally, than is required for healthy growth of the crop. This excess water is as harmful to the growth of crop as lack of water. The natural drainage such as rivers, if existing in the vicinity of the irrigated land, can remove this excess water. However, in the absence of natural drainage, the excess water has to be removed artificially. The artificial removal of the excess water is termed *drainage* which, in general, is complementary to irrigation.

The object of providing irrigation and drainage is to help nature in maintaining moisture in the root-zone soil within the range required for optimum crop production.

1.2 NECESSITY OF IRRIGATION

With increase in the world population, the demand for food and fibre also increases. Rainfall does not always occur in right amount at the time when crops need water. Thus, there is always a need of irrigation in most parts of the world. This is true for India as well due to erratic behaviour of its south-west monsoon and its ever-increasing population.

The average annual rainfall in India is 1,143 mm which varies from 11,489 mm in Cherrapunji region of Assam to 217 mm in Jaisalmer region of Rajasthan. Further, 75 to 90% of the annual rainfall occurs during 25 to 60 rainy days of the four monsoon months from June to September. There is also a large variation from year to year. Since 1801, there have been 37 drought years in India. The severe drought of 1987 and very good monsoon (resulting in floods at several places) in 1988 followed by ten continuous good monsoon seasons are examples of complete uncertainty of south-west monsoon in India. Dependability of rainfall is, therefore, low from agricultural point of view. Also, for a large part of any crop season, the water needs of a crop exceed the available precipitation. These inadequacies of rainfall make irrigation very essential for increasing food and fibre production.

The need and importance of irrigation in India can be appreciated from the facts that

i) about 45 % of agricultural production is still dependant on uncertain rains,
ii) the country would need to produce 277 million tons (against the production of about 200 million tonnes for 1998-99) of food to meet the per capita requirement of 225 kg per year for an estimated population of 1231 million in the year 2030,
iii) about 70% of the country's population is employed in agricultural production, and
iv) the export of agricultural products earns a major part of foreign exchange.

Usefulness and importance of irrigation can be appreciated by the fact that without irrigation it would have been impossible for India to have become self-sufficient in food with its huge population. Primary source of prosperity in Punjab is irrigation.

1.3 IMPACT OF IRRIGATION ON HUMAN ENVIRONMENT

An irrigation project, like any other water resource project, is constructed for the well-being of people, and has definite impact on the environment. The developmental activities cannot be stopped on environmental considerations alone. One should, however, appreciate that both developmental activities and an intact environment are equally important for the sustained well-being of people. Following are the advantages of providing irrigation in an area :

i) It provides protection against famine.

ii) It increases agricultural production and its quality and, thus, adds to the national economy by substituting imports, and generating exports of food and non-food agricultural products.
iii) It reduces rural poverty by creating additional employment in the sectors of main agricultural activities and related activities of input supplies and processing and marketing of agricultural products.
iv) Inspection roads constructed for the irrigation works can be used by the people of the area and, thus, irrigation helps in improving the communication system of the region.
v) Irrigation works can also be used for hydropower generation, inland navigation, industrial and domestic water supply, flood control, *etc.*

As a result of these benefits of irrigation, there are permanent gains in the life-style of rural population due to increased prosperity. However, there are some disadvantages associated with irrigation facilities which cause considerable increase in water-borne and water-related diseases. Excessive surface water irrigation can lead to waterlogging of the cultivable land making it unsuitable for cultivation. There can be some adverse effects on the environment too which may adversely affect the human beings in the long run. With proper planning, these disadvantages can, however, be minimised, if not eliminated completely.

1.4 DEVELOPMENT AND SCOPE OF IRRIGATION IN INDIA

Irrigation has been practised throughout the world since the beginning of civilisation. In India, the Grand Anicut across the river Cauvery was constructed in the second century. There were a large number of water tanks in peninsular India and several inundation canals (such canals draw their supplies from a river only during the high stages of the river) in northern India. The Upper Ganga canal, the Upper Bari Doab canal and the Krishna and the Godavari delta systems were built between 1836 and 1866. The famines of 1876-78, 1897-98 and 1899-1900 led to the setting up of the first Irrigation Commission in 1901. In 1901, the total gross irrigated area was only 13.3 Mha (million hectares) which increased to 22.6 Mha in 1950 as a result of a spurt in protective irrigation schemes. The Bengal famine of 1943 made the authorities appreciate the urgency of increasing agricultural production to meet the needs of the growing population. After independence in 1947, an era of planned development in irrigation started with the first five-year Plan in 1951. Giant projects like the Bhakra-Nangal, Hirakud, Damodar valley, Nagarjunasagar, Rajasthan canal, *etc.*, were taken up. As a result, the irrigated area increased from 22.6 Mha in 1951 to 87.8 Mha in 1995. The total ultimate irrigation potential is estimated at 115.54 Mha of which 58.47 Mha would be from major and medium irrigation schemes, and the remaining from minor irrigation schemes.

Salient details of some major dams of India are given in Table 1.1.

1.5 COMMAND AREA DEVELOPMENT

The irrigation potential created by the construction of a large number of irrigation projects in India has almost quadrupled since independence. It has,

Table 1.1 Salient Details of Major Dams in India

No.	Name of the Dam	Year	River	Nearest City	Type	Height Above L.F.L. (m)	Length (m)	Gross Capacity (m^3)	Project Irr. Pot. (ha)
1.	Nizam Sagar	1931	Manjira	Hyderabad	PG, TE	48	5682	1050000	92536
2.	Nagarjunasagar Dam	1974	Krishna	Hyderabad	TE, PG	125	4865	11550000	506000
3.	Dantiwada Reservoir	1965	Banas	Palanpur	TE, PG	61	4881	464450	54600
4.	Sardar Sarovar Dam	U.C.	Narmada	Rajpipla	PG	137	1210	9492175	3648000
5.	Bhakra Dam	1963	Satluj	Nangal	PG	226	518	9621000	2880000
6.	Gujar Nar Dam	1971	Jhelum	Srinagar	TE	18	115	205	—
7.	Tungabhadra Dam	1957	Tungabhadra	Hospet	PG, TE	49	2449	3767000	364900
8.	Tenughat Dam	1973	Damodar	Ranchi	TE	46	4948	544000	—
9.	Idukki Dam	1974	Periyar	Idukki	VA	169	366	1996000	—
10.	Gandhi Sagar	1960	Chambal	Jhalwar	PG	64	514	7746000	273300
11.	Tawa Dam	1975	Tawa	Hoshangabad	TE, PG	58	1815	2310000	332780
12.	Mula Dam	1974	Mula	Ahmednagar	TE, PG	68	2920	736320	85660
13.	Dudhganga Dam	—	Dudhganga	Kolhapur	TE, PG	89	1264	708260	59933
14.	Hirakud Dam	1957	Mahanadi	Sambalpur	PG, TE	59	4800	8105000	260781
15.	Thein Dam	—	Ravi	Pathankot	ER, TE	47	878	367000	—
16.	Ranapratap Sagar	1967	Chambal	Kota	PG	58	1143	2900000	60700
17.	Mattur Dam	1934	Cauvery	Salem	PG	70	1615	2707200	130550
18.	Tehri Dam	U.C.	Bhagirathi	Tehri	TE, ER	261	570	3539000	—
19.	Kangsabati Kumari Dam	1965	Kangsabati	Bankura	TE	41	10400	1036000	—

TE = EARTH DAM ER = ROCKFILL DAM PG = GRAVITY DAM
L.F.L. = LOWEST FOUNDATION LEVEL U.C. = UNDER CONSTRUCTION VA = ARCH DAM

however, always remained under-utilised, and the optimum benefits by way of increased production have not been fully realised. Against the world average of about 5 tonnes of agricultural production per hectare of irrigated land, India produces only about 2.2 tonnes of crop per hectare of irrigated land. The following have been identified as the main causes for these deficiencies:

i) Need for modernisation of the old irrigation systems.
ii) Lack of adequate drainage which results in waterlogging of the cultivable land.
iii) Inadequate on-farm management of water.
iv) Lack of suitable infrastructure and extension services.
v) Poor coordination amongst the concerned organisations in the command areas.

Gross command area (or command area) of an irrigation system is the total area which can be economically irrigated from the system without considering the limitations on the quantity of available water. For optimising the benefits of available irrigation potential, an integrated command area development is always recommended. The objectives of the command area development programme are as follows:

i) Increasing the area of irrigated land by proper land development and water management.
ii) Optimising yields by adopting the best cropping pattern consistent with the availability of water, soil and other local conditions.
iii) Bringing water to the farmer's fields rather than only to the outlets and, thus, assuring equitable distribution of water and adequate supply to tail-enders.
iv) Avoiding wastage and misuse of water.
v) Optimising the use of scarce land and water resources, including ground water where available, in conjunction with necessary inputs and infrastructure.

The command area development programme includes the following components:

i) Modernisation and efficient operation of the irrigation system.
ii) Development of main drainage system.
iii) Construction of field channels and field drain.
iv) Land shaping/levelling and consolidation of land holdings.
v) Lining of field channels/watercourses.
vi) Exploitation of ground water and installation of tubewells.
vii) Adoption and enforcement of a suitable cropping pattern.
viii) Enforcement of an appropriate rostering system on irrigation.
ix) Making arrangement for timely supply of key inputs like credit, seeds, fertilisers, pesticides and implements.
x) Strengthening of existing extension, training and demonstration organisations.

1.6 PLANNING OF IRRIGATION PROJECTS

An irrigation project is an agricultural establishment which can supply controlled amounts of water to lands for growing crops. Irrigation projects mainly consist of hyraulic structures which collect (from a source), convey and deliver (to farm fields) water for irrigation. A small irrigation project may consist of a small diversion weir (or a pumping plant) with small channels and some minor control structures. A large irrigation project includes a large storage reservoir created by a huge dam (or a long weir or barrage), hundreds of kilometres of canals, branches and distributaries, control structures and other works. Large irrigation projects are generally built as multipurpose projects which also serve to generate hydropower, control floods, and meet water supply and other demands. Assuming other factors (such as enlightened farmer, availability of good infrastructure for supplying input material and marketing the agricultural production) reasonably favourable, the following are the essential conditions for the success of any irrigation project:

i) Suitability of land (with respect to its soil, topography and drainage features) for the purpose of agriculture.
ii) Favourable climatic conditions for proper growth and yield of the crops.
iii) Adequate and economic supply of suitable quality of water.
iv) Good site condition for the construction and operation of engineering works.

A small irrigation project can be developed in a relatively short time. For example, a farmer can develop his own tubewell irrigation system by securing bank loan and, soon after, getting the engineering works constructed. However, development of a large irrigation project is more complicated and time-consuming due to the associated organisational, financial, legal, administrative, environmental and engineering problems. The main stages of a large irrigation project are:

i) the promotional stage,
ii) the planning stage,
iii) the construction stage, and
iv) the settlement stage.

The planning stage itself consists of three sub-stages:

i) preliminary planning, including feasibility studies,
ii) detailed planning of water and land use, and
iii) the design of irrigation structures and canals.

The feasibility of an irrigation project is decided on the basis of preliminary estimates of

i) area of land suitable for irrigation,
ii) water requirements,
iii) available water supplies,

iv) productivity of irrigated land, and
v) required engineering works.

An irrigation project is considered feasible if the total estimated benefits of the project exceed its total estimated cost.

Adequate planning of all aspects (organisational, technical, agricultural, legal, environmental and financial) is always essential for a feasible irrigation project. The process of planning of an irrigation project is divided into the following two stages:

i) Preliminary planning, and
ii) Detailed planning.

Preliminary plans, usually based on available information, are generally approximate, but set the course for detailed planning. Based on preliminary planning, the accurate measurements are taken and, thus, more accurate detailed plans are prepared. The detailed plans may, however, have to be altered at different stages of the project. The following are the main factors which must be determined accurately during the planning stage of an irrigation project:

i) Type of project and general plan of irrigation works.
ii) Location, extent and type of irrigable lands.
iii) Irrigation requirements for profitable crop production.
iv) Available water supplies for the project.
v) Culturable areas which can be economically supplied with water.
vi) Types and locations of necessary engineering works.
vii) Needs for immediate and future drainage.
viii) Feasibility of hydroelectric power development.
ix) Cost of storage, irrigation, power and drainage features.
x) Evaluation of probable power, income and indirect benefits.
xi) Method of financing the project construction.
xii) Desirable type of construction and development.
xiii) Probable annual cost of water to the farmers.
xiv) Cost of land preparations and farm distribution systems.
xv) Feasible crops, costs of crop production and probable crop returns.

The preliminary planning of an irrigation project consists of collecting and analysing all available data for the purpose, securing additional data needed by limited field surveys and determining the feasibility of the proposed development by making preliminary study of major features in sufficient detail. For detailed planning, accurate data on all aspects of the proposed irrigation project are needed to prepare plans and designs of various components, and also to determine their most suitable site locations. There can be different feasible plans and designs possible for a particular project. Merits and demerits of all such possible alternatives must be looked into before arriving at a final plan for the project.

1.7 TYPES OF IRRIGATION SYSTEMS

Irrigation systems are generally classified into two groups:

i) flow irrigation system, and
ii) lift irrigation system.

In the flow irrigation system, the water at its source is at such a level that it can be conveyed to the farm land through canal network by gravity flow alone. When river is the source of irrigation water, the flow irrigation can, usually, be employed. However, when irrigation water is available at a level lower than the land to be irrigated, one has to first lift water to a higher level from which it can flow under gravity upto the land to be irrigated. When ground water is to be used for irrigation, lift irrigation is adopted and ground water is pumped through wells to the ground surface from where it flows, under gravity, upto the farm land. Generally, flow irrigation is carried out through a canal network system and is, therefore, also termed canal irrigation. Sometimes, water has to be lifted from rivers and canals as well for the purpose of irrigation in which case the canal irrigation system may be termed as the lift irrigation system.

1.8 DELIVERY OF WATER TO FARMS

Water can be delivered to farms from a watercourse in one of the following four ways:

i) Continuous delivery system in which water is supplied continuously to farms at a predetermined rate.
ii) Free demand system in which farmers take intermittent delivery at will depending upon the needs of their crop such that the instantaneous withdrawal rate does not exceed the withdrawal rate for which they have subscribed.
iii) Rotation delivery system in which canal authorities supply water to farmers according to a fixed delivery schedule. This method is generally adopted in India and has been described here in detail.
iv) In modified rotation delivery system, priority for delivery is on a rotation basis, but actual delivery may deviate depending upon the actual demand. It combines good features of the free demand system and rotation delivery system but requires much better coordination between farmers and the authorities.

1.8.1 Rotation Delivery System (or Warabandi)

In the rotation delivery system, water is delivered from a watercourse to various farms situated along the watercourse according to a pre-decided time roster. Accordingly, this delivery system is also known as *warabandi* system, which can be defined as an integrated management system from source (river or reservoir) to the farm gate, *i.e., nakka*. The main objective of the warabandi system is to attain high efficiency of water use by imposing water scarcity on every user. The system ensures equitable distribution of water and safeguards the interest of the farmers whose fields are located at the tail end of the conveyance system.

In the warabandi system (Fig 1.1), water from the source is carried by the main canal which feeds two or more branch canals that operate by rotation and may not carry the total required supply. This is the primary distribution system which runs throughout the irrigation season with varying supplies. The secondary distribution system consists of a large number of distributaries which too run by rotation but carry full supply. The branch canals supply water to the distributaries which, in turn, feed watercourses through the outlets. The watercourses form tertiary distribution system and carry their full supply when the supplying distributary is running.

The distributaries generally carry their supplies in eight-day periods. The number of these periods would depend upon the availability of water and

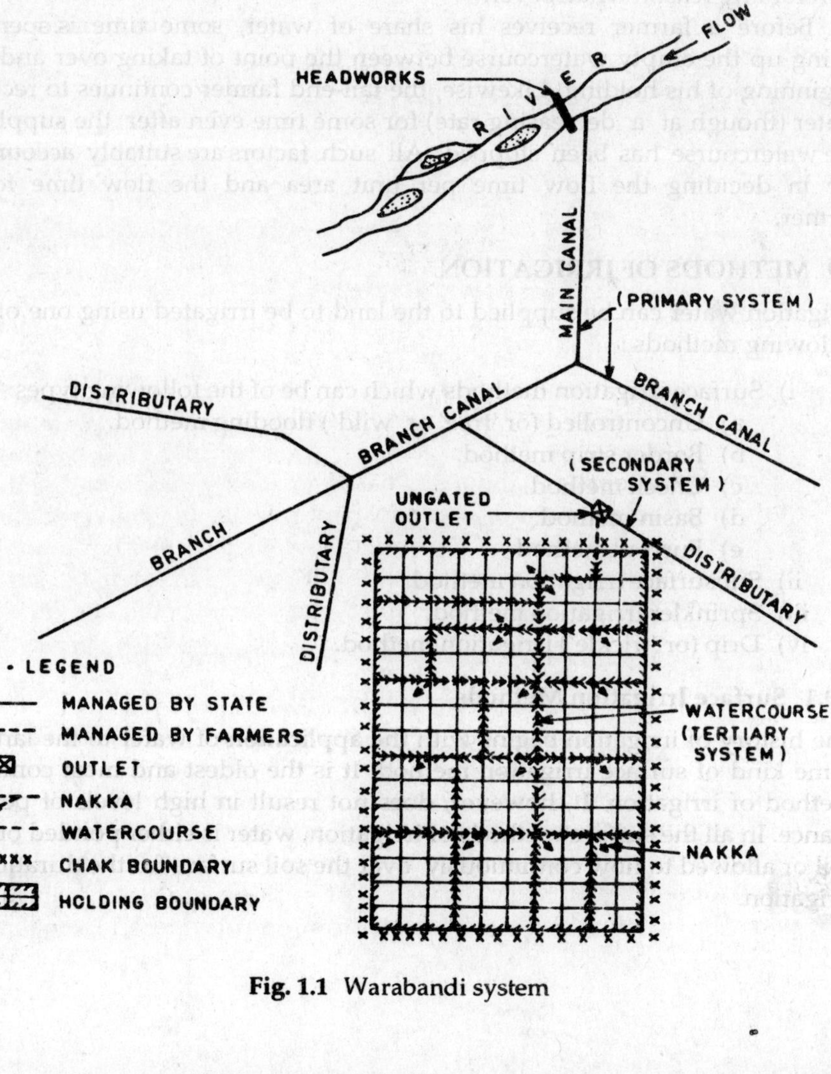

Fig. 1.1 Warabandi system

crop requirements. The eight-day period of distributary running ensures a minimum of seven days running for all watercourses including those which are at the tail-end of the distributary. The distributaries of the Bhakra project generally carry water for 18 periods during the Kharif season and 16 periods during the Rabi season.

The distribution of water flowing in watercourse is done on a seven-day rotation basis with the help of an agreed roster (of turns) which divides 168 hours of seven days in the ratio of holdings of farmers who are to be supplied water by the watercourse.

Whenever a distributary carries water, its watercourses receive their share of water at a constant rate round-the-clock, and water distribution proceeds from head to tail-end of a watercourse. Each cultivator on a watercourse is entitled to receiving the entire water in the watercourse only on a specific weekday and at a specific time (including night time). There is no provision in this system to compensate a defaulting farmer who has failed to utilise his turn for any reason whatsoever.

Before a farmer receives his share of water, some time is spent in filling up the empty watercourse between the point of taking over and the beginning of his holding. Likewise, the tail-end farmer continues to receive water (though at a decreasing rate) for some time even after the supply to the watercourse has been stopped. All such factors are suitably accounted for in deciding the flow time per unit area and the flow time for a farmer.

1.9 METHODS OF IRRIGATION

Irrigation water can be supplied to the land to be irrigated using one of the following methods :

i) Surface irrigation methods which can be of the following types:
   a) Uncontrolled (or 'free' or 'wild') flooding method.
   b) Border strip method.
   c) Check method.
   d) Basin method.
   e) Furrow method.
ii) Subsurface irrigation method.
iii) Sprinkler irrigation method.
iv) Drip (or 'trickle') irrigation method.

1.9.1 Surface Irrigation Methods

The history of irrigation begins with the application of water to the land in some kind of surface irrigation method. It is the oldest and most common method of irrigation. It, however, does not result in high levels of performance. In all the surface methods of irrigation, water is either ponded on the soil or allowed to flow continuously over the soil surface for the duration of irrigation.

(i) Uncontrolled Flooding

In the uncontrolled flooding method of irrigation, water is applied to a field for irrigation without any land preparation and without any levees to guide or restrict the flow of water on the field. Water is simply admitted at one end of the field, thus, letting it flood the entire field without any control. This method generally results in excess irrigation at the inlet region of the field and insufficient irrigation at the outlet region. This method has the advantage of low expenses on land preparation. Its main disadvantage is greater loss of water due to deep percolation and surface runoff. This method is, therefore, suitable when water is available in large quantities, the land surface is irregular, and the crop being grown is unaffected because of excess water.

(ii) Border Strip Method

It is a controlled surface irrigation method in which the farm is divided into a number of strips which are separated from each other by low levees (or 'borders' or 'dikes'). These strips can be 3-20 m wide and 100-400 m long depending upon the unevenness of the land and the size of the supply channel. However, narrow strips would require too many levees which would occupy lot of cultivable land. The length of the strip depends primarily on the infiltration rate of the soil and the slope of the land and is generally 60 to 120 m for more permeable sandy and sandy-loam soil and 150 to 300 m for less permeable clay loam and clay soils. The strips do not have cross slopes but slope along the length depending upon the type of the soil. The strips should have much flatter longitudinal slope for less permeable clay and clay-loam soils, and flatter slope for more permeable sand and sandy-loam soils. Water from the supply channel is diverted to each of these strips along which it flows slowly towards the downstream end and, thus, irrigates the land.

(iii) Check Method

In this method, the land to be irrigated is divided into a number of almost levelled plots *(kiaries)* surrounded by levees. Water is admitted from the farmer's field channels to these plots turn by turn so that the plots are flooded without overtopping the levees. Size of individual plots may vary from as small as one metre square (suitable for growing vegetables) to as large as one hectare or even more. This method is suitable for wide range of soils ranging from very permeable to much less permeable soils. The farmer has good control over the distribution of water in different parts of his farm. The water application efficiency is higher for this method. However, this method requires constant attendance for admitting and closing the supplies to the levelled plots. Also, there is some loss of cultivable area which is occupied by the levees. Sometimes, levees are made sufficiently wide to grow 'row' crops and, thus, compensate to some extent the loss of cultivable area on account of levees.

(iv) Basin Method

It is similar to the check method and is suitable for orchards which are irrigated by constructing a separate basin, usually circular in shape, for every tree. Basins of larger size can also be made in order to accommodate more than one tree. The basins are fed by field channels which receive water from the supply channel.

(v) Furrow Method

Furrows are small field channels having uniform slope and are used to irrigate crops planted in rows. Water infiltrates through the wetted perimeter of the furrows and, thus, raises the moisture content of the root-zone soil of the plants which are planted in rows. The lengths of furrows may vary from 10 m to as much as 500 m, although, 100 to 200 m long furrows are more commonly used to avoid excessive percolation losses and soil erosion in the upstream reach of the furrows. Furrows generally slope between 0.5 and 3.0%. If soil can resist erosion, furrows may have steeper slopes of about 6%. Spacing of furrows is decided by the spacing requirement of the row crops to be irrigated. The furrow water should not come in direct contact with plants or their roots. Furrows in low permeability soil are generally 20 to 30 cm deep, whereas in other soils they are 8 to 12 cm deep. Water is fed to furrows from supply channel either through small openings made in the earthen banks of the supply channel, or by siphoning water from the supply channel to the furrows by means of a small diameter pipe of plastic or rubber.

Furrows wet only about half to one-fifth of the cultivated land and, therefore, reduce evaporation loss considerably. Furrows provide better on-farm water management and, thus, obtain high irrigation efficiency. Following are the disadvantages of furrow method of irrigation:

i) Possibility of increased salinity between furrows.
ii) Loss of water at the downstream end unless end dikes are used.
iii) The necessity of one extra tillage work, *viz.*, furrow construction.
iv) Possibility of increased erosion.
v) Furrow irrigation requires reatively more labour.

1.9.2 Subsurface Irrigation

In subsurface irrigation (or simply subirrigation), the water is supplied to soils directly under their surface. Moisture reaches the plant roots through capillary action. In this method, water is supplied to a network of ditches which are about 0.6 to 0.9 m deep and 0.3 m wide and with vertical sides. These ditches are spaced 45 to 90 m apart. Sometimes, a distribution system of porous pipes is laid in the soil well below the ground surface. Soils which permit free lateral movement of water, rapid capillary movement in the root zone soil and very slow downward movement of water in the subsoil, are very suitable for sub-irrigation by porous pipes. The cost of sub-irrigation is very high, but the water consumption is as low as one-third of the surface irrigation methods. The crop yield also improves. Application efficiencies generally vary between 30 to 80%. An impervious soil layer at about 2 m below the upper permeable soil layer would be favourable to subirrigation methods, if water is scarce.

1.9.3 Sprinkler Irrigation

In this method, water is sprayed into the atmospheric air over the soil surface to be irrigated and allowed to fall on the soil surface at a rate less than the infiltration rate of the soil. Sprinkler irrigation provides controlled uniform application of water for frequent and light irrigation on shallow soils, sloping and undulating lands without having to develop them by land grading or levelling operation.

Rotating sprinkler-head systems are commonly used for sprinkler irrigation. Each rotating sprinkler-head applies water to a specified area size of which is governed by the nozzle size and the water pressure. Alternatively, perforated pipe can be used to deliver water through very small holes which are drilled at close intervals along a segment of the circumference of a pipe. The trajectories of these jets provide fairly uniform application of water over a strip of farm land along both sides of the pipe. Because of the availability of flexible PVC pipes, the sprinkler systems can be made portable too.

Sprinklers have been used on all types of soils on lands of different topography and slopes, and for many crops. Sprinkler irrigation is normally recommended in the command areas where the land is highly undulating, water availability is poor, soils are sandy or shallow and where uniform application of irrigation water is required. The following conditions are favourable for sprinkler irrigation system:

i) Soils with very high infiltration rate.
ii) Shallow soils, the topography of which prevents desired levelling at reasonable costs.
iii) Undulating land and land with steep slopes where surface irrigation may result in excessive erosion.
iv) Water is very scarce.
v) Ground water is the source of irrigation water.

Following are the advantages of sprinkler irrigation :

i) Saving of water and soil (due to no or negligible erosion of soil).
ii) Saving in cost of land preparation.
iii) Better control of soil moisture.
iv) Frequent and light irrigation results in better crop yields.
v) Easy and uniform application of water, fertilizers and pesticides.

Following are the disadvantages of sprinkler irrigation:

i) Higher initial investment.
ii) Higher power requirement.
iii) Unsuitable for soils having low infiltration rate.
iv) Poor application efficiency under high windy conditions and high temperature.
v) Unsuitable for canal irrigation in which water is distributed by rotational supply system.

Because of its advantages, sprinkler irrigation is replacing the surface irrigation methods. In India, the gross area under sprinkler irrigation has increased from 3 lakh hectares in 1985 to 5.80 lakh hectares in 1989, and is expected to further increase to about 20 lakh hectares by the turn of the 20th century.

1.9.4 Trickle (or Drip) Irrigation

In the drip irrigation system, water is applied slowly and frequently to keep the soil moisture in the root-zone soil of the plant within the desired range. The water for irrigation is conveyed from the source to the plant root zone through a system comprising main line (37.5 to 70 mm diameter pipe), submains (25 to 37.5 mm diameter pipe), laterals (6 to 8 mm diameter pipe), valves (to control the flow), drippers or emitters (to supply water at a desired rate of about 1 to 10 litres per hour to the plants), pressure gauges, water meters, filters (to remove all debris, sand and clay to reduce clogging of the emitters), pumps, fertiliser tanks, vacuum breakers and pressure regulators. Flow is controlled manually or set to automatically deliver either

i) desired amount of water for a predetermined time, or
ii) water whenever soil moisture decreases to a predetermined amount.

A line sketch of a typical drip irrigation system is shown in Fig 1.2. Following are the advantages of this method:

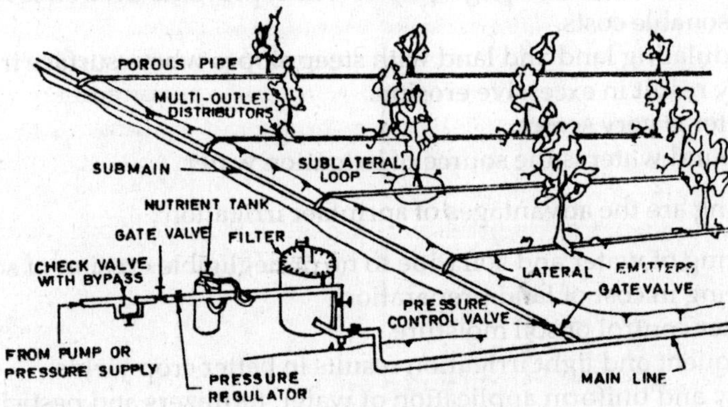

Fig. 1.2 Drip irrigantion system

i) It saves water and improves water penetration.
ii) It reduces weed growth.
iii) Limited soil wetting permits uninterrupted agricultural operations.
iv) Lower operating pressures and lower flow rates require lesser energy for pumping.
v) It enhances plant growth and improves crop yield.
vi) It does not require land preparation.

vii) It does not cause soil erosion.
viii) It improves fertiliser application efficiency.

Following are the main disadvantages of drip irrigation:

i) It requires high skill in its design, installation and maintenance.
ii) Initial investment cost is rather high.
iii) The system is sensitive to clogging because of small openings used in the system.

Because of the obvious advantages of water saving and increased crop yield associated with drip irrigation, India has embarked on a massive programme for popularising this method.

1.10 ASSESSMENT OF CHARGES FOR IRRIGATION WATER

The importance of accurate flow measurement for proper regulation, distribution and charging of irrigation water cannot be overemphasised. There are several flow-measuring devices available for flow measurement in the irrigation systems. Generally weirs, flumes and orifices are used for this purpose. Besides, there are some other indirect methods by which velocities are measured and the discharge computed. In these methods, the channel section is divided into suitable number of compartments and the mean velocity of flow for each of these compartments is measured by using devices such as current meter, surface floats, double floats, velocity rods, etc. The discharge through any compartment is obtained by multiplying the mean velocity of flow with the area of cross-section of the compartment. The sum of all compartmental discharges gives the channel discharge.

Irrigation projects involve huge expenditure for their construction. The operation and maintenance of these projects also require finances. With the introduction of irrigation facilities in an area, the farmers are immensely benefited. Hence, it is only appropriate that they are suitably charged for the irrigation water supplied to them.

Assessment of irrigation water charges can be done in one of the following ways:

i) Assessment on area basis
ii) Volumetric assessment
iii) Assessment based on outlet capacity
iv) Permanent assessment
v) Consolidated assessment.

In the area basis method of assessment, water charges are fixed per unit area of land irrigated for each of the crops grown. The rates of water charges depend on the cash value of crop, water requirement of crop and the time of water demand with respect to the available supplies in the source. Since the water charges are not related to the actual quantity of water used, the farmers (particularly those whose holdings are in the head reaches of the canal) tend to overirrigate their land. This results in uneconomical use of available irrigation water beside depriving the cultivators in the tail reaches of the canal of their due share of irrigation water. However, this method of assessment, being simple and convenient, is generally used for almost all irrigation projects in India.

In the volumetric assessment, the charges are in proportion to the actual amount of water received by the cultivator. This method, therefore, requires installation of water meters at all the outlets (see Art. 7.6) of the irrigation system. Alternatively, modular outlets may be provided to supply a specified discharge of water. This method results in economical use of irrigation water and is, therefore, an ideal method of assessment. But it has several drawbacks. This method requires installation and maintenance of suitable devices for water measurement. These devices require adequate head at the outlet. Further, there is a possibility of water theft by cutting of banks or siphoning over the bank through a flexible hose pipe. Also, the distribution of charges among the farmers, whose holdings are served by a common outlet, may be difficult. Because of these drawbacks, the method has not been adopted in India.

Assessment of canal water charges based on outlet capacity is a simple method and is workable if the outlets are rigid or semi-modular and the channel may run within outlet's designed range of parameters.

In some regions, artificial irrigation, though not essential, has been provided to meet the water demand only in drought years. Every farmer of such a region has to pay a fixed amount. The farmers have to pay these charges even for the years in which they do not take any water.

A farmer has also to pay tax on the land owned by him. In the consolidated assessment method, both the land revenue and the water charges are combined, and the cultivators are accordingly charged.

EXERCISES

1. What is irrigation ? What has been its impact on human environment ?
2. Justifying the need of irrigation in India, describe its development in India.
3. What are the requirements for the success of an irrigation project? How is an irrigation project planned?
4. What are the objectives of command area development ? How are these achieved through command area development programmes?
5. In what possible ways irrigation water can be delivered to various farms once it has been brought upto the watercourse. Discuss the salient features of these methods.
6. Describe various irrigation methods mentioning their advantages, disadvantages and applicability to different field conditions.
7. How is water distribution managed in 'Warabandi' system?

Chapter 2

Hydrology

2.1 GENERAL

Hydrology is the science of water which deals with the spatial and temporal characterstics of the earth's water. In other words, *hydrology* is the study of water in all its phases, including the occurrence, movement, distribution, circulation, storage, exploration, development and management.

The atmospheric air always contains moisture. Under favourable conditions, this moisture gets condensed and water drops are formed. These water drops ultimately fall on the earth's surface as precipitation in the form of rain, snow, fog, drizzle, dew, hail (frozen rain drops) and sleet (snow mixed with rain). *Rainfall* is the water that reaches the surface of the earth from the atmosphere due to the condensation of the atmospheric vapour.

Part of the natural precipitation (*i.e.*, rainfall) is transported on the earth's surface through natural surface channels which are known as streams or rivers. This is known as runoff which includes :

i) surface runoff or overland flow received in a stream immediately after rain,
ii) interflow, *i.e.* the portion of soil moisture which flows through the upper soil layers and joins the stream, and
iii) delayed runoff which includes part of rain water which enters the stream after flowing through deeper portions of the ground, and that part of the runoff which has been temporarily stored in natural lakes or as snow cover.

Overland flow and interflow together are termed *direct runoff*, while the ground water flow that enters a stream is termed *base flow* (or *base runoff*).

Thus, *runoff* is the total quantity of water received by a stream from its drainage basin (or watershed or catchment). A *drainage basin* of a stream is defined as that part of the earth's surface which diverts all its runoff to the same stream (*i.e.*, drainage outlet). Characteristics of a drainage basin such as size, shape, surface characteristics, topography and geology and those of rain (like its intensity and duration) considerably affect the runoff. In general, a

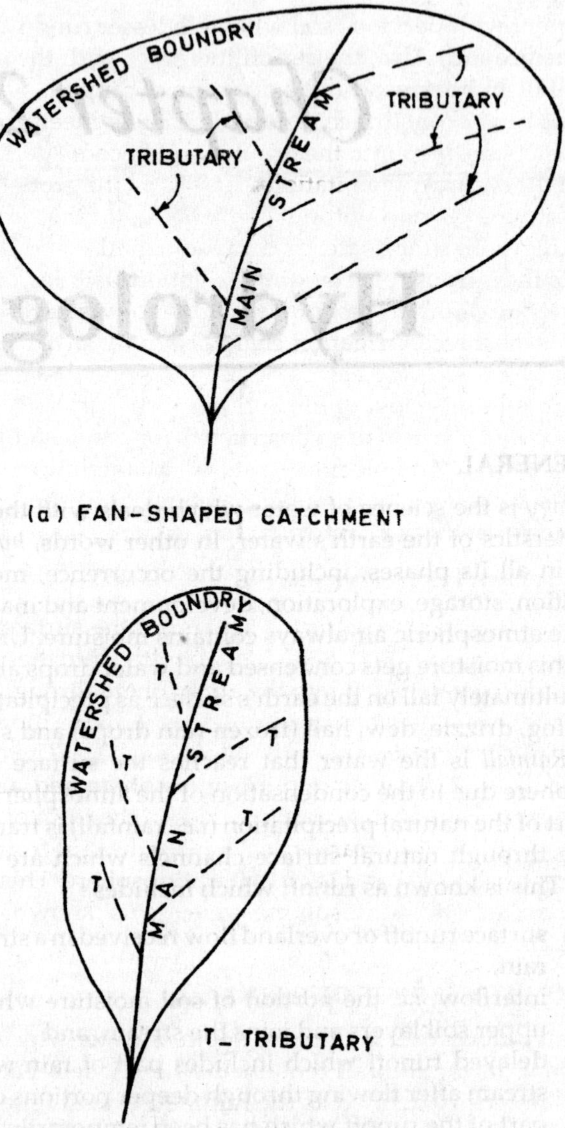

Fig. 2.1 Shapes of catchments

larger catchment would yield higher runoff. A fan-shaped catchment (Fig. 2.1) produces larger runoff compared to that produced by fern-shaped catchment. Similarly, a catchment with vegetal cover yields lesser runoff compared to that yielded by a catchment with paved surface or no vegetal cover. A steeply sloping catchment will result in higher runoff. Again, a catchment with pervious soil will yield lesser runoff due to larger infiltration into the ground. Also, the runoff increases with the increase in the intensity of rainfall and decrease in the duration of rainfall.

The runoff (or surface runoff) ultimately meets the sea. Part of the runoff may percolate deep into the ground and become part of ground water just as part of the natural precipitation that falls on the ground may percolate directly deep into the ground without contributing to the runoff. Part of this ground water may join runoff later as delayed runoff.

For the purpose of providing irrigation facilities, one has to plan, construct and operate different types of irrigation (or water resources) structures, such as dams, barrages, irrigation channels, canal structures, *etc.* Besides, bridges have to be constructed across rivers, and several types of measures have to be taken to minimise loss of life and property due to floods in rivers. Likewise, hydropower projects are constructed for the benefit of mankind. All such projects require knowledge about the stream flow and its behaviour. It is this (*i.e.*, the behaviour of a stream) and related aspects which make study of hydrology useful and important for irrigation engineers.

2.2 HYDROLOGIC CYCLE

Streams transport water to the sea. From the surface of the oceans, streams and lakes (or reservoirs) water is evaporated into the atmosphere. In addition, water is also evaporated into the atmosphere through plants and trees which take water from their root-zone soil. Furthermore, moisture in the upper layers of ground also evaporates into the atmosphere. The evaporated water (from the earth's surface) goes into the atmosphere and, under favourable conditions, comes back to the earth's surface in the form of precipitation. Thus, the same water has been transferred time and again from the atmosphere to the land and then to sea and back to the atmosphere. This cycle of water amongst earth, ocean and atmospheric systems is known as the *hydrologic cycle* (Fig. 2.2).

2.3 MEASUREMENT OF RAINFALL

Rainfall is measured in terms of depth of water which would result on a land surface if all the rainfall remained where it fell. For measuring rainfall (or rainfall intensity defined as the rainfall per unit time), rain gauges are used. The rain gauges are classified as either non-recording or recording.

Non-recording rain gauges only collect rain water which, when measured suitably, gives the total amount of rainfall at the rain gauge station during the measuring interval. The Indian Meteorological Department has adopted Symon's rain gauge (Fig. 2.3). A glass bottle and funnel with brass rim are put in a metallic cylinder such that the top of the cylinder is 30.5 cm above the ground level. Rain water falls into the glass bottle through the funnel. The water collected in the bottle is measured with the help of a standard measuring glass jar which is supplied with the rain gauge. The jar measures rainfall in millimetres. At each station, rainfall observations are taken twice daily at 8.30 am and 5.30 pm.

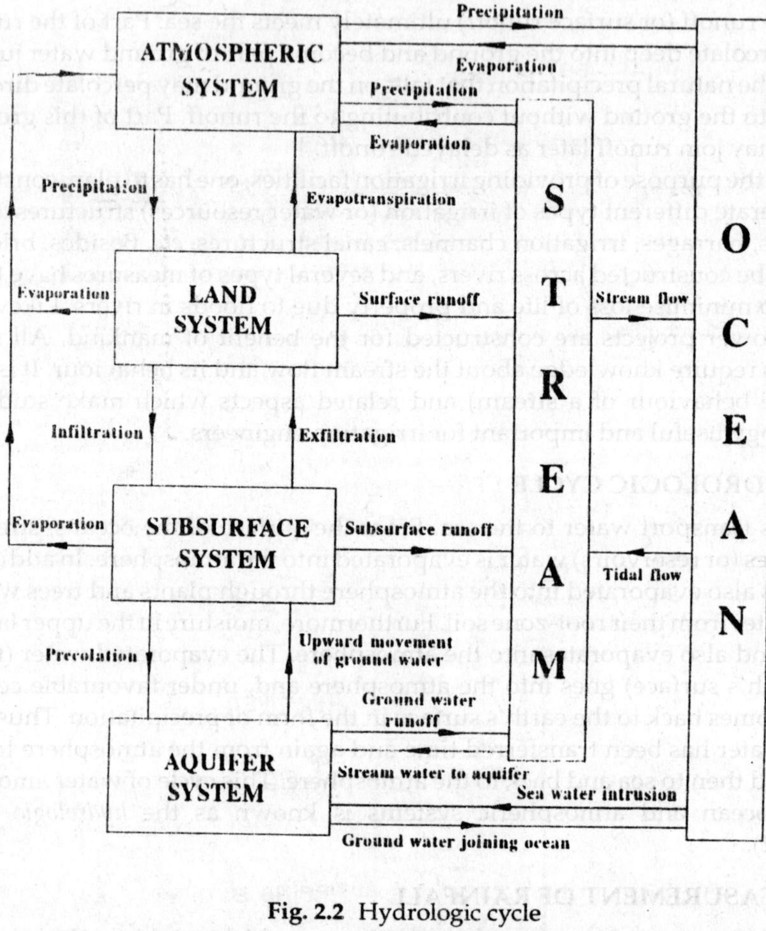

Fig. 2.2 Hydrologic cycle

Recording rain gauges automatically record the intensity of rainfall and the time of its occurrence in the form of a trace (or graph) marked on a graph paper wrapped round a revolving drum. Following three types are the most widely used recording rain gauges :

i) Tipping bucket rain gauge,
ii) Weighing bucket rain gauge, and
iii) Siphon rain gauge.

i) Tipping bucket rain gauge: A 300 mm diameter funnel collects rain water and conducts it to one of the two small buckets (Fig. 2.4) which are so designed that when 0.25 mm of rainfall is collected in a bucket it tilts and empties its water into a bigger storage tank and simultaneously moves the other bucket below the funnel. When any of the two buckets tilts, it actuates

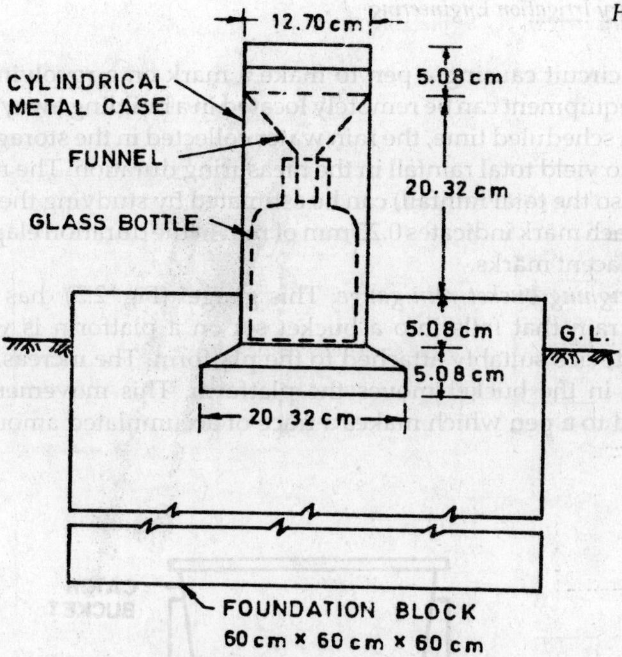

Fig. 2.3 Symon's rain gauge

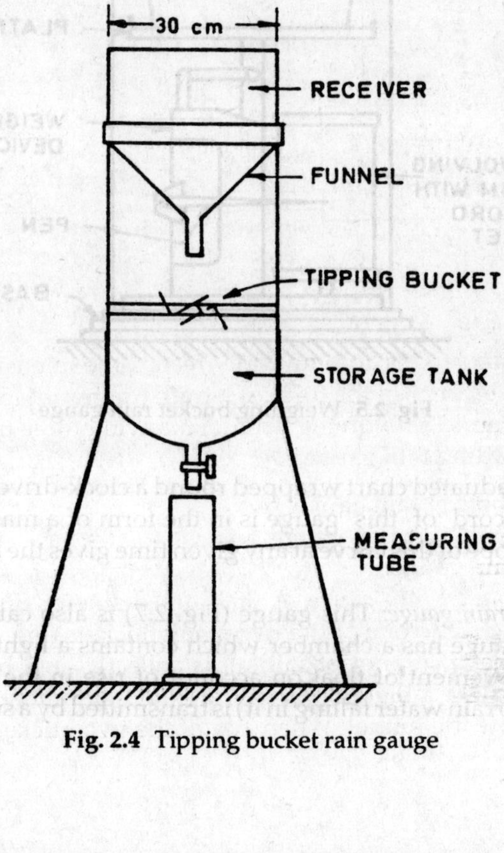

Fig. 2.4 Tipping bucket rain gauge

an electric circuit causing a pen to make a mark on a revolving drum. The recording equipment can be remotely located in a building away from the rain gauge. At a scheduled time, the rain water collected in the storage tank can be measured to yield total rainfall in the measuring duration. The rainfall intensity (and also the total rainfall) can be estimated by studying the record sheet on which each mark indicates 0.25 mm of rain in the duration elapsed between the two adjacent marks.

ii) Weighing bucket rain gauge: This gauge (Fig. 2.5) has a system by which the rain that falls into a bucket set on a platform is weighed by a weighing device suitably attached to the platform. The increasing weight of rain water in the bucket moves the platform. This movement is suitably transmitted to a pen which makes a trace of accumulated amount of rainfall

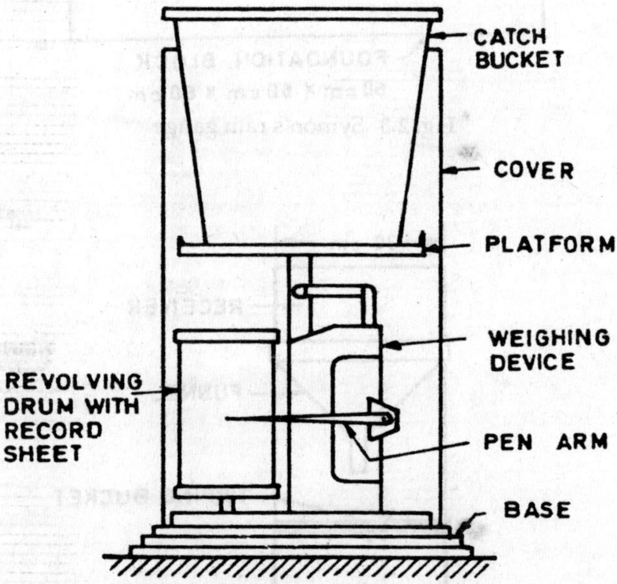

Fig. 2.5 Weighing bucket rain gauge

on a suitably graduated chart wrapped round a clock-driven revolving drum. The rainfall record of this gauge is in the form of a mass curve of rainfall (Fig. 2.6). The slope of this curve at any given time gives the intensity of rainfall at that time.

iii) Siphon rain gauge: This gauge (Fig. 2.7) is also called float type rain gauge as this gauge has a chamber which contains a light and hollow float. The vertical movement of float on account of rise in the water level in the chamber (due to rain water falling in it) is transmitted by a suitable mechanism

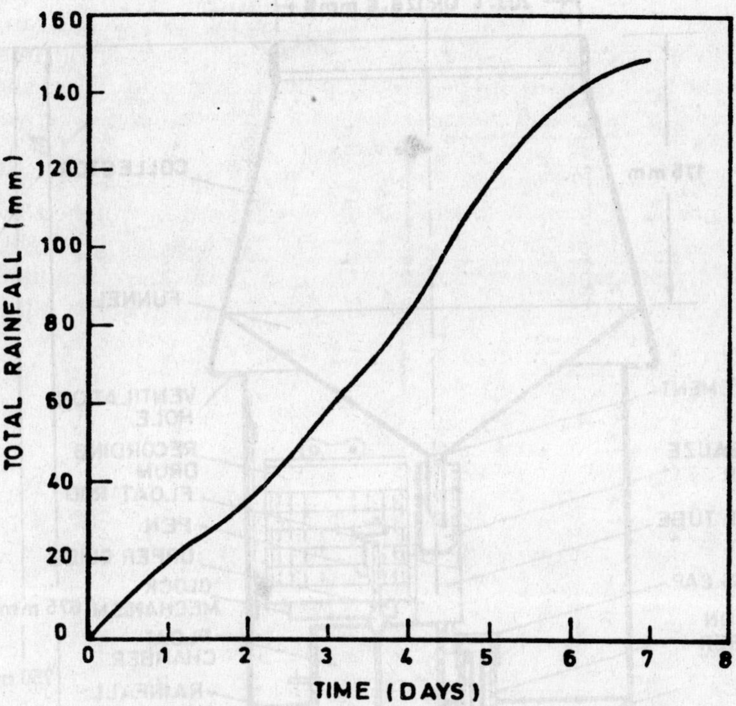

Fig. 2.6 Rainfall record of weighing bucket rain gauge

to move a pen on a clock-driven revolving chart. The record of rainfall is in the form of a mass curve of rainfall and, hence, the slope of the curve gives the intensity of rainfall.

2.4 AVERAGE DEPTH OF RAINFALL

The depth of rainfall measured by a rain gauge is valid for that rain gauge station and in its immediate vicinity. Over a large area like watershed (or catchment) of a stream, there will be several such stations, and the average depth of rainfall over the entire area can be estimated by one of the following methods:

2.4.1 Arithmatic Mean Method

This is the simplest method in which average depth of rainfall is obtained by obtaining the sum of the depths of rainfall (say $P_1, P_2, P_3, P_4 .... P_n$) measured at stations 1, 2, 3 ....n^{th} and dividing the sum by total number of stations *i.e.* n. Thus,

$$P = \frac{P_1 + P_2 + P_3 + ...P_n}{n} = \frac{1}{n}\sum_{i=1}^{n} P_i \qquad \ldots (2.1)$$

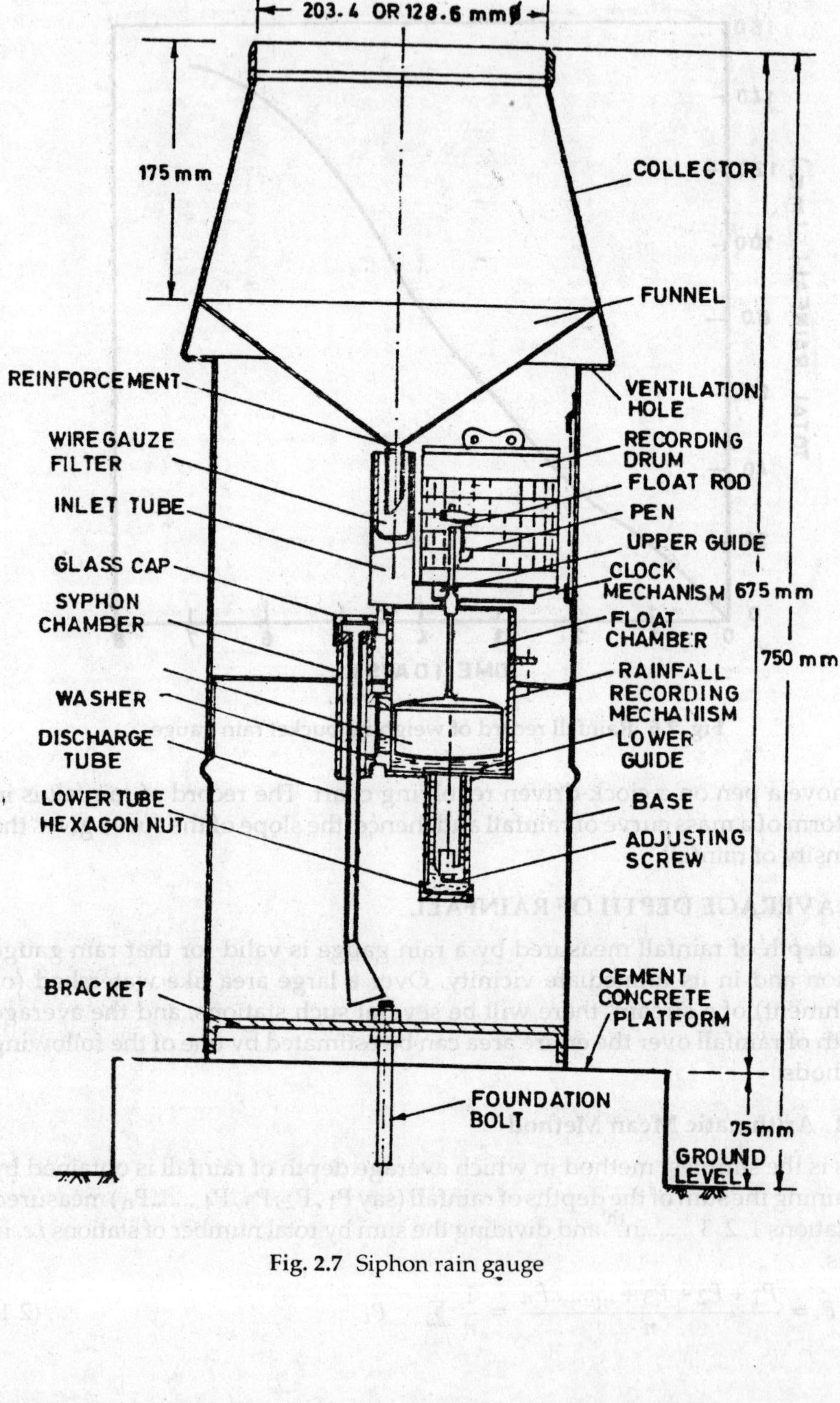

Fig. 2.7 Siphon rain gauge

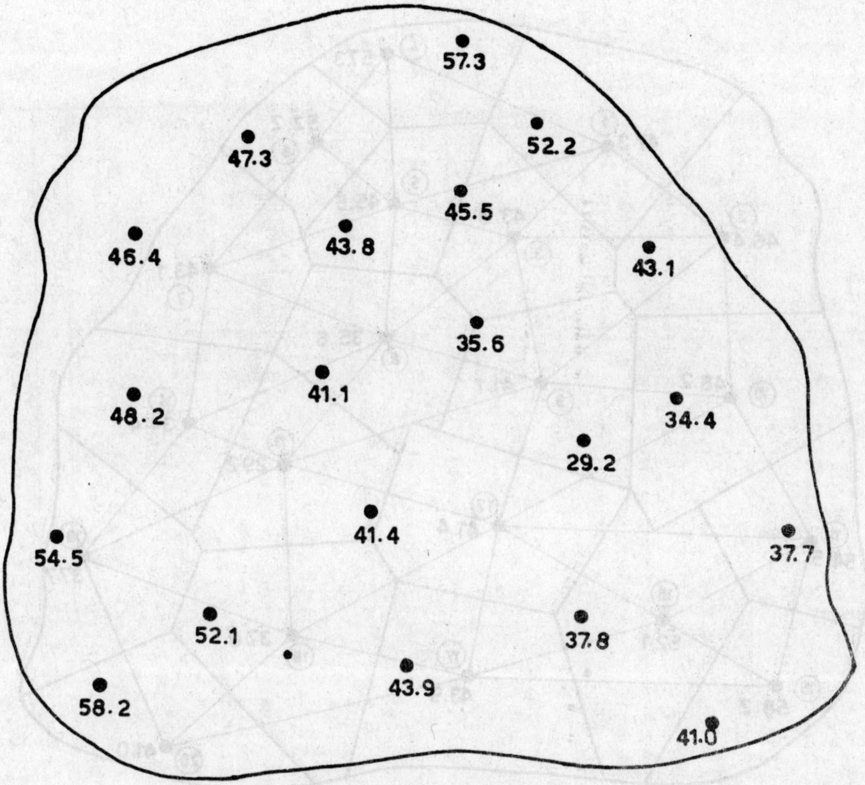

Fig. 2.8(a) Watershed for Example 2.1

This method is suitable if the rain gauge stations are uniformly distributed over the entire area and the rainfall variation in the area is not large.

2.4.2 Theissen Polygon Method

In this method, the entire area is divided into number of triangular areas by joining adjacent rain gauge stations with straight lines, as shown in Fig. 2.8 (a and b). If a bisector is drawn on each of the lines joining adjacent rain gauge stations, there will be number of polygons and each polygon, within itself, will have only one rain gauge station. Assuming that rainfall P_i recorded at any station i is representative rainfall of the area A_i of the polygon i within which rain gauge station is located, their average depth of rainfall P is given as

$$P = \frac{1}{A} \sum_{i=1}^{n} P_i \, A_i \tag{2.2}$$

where

$$A = \sum_{i=1}^{n} A_i = A_1 + A_2 + A_3 + \ldots\ldots\ldots\ldots\ldots A_n$$

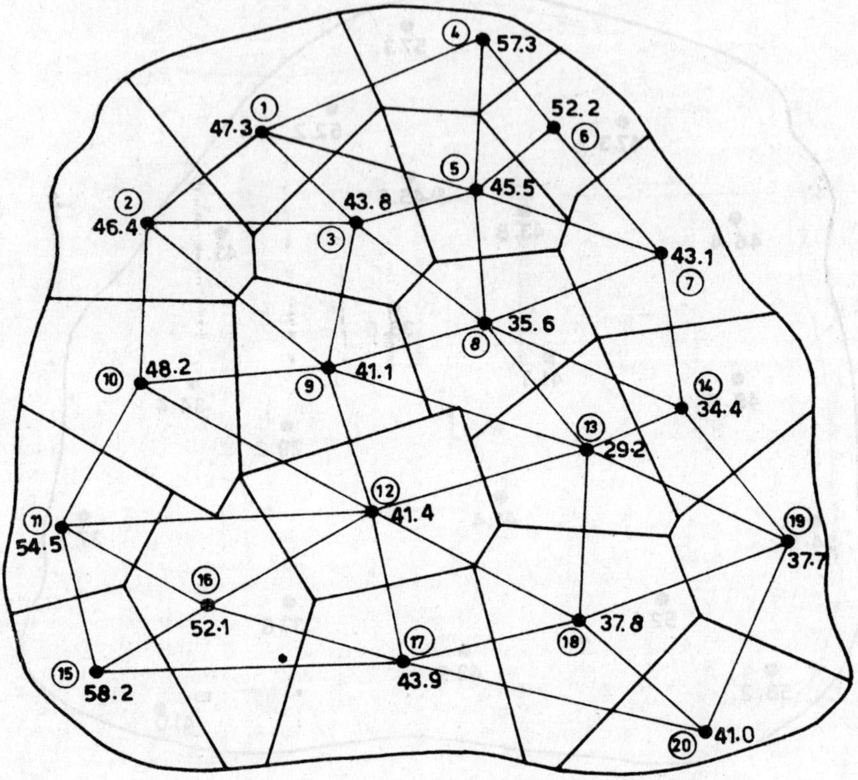

Fig. 2.8(b) Theissen polygon of rain gauge stations of watershed of Example 2.1

2.4.3 Isohyetal Method

An isohyet is a contour of equal rainfall. Knowing the depths of rainfall at each rain gauge station of an area and assuming linear variation of rainfall between any two adjacent stations, one can draw a smooth curve passing through all points indicating the same value of rainfall, Fig. 2.8(c). The area between two adjacent isohyets is measured with the help of a planimeter. The average depth of rainfall P for the entire area A is given as

$$P = \frac{1}{A} \sum \text{Area between two adjacent isohyets} \times \text{mean of the two adjacent isohyet values} \quad \ldots (2.3)$$

Since this method considers actual spatial variation of rainfall, it is considered as the best method for computing average depth of rainfall.

Example 2.1: Figure 2.8(a) shows annual rainfall in centimetres at the corresponding rain gauge stations of a watershed. Determine the average depth of annual precipitation using (i) the arithmetic mean method, (ii) Theissen polygon method, and (iii) isohyetal method.

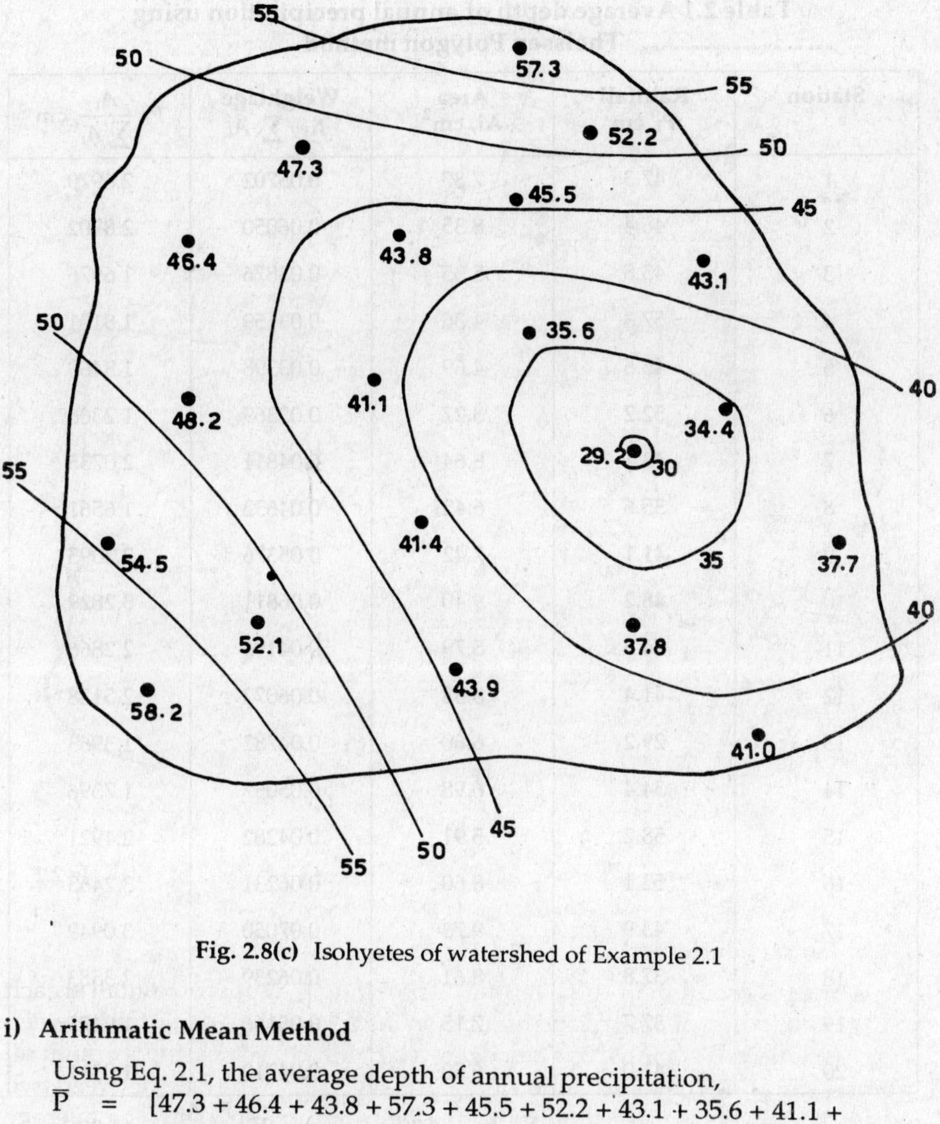

Fig. 2.8(c) Isohyetes of watershed of Example 2.1

i) Arithmatic Mean Method

Using Eq. 2.1, the average depth of annual precipitation,

$$\overline{P} = [47.3 + 46.4 + 43.8 + 57.3 + 45.5 + 52.2 + 43.1 + 35.6 + 41.1 + 48.2 + 54.5 + 41.4 + 29.2 + 34.4 + 58.2 + 52.1 + 43.9 + 37.8 + 37.7 + 41.0\,] \times \tfrac{1}{20}$$

$$= \frac{1}{20}\ (890.7)$$

$$= 44.535 \text{ cm}$$

ii) Theissen Polygon Method

Theisson polygons for the given problem have been shown in Fig. 2.8(b) after making suitable adjustments. The calculations for the average depth of annual precipitation are shown in Table 2.1.

Table 2.1 Average depth of annual precipitation using Theissen Polygon method

Station	Rainfall P_i, cm	Area A_i, cm^2	Weightage $A_i / \sum A_i$	$P_i \dfrac{A_i}{\sum A_i}$, cm
1	47.3	7.87	0.05702	2.6970
2	46.4	8.35	0.06050	2.8702
3	43.8	5.35	0.03876	1.6976
4	57.3	4.36	0.03159	1.8101
5	45.5	4.69	0.03398	1.5460
6	52.2	3.27	0.02369	1.2366
7	43.1	6.64	0.04811	2.0735
8	35.6	6.42	0.04652	1.6561
9	41.1	7.42	0.05376	2.2095
10	48.2	9.40	0.06811	3.2829
11	54.5	5.79	0.04196	2.2866
12	41.4	8.38	0.06072	2.5138
13	29.2	6.60	0.04782	1.3963
14	34.4	6.98	0.05057	1.7396
15	58.2	5.91	0.04282	2.4921
16	52.1	8.60	0.06231	3.2463
17	43.9	9.73	0.07050	3.0949
18	37.8	8.61	0.06239	2.3583
19	37.7	7.13	0.05166	1.9475
20	41.0	6.50	0.04710	1.9311
		$\sum A_i = 138$		$\sum \dfrac{P_i A_i}{A_i} = 44.023$ cm

$$\overline{P} = \frac{\sum P_i A_i}{\sum A_i} = 44.023 \text{ cm.}$$

iii) Isohyetal Method

The isohyetes have been drawn as shown in Fig. 2.8(c). The calculations for the average depth of annual precipitation are shown in Table 2.2.

Table 2.2 Average depth of annual precipitation using isohyetal method

Isohyetes x, cm	Area between adjacent isohyetes y, cm^2	xy
55	6.85	376.75
55	3.48	191.4
$\left(\frac{50+55}{2}\right)$	12.52	657.3
$\left(\frac{50+55}{2}\right)$	7.68	403.2
$\left(\frac{50+45}{2}\right)$	33.78	1604.55
$\left(\frac{45+40}{2}\right)$	33.05	1404.625
$\left(\frac{40+35}{2}\right)$	30.16	1131.000
$\left(\frac{35+30}{2}\right)$	10.22	332.15
30	0.26	7.8

Total Area = 138 km^2, $\sum xy = 6108.775$

$$\overline{P} = \frac{\sum xy}{\sum A} = \frac{6108.775}{138} = 44.266 \text{ cm}$$

2.5 ESTIMATION OF PEAK FLOOD DISCHARGE

The design of structures on a river, such as dams, spillways, earthen embankments, flood control reservoirs, *etc.*, requires information about the maximum (or peak) flood discharge in the river. For gauged watersheds, one can use the collected data and analyse them to get peak flood in the river. But, for ungauged watersheds, one has to use empirical relations. In 1985, Dickens made the first attempt in India to obtain an empirical formula for determining the maximum flood dischange Q (m^3/sec) in a river. Dicken's formula is written as

$$Q = CA^{3/4} \qquad \ldots (2.4)$$

in which A is the area of catchment in sq. Km (*i.e.*, Km^2) and C is a constant whose value varies widely between 2.8 to 5.6 for catchments in plains and 14 to 28 for catchments in hills, depending upon the catchment characteristics. Dicken's formula is used for catchments in north India and central India. For catchments in south India, Ryve's formula is preferred. Ryve's formula is expressed as

$$Q = CA^{2/3} \qquad \ldots (2.5)$$

The value of C varies widely between 6.8 (for flat or plain catchments) and 42.40 (for western coast region).

A rational method for estimating peak flood discharge of a river includes intensity of rainfall in the relation for peak flood discharge which is expressed as

$$Q = CIA \qquad \ldots (2.6)$$

in which I is the intensity of rainfall (in m/hour) and C is the runoff coefficient whose value varies between 0.20 for flat catchment with sandy soil to 0.8 for relatively less pervious catchment.

2.6 STREAM GAUGING

For planning of any water resource project, one needs to know the magnitude of the stream flow which is measured in terms of its discharge, *i.e.*, the quantity (volume) of water flowing past a section per unit time. It is expressed in m^3/sec. Most commonly used methods for stream gauging are:

i) Area-velocity method,
ii) Area slope method, and
iii) Discharge measuring structures.

2.6.1 Area-Velocity Method

It should be noted that depthr of flow varies in a section of a stream across the main flow direction. Likewise, the velocity of flow too varies from point to point within a cross-sectional area of the stream. The best method for stream flow measurement would, therefore, be to determine the velocity variation at a channel section and then integrate (*i.e.*, sum) the products of velocity in a small individual elemental area with that area for the whole flow cross-section. However, this may not be possible most of the times and, hence, other simpler measurements are made to estimate the stream flow.

For example, a flow section can be divided into a suitable number of vertical strips the average depths of which are measured. In each of these strips, velocities at 0.2 h and 0.8 h depths below the free surface are measured using a current meter. Here, h is the depth of flow in the strip. The average of these two values for any given strip gives approximately the average velocity of flow in that strip. The total discharge in the stream can be obtained by obtaining the sum of products of the average velocity and area of the strip for all the individual strips, *i.e.*,

$$Q = \sum_{i=1}^{N} Q_i = \sum_{i=1}^{N} B_i h_i v_i \qquad \ldots (2.7)$$

in which B_i, h_i, v_i and Q_i are width, average depth, average velocity and discharge of ith strip and the flow cross-section has been divided into N strips.

For obtaining the average velocity in a strip, one can, alternatively, measure velocity only at 0.6 h depth below the free surface and take it equal to the average velocity in the strip. Or, one can measure surface velocity within the strip and multiply it by 0.9 to get an approximate average velocity.

2.6.2 Area-Slope Method

During floods, it is generally difficult to identify peak flow conditions and then make velocity measurements within peak flow duration. It is relatively simpler to install two gauges with the same datum at some distance apart. During flood, water surface levels in these gauges are read. At times, flood level marks on the banks can also be used for this purpose. Knowing the river cross-section, one can determine the area of flow cross-section at the two gauge locations and an average value of area A is determined. Likewise, the hydraulic radius R can also be obtained. Water surface slope S can also be computed using the gauge level readings and the distance between the two gauge stations. Assigning a suitable value to the Manning's n, one can predict discharge Q in the stream by using the Manning's equation,

$$Q = \frac{1}{n} AR^{2/3} S^{1/2} \qquad \text{... (2.8)}$$

2.6.3 Discharge Measuring Structures

The most commonly used structure for the purpose of discharge measurement in a river is a weir which is, generally, either triangular (for relatively small discharges) or rectangular (for relatively large discharges) in shape. These weirs are in the form of an obstruction constructed across a river. The discharge Q flowing over a weir is related to the head over the weir, *i.e.* H and the weir characteristics. For example, for a triangular weir having its notch angle θ, the discharge Q is expressed as

$$Q = \frac{8}{15} C_d \sqrt{2g}\, H^{5/2} \tan \theta/2 \qquad \text{... (2.9)}$$

Likewise, for rectangular sharp-crested weir

$$Q = \frac{2}{3} C_d B \sqrt{2g}\, H^{3/2} \qquad \text{... (2.10)}$$

in which C_d is the Coefficient of discharge, B the length of weir and g is the acceleration due to gravity.

EXERCISES

1. Describe the hydrologic cycle.
2. Discuss different methods of computing average depth of rainfall.
3. How is rainfall measured? Describe the use of different rain gauges.
4. How is stream gauging carried out?

Chapter 3

Water Requirement of Crops

3.1 COMMAND AREAS

The area which can be served (or commanded) for irrigation by an irrigation system (usually a canal system) is referred to as *command area* of the system.

Gross command area (or GCA) is the total area which can be economically irrigated by an irrigation system without considering any limitation of the quantity of available water. GCA includes the areas which are, otherwise, uncultivable. For example, uncultivable areas such as roads, barren land, ponds and residential areas of a command area are included in the GCA.

An irrigation canal system usually lies in a doab. *Doab* is the area between two drainages (or rivers). Flow irrigation would not be possible if an irrigation system in a doab is used to irrigate land beyond the drainages of the doab. Thus, the boundaries of GCA is fixed by the drainages on either side of the irrigation canal system.

The area of the cultivable land in the gross command area of an irrigation system is called *cultivable command area* (CCA) which includes all land of gross command on which cultivation is possible. However, at a given time all the cultivable land, i.e., CCA may not be under cultivation. Therefore, the CCA can be further divided into two categories:

i) Cultivated CCA, and
ii) Uncultivated CCA.

3.2 ROOT-ZONE SOIL WATER RELATIONSHIPS

Any given volume, V of soil (Fig. 3.1) consists of (i) volume of solids V_s (ii) volume of liquid (water) V_w, and (iii) volume of gas (air) V_a. The porosity n, the volumetric moisture content w and the saturation s are defined as

$$n = \frac{V_v}{V}$$

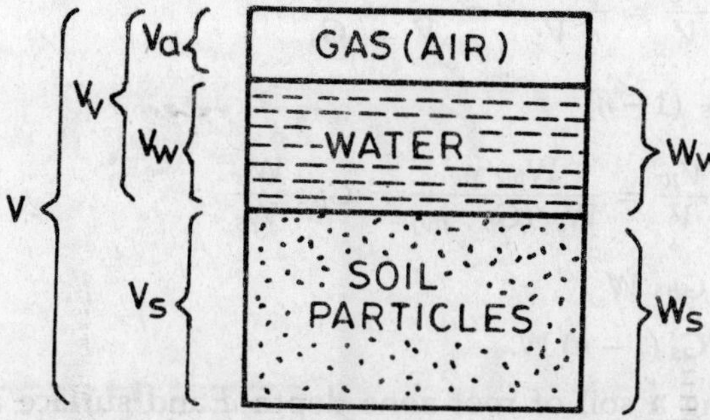

Fig. 3.1 Occupation of Space in a Soil Sample

$$w = \frac{V_w}{V}$$

$$s = \frac{V_w}{V_v}$$

$$V_v = V_w + V_a$$

Obviously, $w = s.n.$ (3.1)

Further, if the weight of water in a wet soil sample is W_w and the dry weight of the sample is W_s, then the dry weight moisture fraction, W is expressed as

$$W = \frac{W_w}{W_s} \tag{3.2}$$

The bulk density (or the bulk specific weight or the bulk unit weight) of a soil mass is then dry weight of the soil per unit bulk volume, i.e., W_s/V (Fig. 3.1). The specific weight (or the unit weight) of the soil particles is the ratio of dry weight of the soil particles W_s to the volume of the soil particles V_s, *i.e.*, W_s/V_s. Thus,

$$G_b \cdot \gamma_w = \frac{W_s}{V}, \quad i.e., V = \frac{W_s}{G_b \cdot \gamma_w}$$

and $$G_s \cdot \gamma_w = \frac{W_s}{V_s}, \quad i.e., V_s = \frac{W_s}{G_s \cdot \gamma_w}$$

$$\therefore \frac{V_s}{V} = \frac{G_b}{G_s}. \tag{3.3}$$

Here, γ_w is the unit weight of water and G_b and G_s are, respectively, bulk specific gravity of the soil and relative density of soil grains. Further,

$$1 - n = 1 - \frac{V_v}{V} = \frac{V - V_v}{V} = \frac{V_s}{V} = \frac{G_b}{G_s}$$

$$\therefore\ G_b = G_s\ (1 - n) \tag{3.4}$$

$$\text{Also, } w = \frac{V_w}{V} = \frac{W_w/\gamma_w}{W_s/(G_b \cdot \gamma_w)} = G_b \cdot \frac{W_w}{W_s}$$

$$\therefore\ w = G_b \cdot W \tag{3.5}$$

$$\text{and}\quad w = G_s\,(1 - n)\,W.$$

Considering a soil of root zone depth *d* and surface area A (*i.e.*, bulk volume = *Ad*),

$$W_s = V_s \cdot G_s \cdot \gamma_w$$

$$= \text{A}d\,(1 - n) \cdot G_s \cdot \gamma_w$$

$$\therefore\ \text{Dry weight moisture fraction, } W = \frac{W_w}{W_s}$$

$$= \frac{V_w \cdot \gamma_w}{Ad\ (1 - n)\ G_s \cdot \gamma_w}$$

∴ Volume of water in the root-zone soil,

$$V_w = W\,Ad\,(1 - n)\,G_s. \tag{3.6}$$

This volume of water can also be expressed in terms of depth of water which would be obtained when this volume of water is spread over the soil surface area A.

$$\therefore\ \text{Depth of water, } d_w = \frac{V_w}{A}$$

$$\therefore\qquad d_w = G_s\ (1 - n)\ Wd \tag{3.7}$$

$$\text{or}\qquad d_w = w \cdot d \tag{3.8}$$

Crop growth (or yield) is directly affected by the soil-moisture content. Both excessive water (which results in waterlogging) and deficient water retard the crop growth and reduce the crop yield.

Soil water can be divided into three categories (Fig. 3.2):

i) Gravity (or free) water.
ii) Capillary water.
iii) Hygroscopic water.

Gravity water is that water which drains away under the influence of gravity. Soon after irrigation (or rainfall), this water remains in the soil and saturates the soil, thus, preventing circulation of air in the void spaces.

The *capillary water* is held within soil pores due to the surface tension forces (against gravity) which act at the liquid-vapour (or water-air) interface.

Water attached to soil particles through loose chemical bonds is termed *hygroscopic water*. This water can be removed by heat only. But the plant roots can use a very small fraction of this soil moisture under drought conditions.

When an oven-dry (heated to 105°C for zero per cent moisture content) soil sample is exposed to atmosphere, it takes up some moisture called *hygroscopic moisture*. This moisture can be removed by heat only. If more water is made available, it can be retained as capillary moisture due to surface tension (*i.e.*, intermolecular forces). Any water, in excess of maximum capillary moisture, flows down freely and is gravitational water.

The water remaining in the soil after removal of gravitational water is called the field capacity. *Field capacity* of a soil is defined as the moisture fraction, W_{fc} (= W_w/W_s) of the soil when free drainage (at rapid rate) has essentially stopped and further drainage, if any, occurs at a very slow rate. An irrigated soil may take approximately one (in case of sandy soil) to three (in case of clayey soil) days for the rapid drainage to stop. Obviously, the field capacity depends on porosity and soil-moisture tension. The volumetric moisture content at the field capacity, W_{fc} becomes equal to G_b W_{fc}.

A plant wilts when it is incapable of extracting sufficient moisture from the soil to meet its water requirements. *Permanent wilting point* is defined as the soil-moisture fraction, W_{wp} at which the plant leaves wilt (or droop) permanently and applying additional water after this stage will not relieve the wilted condition. The moisture content at the permanent wilting condition will be higher in the hot climate than in the cold climate. Similarly, the percentage of soil moisture at the permanent wilting point of a plant will be larger in clayey soil than in sandy soil. The permanent wilting point is, obviously, at the lower end of the available moisture range and can be approximately estimated by dividing the field capacity by a factor varying

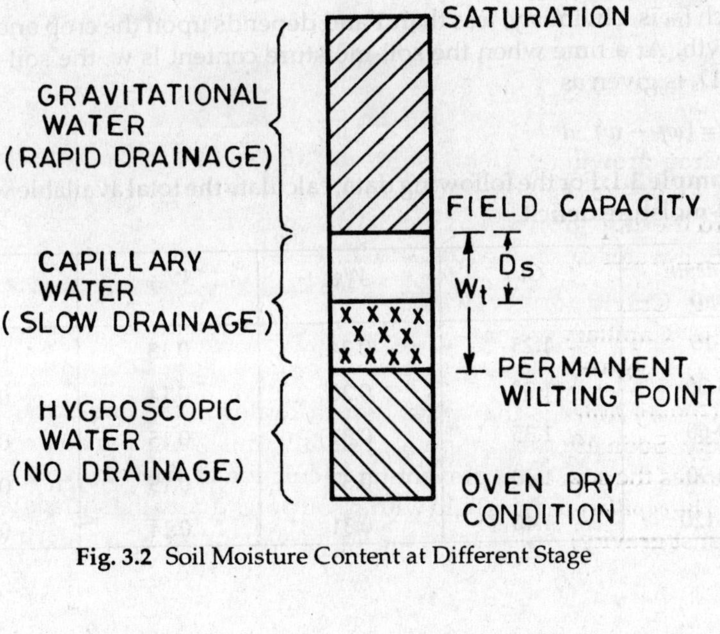

Fig. 3.2 Soil Moisture Content at Different Stage

from 2.0 (for soils with low silt content) to 2.4 (for soils with high silt content). The permanent wilting point also depends upon the nature of crop. The volumetric moisture content at the permanent wilting point, w_{wp} becomes $G_b . W_{wp}$. Figure 3.2 shows the different stages of soil-moisture content and the corresponding conditions.

The difference in the moisture content of the soil between its field capacity and the permanent wilting point within the root zone of the plants is termed as the *available* moisture. It represents the maximum moisture which can be stored in the soil for the plant use. It should be noted that the soil moisture content near the wilting point is not easily extractable by the plants. Hence, the term *readily available moisture* is used to represent that fraction of the available moisture which can be easily extracted by the plants. Readily available moisture is approximately 75% of the available moisture.

The total available moisture W_t (in terms of depth) for a plant (or soil) is given by

$$W_t = (w_{fc} - w_{wp}) . d \tag{3.9}$$

in which d is the depth of the root zone.

It is obvious that soil moisture can vary between the field capacity (excess amount would drain away) and the permanent wilting point. However, depending upon the prevailing conditions, soil moisture can be allowed to be depleted below the field capacity (but not below the permanent wilting point in any case) before the next irrigation is applied. This permissible amount of depletion is referred to as the *management allowed deficit* D_m which primarily depends on the type of crop and its stage of growth. Thus,

$$D_m = f_m W_t \tag{3.10}$$

in which f_m is, obviously, less than 1 and depends upon the crop and its stage of growth. At a time when the soil-moisture content is w, the soil-moisture deficit D_s is given as

$$D_s = (w_{fc} - w) . d \tag{3.11}$$

Example 3.1: For the following data, calculate the total available water and the soil-moisture deficit.

Soil depth (cm)	G_b	W_{fc}	W_{wp}	W
0-15	1.25	0.24	0.13	0.16
15-30	1.30	0.28	0.14	0.18
30-60	1.35	0.31	0.15	0.23
60-90	1.40	0.33	0.15	0.26
90-120	1.40	0.31	0.14	0.28

Solution:

Depth of soil layers d (mm)	$w_{fc} = G_b . W_{fc}$	$w_{wp} = G_b . W_{wp}$	$W_t = (w_{fc} - w_{wp})d$ (mm)	$w = G_b . W$	$D_s = (w_{fc} - w)d$ (mm)
150	0.3	0.1625	20.625	0.2	15.0
150	0.364	0.182	27.300	0.234	19.5
300	0.4185	0.2025	64.800	0.3105	32.4
300	0.462	0.21	75.600	0.364	29.4
300	0.434	0.196	71.400	0.392	12.6
		Total	259.725		108.9

∴ Total available water = 259.725 mm ≈ 260 mm
and the soil moisture deficit = 108.9 mm ≈ 109 mm

3.3 ESTIMATION OF IRRIGATION REQUIREMENT

It is usually not possible to irrigate entire CCA because of the limitations on the quantity of water available for irrigation. Also, one would like to extend irrigation to a much larger area than could be supported by the lowest available supply and, therefore, it is usually not possible to irrigate entire CCA. The percentage of CCA which is proposed to be provided irrigation in a year by an irrigation system is termed the *intensity of irrigation.* Till recently, the intensity of irrigation in India generally varied between 40 and 60%. This needs to be raised to the range of 100 to 180% by cultivating parts of CCA for more than one crop in a year and through improved management of the existing system.

The CCA multiplied by the intensity of irrigation (in fraction) gives the actual area to be irrigated.

For estimating the design discharge of irrigation canal system, the designer has to decide irrigation requirement of the command area of the system. One of the following two methods is generally used for this purpose.

3.3.1 Method Based on 'Duty of Water'

In this method, the designer has to first decide the duty of water for different crops in the command area of the system. *Duty of water* (or simply *duty*) for a given crop is defined as the area irrigated by the unit discharge of water flowing continuously for the duration of the base period of the crop. The *base period* of a crop is the time duration between the first watering at the time of sowing and the last watering prior to the harvesting of the crop. On the other hand, *crop period* of a crop is defined as the total time duration between the sowing and harvesting of the crop. This means that the base period of a crop is smaller than its crop period. The duty is measured in hectares per cubic metre per second and depends on

i) the crop,

ii) type of soil,
iii) irrigation and cultivation methods,
iv) climatic factors, and
v) channel conditions.

As water flows in a canal, there is loss of water due to evaporation and percolation. Therefore, duty is different at different points of a canal system. The duty at the headworks of a canal system is less than the duty at an outlet or in the tail end region of the canal. Duty is usually calculated for the head discharge of a canal. Duty calculated on the basis of the outlet discharge is called *outlet discharge factor* or simply *outlet factor* which excludes all losses in the system.

The volume of water needed for the growth of a crop during its entire crop-growing period is known as the water requirement of the crop. This requirement varies at different stages of the growth of the plant. The water requirement of a crop expressed in volume divided by the cultivated area would result in depth of water which term is usually used as a measure of water requirement of a crop. Any irrigation system should be capable of supplying peak requirement of the crops being grown in the command area. One of the methods to decide the water requirement of a crop is on the basis of *kor* watering.

When a plant is only a few centimetres high, it needs to be given its first watering which is called the *kor* watering in a limited period of time which is known as the *kor* period. If the plants do not receive water during the *kor* period, their growth is retarded and the crop yield reduces considerably. The *kor* watering depth and *kor* period vary depending upon the crop and the climatic factors of the region. For example, in UP, the *kor* watering depth for wheat is 13.5 cm and the *kor* period varies from 8 weeks in north-east UP (a relatively dry region) to 3 weeks in the hilly region which is relatively humid. For rice, the *kor* watering depth is 19 cm, and the *kor* period varies from 2 to 3 weeks.

If D represents the duty (measured in hectares/m^3/sec), then, by definition,

1 m^3/s of water flowing for *b* (*i.e.*, base period) days irrigates D hectares.

∴ 1 m^3/s of water flowing for 1 day (*i.e.*, 86400 m^3 of water) irrigates D/b hectares.

This volume (*i.e.*, 86400 m^3) of water spread over D/*b* hectares of land gives the water depth, Δ.

$$\therefore \Delta = \frac{86400}{(D/b) \times 10^4} = \frac{8.64b}{D} \text{ (in metres)} \tag{3.12}$$

For the purpose of designing on the basis of the keenest demand (*i.e.*, the *kor* period requirement), the base period b and the water depth Δ are replaced by the *kor* period and the *kor* watering requirement, respectively.

Example 3.2: The culturable command area for a distributary channel is 15,000 hectares. The intensity of irrigation is 35% for wheat and 20% for rice. The *kor* periods for wheat and rice are 4 and 3 weeks, respectively. The *kor* watering depths for wheat and rice are 135 and 190 mm, respectively. Estimate the distributary discharge.

Solution:

Quantity	*Wheat*	*Rice*
Area to be irrigated (hectares)	0.35×15000 $= 5250$	0.20×15000 $= 3000$
Duty of water in the distributary, (in hectares/m^3/s)	$\frac{8.64\ (4 \times 7)}{0.135}$ $= 1792$	$\frac{8.64\ (3 \times 7)}{0.190}$ $= 954.95$
Distributary discharge (m^3/s)	$\frac{5250}{1792} = 2.93$	$\frac{3000}{954.95} = 3.14$

Since the water demands for wheat and rice are at different times, these are not cumulative. Therefore, the distributary channel should be designed for higher of the two values, *i.e.*, 3.14 m^3/s.

The *kor* period for a given crop in a region depends on the duration during which there is likelihood of the rainfall being smaller than the corresponding water requirement. Accordingly, the *kor* period is least in humid regions and more in dryer regions. The *kor* depth requirement must be met within the *kor* period. As such, the channel capacity designed on the basis of *kor* period would be large in humid regions and small in dry regions. Obviously, this method of determining the channel capacity is, therefore, not logical and rational.

A more rational method for determining the channel capacity would be to compare evopotranspiration (or consumptive use) and the corresponding effective rainfall for, say, 10-day or 15-day or 30-day periods of the entire year and determine the water requirement for each of these periods. The channel capacity can then be determined on the basis of peak water requirement of those periods.

3.3.2 Method Based on Consumptive Use

During the crop period of a crop, there is continuous movement of water from soil into roots, up the stem and leaves, and out of leaves to the atmosphere. This movement of water is necessary for carrying plant food from the soil to the various parts of the plant. Only a very small portion (less than 2%) of water absorbed by the roots is retained in the plant and the rest of the absorbed water, after performing its tasks, gets evaporated to the atmosphere mainly through the leaves and stem. This process is called *transpiration*. In addition, some water gets evaporated to the atmosphere directly from the adjacent soil and water surfaces and from surfaces of the plant leaves. The water needs of a crop, thus, consist of transpiration and evaporation, and is called consumptive use or evopotranspiration. *Evopotranspiration or consumptive* use can be defined as the amount of water needed to meet the water loss through evaporation and transpiration. Consumptive use can be expressed in terms of volume per unit area or simply the depth of water. Consumptive use helps determine the irrigation requirement (at a farm) which should, obviously, be the difference between the consumptive use and the effective precipitation.

Consumptive use (or evopotranspiration) depends on

i) Crop and its stage of growth;
ii) Climatic conditions such as temperature, humidity and wind movement, and
iii) Physical and chemical properties of soil.

Since pan evaporation (a measure of evaporation due to atmospheric temperature) and evopotranspiration depend on climatic factors, evopotranspiration D_{et} can be correlated to the pan evaporation E_p as

$$D_{et} = KE_p \tag{3.13}$$

in which K is the crop factor for the period under consideration. Pan evaporation data for different parts of India during different periods are published by the meteorological department. The crop factor K depends on the crop as well as its stage of growth (Table 3.1).

Table 3.1 Values of crop factor K

% of crop period since sowing	*Maize, Cotton, Potatoes, Peas, and Sugarbeets*	*Wheat, Barley, and other small grains*	*Sugarcane*	*Rice*
0	0.20	0.08	0.50	0.80
10	0.36	0.15	0.60	0.95
25	0.75	0.33	0.75	1.10
50	1.00	0.65	1.00	1.30
75	0.85	0.90	0.85	1.15
100	0.20	0.20	0.50	0.20

In the absence of pan evaporation data, the consumptive use u can be estimated using Blaney-Criddle formula expressed as

$$u = 25.4\,kf \tag{3.14}$$

in which u = consumptive use of crop in mm,

k = empirical crop consumptive use coefficient (Table 3.2),

f = consumptive use factor,

$$= \frac{p}{100}(1.8t + 32) \tag{3.15}$$

t = mean temperature in °C for the chosen period, and

p = percentage of daylight hours of the year occurring during the period (Table 3.3).

Table 3.2 Consumptive Use Coefficient

Crop	*Length of normal growing season or period*	*Consumptive use coefficient, k*	
		*for the growing period**	*Monthly (Maximum value) ***
Corn (Maize)	4 months	0.75 to 0.85	0.80 to 1.20
Cotton	7 months	0.60 to 0.70	0.75 to 1.10
Potatoes	3-5 months	0.65 to 0.75	0.85 to 1.00
Rice	3-5 months	1.00 to 1.10	1.10 to 1.30
Small grains	3 months	0.75 to 0.85	0.85 to 1.00
Sugarbeet	6 months	0.65 to 0.75	0.85 to 1.00
Sorghums	4-5 months	0.70 to 0.80	0.85 to 1.00
Orange and Lemon	1 year	0.45 to 0.55	0.65 to 0.75

* The lower values are for more humid areas, and the higher values are for more arid climates.

** Dependent upon mean monthly temperature and stage of growth of crop.

Table 3.3 Per cent Daylight Hours per month for Northern Hemisphere (0 - 50° latitude)

Latitude North (in degrees)	*Jan*	*Feb*	*Mar*	*Apr*	*May*	*June*	*July*	*Aug*	*Sep*	*Oct*	*Nov*	*Dec*
0	8.50	7.66	8.49	8.21	8.50	8.22	8.50	8.49	8.21	8.50	8.22	8.50
5	8.32	7.57	8.47	8.29	8.65	8.41	8.67	8.60	8.23	8.42	8.07	8.30
10	8.13	7.47	8.45	8.37	8.81	8.60	8.86	8.71	8.25	8.34	7.91	8.10
15	7.94	7.36	8.43	8.44	8.98	8.80	9.05	8.83	3.28	8.26	7.75	7.88
20	7.74	7.25	8.41	8.52	9.15	9.00	9.25	8.96	3.30	8.18	7.58	7.66
25	7.53	7.14	8.39	8.61	9.33	9.23	9.45	9.09	8.32	8.09	7.40	7.42
30	7.30	7.03	8.38	8.72	9.53	9.49	9.67	9.22	8.33	7.99	7.19	7.15
32	7.20	6.97	8.37	8.76	9.62	9.59	9.77	9.27	8.34	7.95	7.11	7.05
34	7.10	6.91	8.36	8.80	9.72	9.70	9.88	9.33	8.36	7.90	7.02	6.92
36	6.99	6.85	8.35	8.85	9.82	9.82	9.99	9.40	8.37	7.85	6.92	6.79
38	6.87	6.79	8.34	8.90	9.92	9.95	10.10	9.47	8.38	7.80	6.82	6.66
40	6.76	6.72	8.33	8.95	10.02	10.08	10.22	9.54	8.39	7.75	6.72	6.52

42	6.63	6.65	8.31	9.00	10.14	10.22	10.35	9.62	8.40	7.69	6.62	6.37
44	6.49	6.58	8.30	9.06	10.26	10.38	10.49	9.70	8.41	7.63	6.49	6.21
46	6.34	6.50	8.29	9.12	10.39	10.54	10.64	9.79	8.42	7.57	6.36	6.04
48	6.17	6.41	8.27	9.18	10.53	10.71	10.80	9.89	8.44	7.51	6.23	5.86
50	5.98	6.30	8.24	9.24	10.68	10.91	10.99	10.00	8.46	7.45	6.10	5.65

The consumptive use is generally determined on a monthly basis and the irrigation system is designed for the maximum monthly water needs.

Example 3.3: Using the Blanrey-Criddle formula, estimate the yearly consumptive use of water for sugarcane for the data given in the first four columns of Table 3.4.

Solution : Using Eqs. (3.14) and (3.15),

$$u = 25.4k \frac{p}{100} (1.8t + 32)$$

Table 3.4 Data and Solution for Example 3.2

Month	*Mean monthly temp. t °C*	*Monthly Crop Consumptive Coefficient, k*	*Per cent sunshine hours, p*	*Monthly Consumptive use, u (mm)*
Jan	13.10	0.75	7.38	78.14
Feb	15.70	0.80	7.02	85.96
Mar	20.70	0.85	8.39	125.46
Apr	27.00	0.85	8.69	151.22
May	31.10	0.90	9.48	190.66
June	33.50	0.95	9.41	209.58
July	30.60	1.00	9.60	212.34
Aug	29.00	1.00	9.60	205.31
Sep	28.20	0.95	8.33	166.35
Oct	24.70	0.90	8.01	140.01
Nov	18.80	0.85	7.25	103.06
Dec	13.70	0.75	7.24	78.15

Values of monthly consumptive use calculated from the above formula have been tabulated in the last column of Table 3.4. Thus, yearly consumptive use

$= \Sigma u = 1.75$m.

The growth of all plants can be divided into three stages, *viz.*, vegetation, flowering and fruiting. Different crops are harvested during different stages of crop growth. The consumptive use increases during the vegetative stage and attains the peak value around the flowering stage and, thereafter, the consumptive use decreases.

At each rainfall (or precipitation), some water is added to the crop field. However, the entire rainfall cannot be stored within the root zone of the soil. The part of the rainfall, which contributes to the soil moisture in the root zone soil, is effective precipitation (or rainfall) and is obtained by subtracting the sum of runoff, evaporation and deep percolation from total rainfall.

If for a given period, the consumptive use (D_{et}) exceeds the effective rainfall (D_p - D_{pl}), the difference (*i.e.*, the net irrigation requirement (NIR)) has to be supplied by the irrigation system. Thus, the field irrigation requirement (FIR) is given by

$$\text{FIR} = \frac{NIR}{E_a} = \frac{D_{et} - (D_p - D_{pl})}{E_a} \tag{3.16}$$

in which D_{et} = depth of evopotranspiration (or consumptive use),

D_p = depth of total rainfall (precipitation),

D_{pl} = depth of precipitation that goes as surface runoff and/or infiltrates into the ground and/or that intercepted by the plants, and

E_a = irrigation efficiency or application efficiency

Example 3.4: Using the data given in the first four columns of Table 3.5 for a given crop, determine the field irrigation requirement for each month assuming irrigation efficiency to be 60%.

Table 3.5 Data and Solution for Example 3.3

Month	*Crop Factor K*	*Pan Evaporation E_p (mm)*	*Effective Rainfall $D_p - D_{pl}$ (mm)*	*Consumptive Use D_{et} (mm) [Eqs. (3.13)]*	*FIR (mm) [Eqs. (3.16)]*
Nov	0.20	118.0	6.0	23.60	29.33
Dec	0.36	96.0	16.0	34.56	30.93
Jan	0.75	90.0	20.0	67.50	79.17
Feb	0.90	105.0	15.0	94.50	132.50
Mar	0.80	140.0	2.0	112.00	183.33

Field irrigation requirement for each month of the crop growing season has been calculated using Eqs. 3.13 and 3.16 and tabulated in the last column of Table 3.5.

3.4 CROP SEASONS

In India, there are two main crop seasons : *Kharif* and *Rabi*. The Kharif crops are sown in June/July and harvested in September/October. The Rabi crops are sown in October and harvested in March. Crops grown between March and June are known as *'Zaid'* crops or hot-weather crops. The sowing and harvesting time of crops of any crop season may vary depending upon the type of crop and the climatic characteristics of the region. In addition, there are crops such as sugarcane and cotton which take much longer than any of the crop seasons.

Main crops of Kharif season are rice, maize, *jawar, bajra,* groundnut and other crops. Main crops of Rabi season are wheat, barley, gram, *etc.*

Table 3.6 gives salient details of different crops.

Table 3.6 Salient Details of Some Crops of North India (Plains)

Crop	*Sowing Time*	*Harvesting Time*	*Seed Requirement (kg/ha)*	*Average Yield Under Normal Conditions (q/ha)*	*Average Water Depth (mm)*
Rice	June-July	Oct-Nov	40-50	20-40	1500-2000
Maize	June-July Jan- Feb	Sep-Oct	40-50	15-30	150-200
Sorghum (*Jawar*)	June-July	Oct-Nov	20-30	15-30	150-200
Spiked Millet (*Bajra*)	July	Oct-Nov	5-10	15-30	150-200
Groundnut	June-July	Nov-Dec	100-120	20-25	200-250
Cotton	Apr-May	Nov-Jan	15-20	2-5 (with seeds)	500-700
Wheat	Nov-Dec	Apr-May	100-120	20-40	300-400
Barley	Oct-Nov	Mar-Apr	80-100	20-40	250-300
Gram	Oct-Nov	Mar-Apr	30-40	15-30	250-300
Sugarcane	Oct-Nov Feb-Mar	Oct-Apr	3000-4000	8000-10,000	1500-2000
Potatoes	Sep-Dec	Nov-Feb	1500-2500	25,000-30,000	400-500

EXERCISES

1. What are the crop seasons and main crops thereof in India?
2. What is the meaning of consumptive use? On what factors does it depend? How would one calculate the consumptive use for a given crop?
3. The consumptive use for a given crop is 90 mm. Determine the field irrigation requirement if the effective rainfall and the irrigation efficiency in the area are 15 mm and 60 per cent respectively.
4. What is meant by 'duty' of canal water? Obtain an expression for 'duty' in terms of water depth. Distinguish between 'duty' and 'outlet discharge factor'.

5. An outlet is required to serve 6000 ha of CCA. Determine the discharge for which the outlet should be designed for the following data:

	Wheat	Rice
Intensity of irrigation	20%	10%
Kor period	3 weeks	2 weeks
Kor water depth	90 mm	250 mm

6. An outlet has a gross commanded area of 500 ha out of which only 80% is culturable. The intensity of irrigation for the Rabi season is 65% while it is 30% for the Kharif season. Assuming losses in conveyance system as 6 per cent of the outlet discharge, determine the discharge at the head of the irrigation channel. Assume outlet discharge factor for the Rabi season as 1500 ha/m^3/s and for the Kharif season as 800 ha/m^3/s.
7. The maximum discharge available at an outlet of an irrigation channel is 1.33 m^3/s. The culturable command area for the outlet is 8000 ha. What percentage of this area can be irrigated for wheat if the kor period is 3 weeks and the kor water depth is 13.5 cm?

Chapter 4

Well Irrigation

4.1 GENERAL

The amount of water stored in the earth's crust is estimated to be around 8 billion cubic kilometres, half of which is at depths less than 800 metres. This volume of water is about 35 times the combined storage of all the world's rivers, fresh water lakes, reservoirs and inland seas. Ground water is that part of the subsurface water which occurs within the saturated zone of the earth's crust where all voids (or pores) are filled with water. The estimate of the present ground water resources in India is of the order of 650 cubic km (as against 1780 cubic km for surface water resources) out of which utilisable ground water is assessed at around 420 cubic km (as against 690 cubic km for surface water resources). In view of the large amount of utilisable ground water, its quality and also better agricultural yields with well irrigation, it is only logical to develop ground water resources for irrigation and other activities. A hole or shaft, usually vertical, is excavated in the earth to lift ground water to the earth's surface and is termed a *well.* Following are the main requirements for the success of well irrigation.

i) Presence of a suitable aquifer which can yield good quality water in sufficient quantity.
ii) Availability of energy preferably electric power for pumps.
iii) Well distributed demand for irrigation throughout the year.
iv) Suitable configuration of command area with the highest ground around the centre of the command area.

In general, well irrigation is more efficient than canal irrigation. Following are the comparative features of the two types of irrigation:

i) In canal irrigation system, major structures, such as headworks, main and branch canals, *etc.*, must be constructed prior to the start of proportionate agricultural activity which grows gradually because of the availability of irrigation facility. But wells can be constructed gradually to keep pace with the development of the agricultural activities in the area.

ii) Transit losses in well irrigation are much less than in canal irrigation system.
iii) Isolated patches of high lands can be better served by well irrigation.
iv) Well irrigation offers an effective anti-waterlogging measure for the affected lands, and reduces the chances of waterlogging of canal-irrigated lands.
v) Well irrigation ensures relatively more reliable supply of water at the time of need. This results in better yield. Besides, farmers can switch over to more remunerative crops due to the availability of the assured supply.
vi) Well irrigation needs energy for pumping. Installation and maintenance of pumps and the cost of running the pumps make well irrigation relatively costlier.
vii) Failure of power supply at the time of the keenest demand may adversely affect the yield in case of well irrigation systems.

It is, thus, obvious that both irrigation systems have advantages as well as disadvantages. Therefore, both must be used in a judicious manner (Conjunctive use) to obtain maximum benefits such that there is no waterlogging and the ground water resource can be maintained indefinitely.

4.2 OCCURRENCE OF GROUND WATER

The subsurface medium within which ground water occurs is either porous or fractured or both. The subsurface occurrence of ground water can be divided into two zones (Fig. 4.1): (i) Vadose zone or unsaturated zone or zone of aeration, and (ii) Phreatic zone or saturated zone or zone of saturation. In the saturated zone, all pores or voids are filled with water, whereas in the unsaturated zone, pores contain gases (mainly air and water vapours) in addition to water. The water table is defined as the upper limit of saturation at atmospheric pressure in the saturated zone.

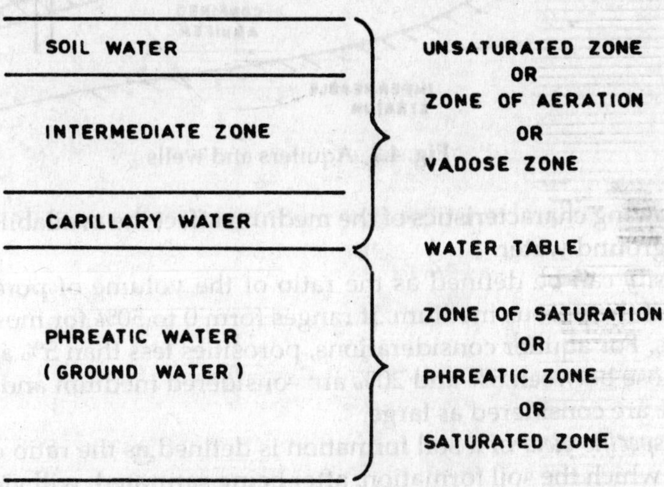

Fig. 4.1 Vertical distribution of sub-surface water

A saturated geological formation capable of yielding water economically in sufficient quantity is known as an *aquifer* (or water-bearing formation or ground water reservoir). Ground water is constantly moving through an aquifer under local hydraulic gradients. Thus, aquifers perform storage as well as conduit functions. Ground water may exist in aquifers in two different manners: (i) unconfined, and (ii) confined. The unconfined condition occurs when the water table is under atmospheric pressure and is free to rise or fall with changes in the volume of the stored water. An aquifer with unconfined conditions is referred to as an unconfined or watertable aquifer. An aquifer which is separated from the unsaturated zone by an impermeable or very less permeable formation is known as confined aquifer (or artesian aquifer or pressure aquifer). Ground water in confined aquifer is under pressure which is greater than the atmospheric pressure. The water level in a well penetrating a confined aquifer indicates the piezometric pressure at that point and will be above the bottom of the upper confining formation. Such wells are known as artesian wells, and if the water level rises above the land surface, a flowing well results (Fig. 4.2).

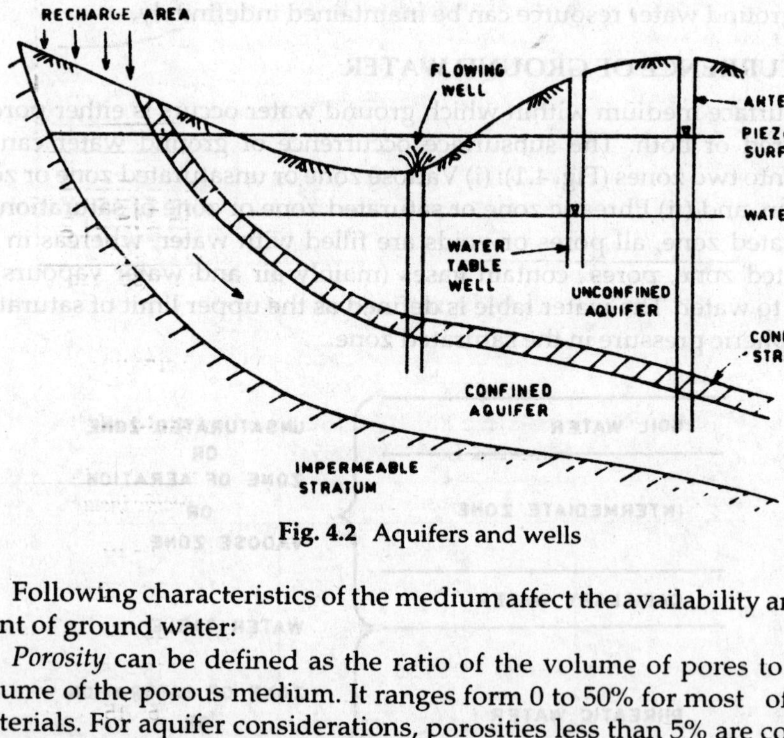

Fig. 4.2 Aquifers and wells

Following characteristics of the medium affect the availability and movement of ground water:

Porosity can be defined as the ratio of the volume of pores to the total volume of the porous medium. It ranges form 0 to 50% for most of the rock materials. For aquifer considerations, porosities less than 5% are considered small, those between 5% and 20% are considered medium and those greater than 20% are considered as large.

The *specific yield* of a soil formation is defined as the ratio of the volume of water which the soil formation, after being saturated, will yield by gravity to the volume of the soil formation.

The *specific retention* of a soil formation is defined as the ratio of the volume of water which the soil formation, after being saturated, will retain against the pull of gravity to the volume of the soil formation.

Obviously, the sum of the specific yield and the specific retention would be equal to the porosity of the given soil formation. The product of the average specific yield of a saturated water-bearing formation and its total volume gives the volume of water which can be recovered from the formation by gravity drainage. Fine-grained materials may have lesser specific yield than coarse material even though their porosity may be greater (Fig. 4.3) and Table 4.1.

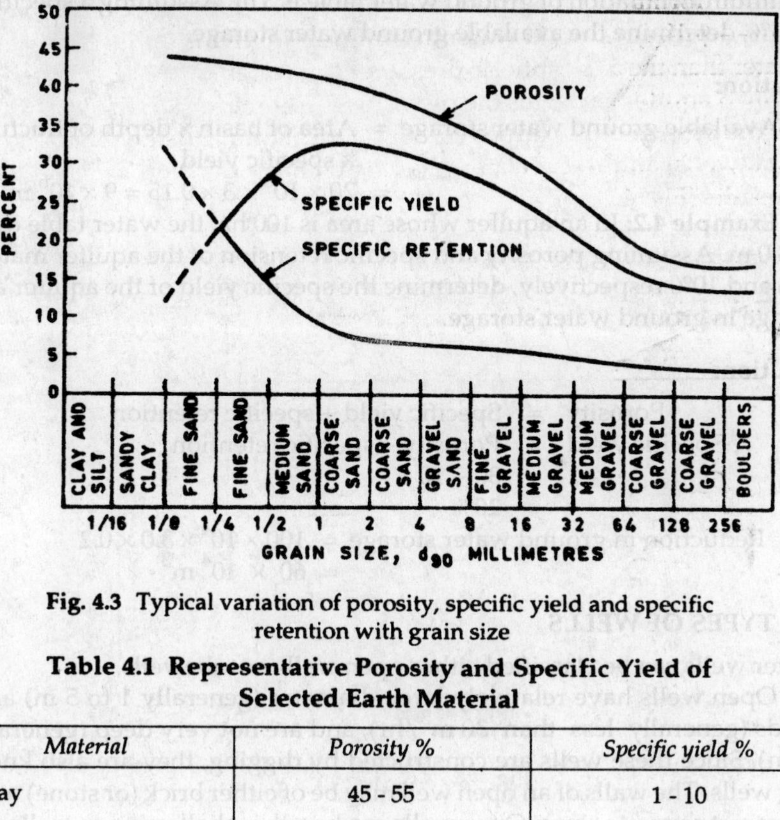

Fig. 4.3 Typical variation of porosity, specific yield and specific retention with grain size

Table 4.1 Representative Porosity and Specific Yield of Selected Earth Material

Material	*Porosity %*	*Specific yield %*
Clay	45 - 55	1 - 10
Sand	25 - 40	10 - 30
Gravel	25 - 40	15 - 30
Sand and gravel	10 - 35	15 - 25
Sandstone	5 - 30	5 - 15
Shale	0 - 10	0.5 - 5
Limestone	1 - 20	0.5 - 5

In case of confined aquifers, there is no dewatering or draining of the material unless the hydraulic head drops below the top of the aquifer. Therefore, the concept of specific yield does not apply to confined aquifers and an alternative term, storage coefficient or storativity is used for confied aquifers. *Storativity* or *storage coefficient* is defined as the volume of water an aquifer would release from, or takes into storage per unit surface area of the aquifer for a unit change in head. Its value is of the order of 5×10 to 1×10^{-5}. For the same drop in head, the yield from an unconfined aquifer is much greater than that from a confined aquifer.

Example 4.1: A ground water basin consists of 20 km^2 of plains. The maximum fluctuation of ground water table is 3 m. Assuming a specific yield of 15%, determine the available ground water storage.

Solution:

Available ground water storage = Area of basin × depth of fluctuation × specific yield

$$= 20 \times 10^6 \times 3 \times 0.15 = 9 \times 10^6 \text{ m}^3.$$

Example 4.2: In an aquifer whose area is 100 ha, the water table dropped by 3.0 m. Assuming porosity and specific retension of the aquifer material as 30% and 10% respectively, determine the specific yield of the aquifer and the change in ground water storage.

Solution:

Porosity = Specific yield + specific retention

∴ Specific yield = Porosity – specific retention

= 30 – 10

= 20%

Reduction in ground water storage $= 100 \times 10^4 \times 3.0 \times 0.2$

$= 60 \times 10^4 \text{ m}^3$

4.3 TYPES OF WELLS

Water wells can be classified either open wells or tubewells.

Open wells have relatively large diameter (generally 1 to 5 m) and low yields (generally less than 30 m^3/hr), and are not very deep (generally 3 to 15 m). Since these wells are constructed by digging, they are also known as dug wells. The walls of an open well may be of either brick (or stone) masonry or precast concrete rings. Open wells can be either shallow open wells or deep open wells. A shallow open well drains its supplies only from the top upper aquifer. But deep open wells are those which rest on an impervious stratum and draw their supplies from the pervious water-bearing stratum lying below the impervious stratum through a bore hole made in the impervious stratum. As shown in Fig. 4.4, a deep open well can have its depth smaller than a shallow open well in the vicinity.

A tube well is in the form of a long pipe with holes (or slots) at suitable locations and which is sunk into the ground intercepting one or more aquifers. The diameter of a tube well is usually in the range of about 8 to 60 cm. The

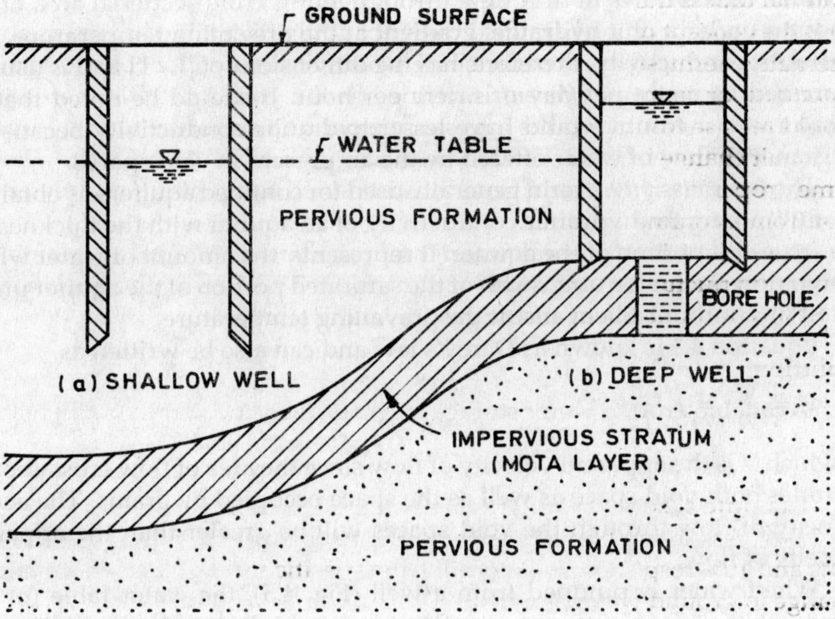

Fig. 4.4 Shallow and deep open wells

depth of a shallow tube well is usually limited to about 30 m. A deep tube well can have depths upto about 600 m.

4.4 WELL HYDRAULICS

Flow of ground water through porous medium is governed by well-known Darcy's law which states that the rate of flow, Q through a saturated porous medium is

i) proportional to the difference in hydraulic head Δh between the two flow sections,
ii) proportional to the area of flow cross-section A, and
iii) inversely proportional to the length, L between the two sections. Thus,

$$Q = KA\frac{\Delta h}{L} \tag{4.1}$$

Here, K is a constant of proportionality and is equal to the hydraulic conductivity (or coefficient of permeability). The *permeability* of a porous medium describes the ease with which a fluid will pass through it. Therefore, it depends on the characteristics of the medium as well as the flowing fluid. The permeability of a medium is measured in terms of hydraulic conductivity (also known as the coefficient of permeability) which is equal to the volume of water which flows in unit time through a unit cross-sectional area of the medium under a unit hydraulic gradient at the prevailing temperature. The hydraulic conductivity, therefore, has the dimensions of [L/T] and is usually expressed as metre per day or metre per hour. It should be noted that an unsaturated medium would have lesser hydraulic conductivity because of resistance to flow of water offered by the air present in void spaces.

The *transmissivity*, a term generally used for confined aquifers, is obtained by multiplying the hydraulic conductivity of an aquifer with the thickness of the saturated portion of the aquifer. It represents the amount of water which would flow through a unit width of the saturated portion of the aquifer under a unit hydraulic gradient and at the prevailing temperature.

Equation 4.1 is known as Darcy's law and can also be written as

$$V = \frac{Q}{A} = K\frac{\Delta h}{L}$$

in which V is the apparent velocity of flow since the area of flow cross-section includes both void space as well as the space occupied by grains. The actual velocity of flow through the void spaces will be greater than the apparent velocity of flow.

When water is pumped from a well (Fig. 4.5), the water table (or the piezometric surface in case of a confined aquifer) is lowered around the well. The surface of a lowered water table resembles a cone and is, therefore, called

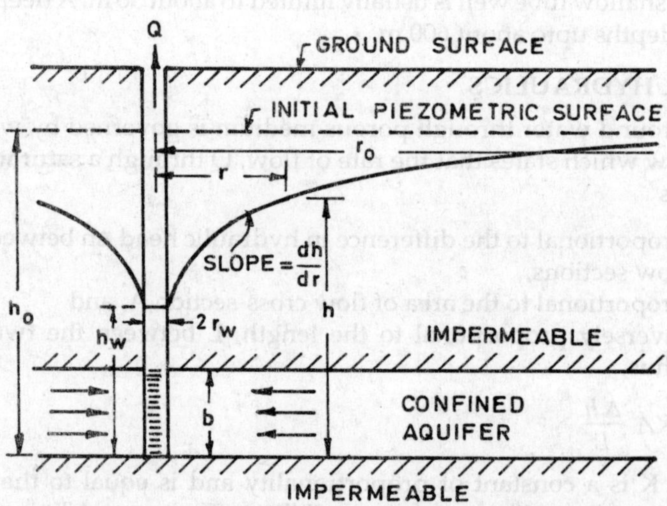

Fig. 4.5 Radial flow towards a well in a confined aquifer

the cone of depression. The vertical distance between the initial position of stable water table and the lowered water table due to pumping is known as the drawdown. The drawdown decreases with increase in the distance from the well. The distance between the well and the location at which the draw-down is negligible is termed the radius of influence of the well. Well yield is defined as the volume of water discharged, either by pumping or free flow, per unit time.

With continued pumping of a well, the cone of depression continues to expand in an extensive aquifer until the pumping rate is balanced by the recharge rate. When pumping and recharging rates balance each other, a steady or equilibrium condition exists and there is no further increase in drawdown with continued pumping. For a confined aquifer, the well discharge Q, under equilibrium condition, is obtained as

$$Q = -2\pi kB \frac{h_o - h_w}{\log_e^{r_o}/r_w} \tag{4.2}$$

and the variation of h is expressed as

$$h = h_o + \frac{Q}{2\pi kB} \log_e (r_o/r) \tag{4.3}$$

$$h = h_w - \frac{Q}{2\pi kB} \log_e (r/r_w) \tag{4.4}$$

and the drawdown s at any radius r is expressed as

$$s = h_o - h = -\frac{Q}{2\pi kB} \log_e (r_o/r) \tag{4.5}$$

Therefore, drawdown in the well (*i.e.*, $r = r_w$) s_w is given as

$$s_w = h_o - h_w = -\frac{Q}{2\pi kB} \log_e (r_o/r_w) \tag{4.6}$$

For unconfined aquifers, Eqs. 4.2 to 4.6 attain the following form:

$$Q = -\pi k \frac{H_o^2 - H_w^2}{\log_e r_o/r_w} \tag{4.7}$$

$$H^2 = H_o^2 + \frac{Q}{\pi k} \log_e (r_o/r) \tag{4.8}$$

$$H = H_w^2 - \frac{Q}{\pi k} \log_e (r/r_w) \tag{4.9}$$

$$H_o^2 - H^2 = -\frac{Q}{\pi k} \log_e (r_o/r) \tag{4.10}$$

$$H_o^2 - H_w^2 = -\frac{Q}{\pi k} \log_e (r_o/r_w) \tag{4.11}$$

In Eqs. 4.2 to 4.11, the value of the discharge Q for a pumping well is substituted with a negative sign.

4.5 METHODS OF WELL CONSTRUCTION

Shallow wells, generally less than about 15 m, are constructed by digging, boring, driving or jetting. Deep wells are constructed using drilling methods. Wells for irrigation purposes are generally deep wells.

4.5.1 Digging

Wells in shallow and unconsolidated glacial and alluvial aquifers can be dug by hand using a pick and shovel. Loose material is brought to the surface in a container by means of rope and pulleys. The depth of a dug well may vary from about 3 to 15 m depending upon the position of the water table. Dug wells usually have large diameter ranging from about 1 to 5 m. Dug wells penetrate about 4 to 6 m below the water table. The yield of the dug wells is generally small and is of the order of about 500 litres per minute.

4.5.2 Boring

Hand-operated or power-driven earth augers are used for boring a well in shallow and unconsolidated aquifers. A simple auger has a cutting edge at the bottom of a cylindrical container (or bucket). The auger bores into the ground with rotary motion. When the container is full of excavated material, it is raised and emptied. Hand-bored wells can be upto about 20 cm diameter and about 15 m deep. Power-driven augers can bore holes upto about one metre in diameter and 30 m in depth.

4.5.3 Driving

In this method, a series of connected lengths of pipe is driven by repeated impacts into the ground to below the water table. Water enters the well through a screened cylindrical section which is protected during driving by a steel cone at the bottom. Driven wells can be installed only in unconsolidated formation which are relatively free of cobbles or boulders. The diameters of driven wells are in the range of about 3 to 10 cm. Such wells can be constructed upto about 10 m, if hand driven, and upto about 15 m when heavy hammers of about 300 kg are used. The maximum yield of driven wells is usually around 200 litres per minute. The main advantage of a driven well is that it can be constructed in a short time, at minimum cost and by one man.

4.5.4 Jetting

Jetting (or jet drilling) method uses a chisel-shaped bit attached to the lower end of a pipe string. Holes on each side of the bit serve as nozzles. Water jetting through these nozzles keeps the bit clean and helps loosen the material being drilled. The fluid circulation system is similar to that of direct rotary drilling method. With water circulation maintained, the drill rods and the bit are lifted and dropped in a manner similar to cable tool drilling but with shorter strokes. Jet drilling is limited to drilling of about 10 cm diameter wells to depths of about 60 m although larger diameter wells have been drilled upto about 300 m by this method. Other drilling methods have displaced the jet drilling for deep and large diameter wells.

4.5.5 Cable Tool Drilling

It is the earliest drilling method developed by the Chinese some 4000 years ago. A cable tool drilling equipment mainly consists of a drill bit, drill stem, drilling jars, swivel socket and cable (Fig. 4.6). The cable tool drill bit is very heavy (about 1500 kg) and crushes all types of earth materials. The drill stem provides additional weight to the bit and its length helps in maintaining a straight vertical hole while drilling in hard rock. The length of the drill stem varies from about 2 to 10 m and its diameter varies from 5 to 15 cm. It weighs about 50 to 1500 kg. Drilling jars consist of a pair of linked steel bars and help in loosening the tools when these stick in the hole. Under normal tension of the drilling line, the jars are fully extended. When tools get stuck, the drilling line is slackened and then lifted upward. This causes an upward blow to the tools which, as a result, are released. Swivel socket (or rope socket) connects the string of tools to the cable. The wire cable (about 25 mm in diameter), which carries and rotates the drilling tool on each upstroke, is called the drill line. The cable tool drilling rig mainly consists of a mast, a multiline hoist, a walking beam, and an engine. Drill cuttings are removed from the well by means of bailers having capacities of about 10 to 350 litres. A bailer is simply a pipe with a valve at the bottom and a ring at the top for attachment to the bailer line. The valve allows the cuttings to enter the bailer but prevents them from escaping. Another type of bailer is called the sand pump or suction bailer which is fitted with a plunger. An upward pull on the plunger produces a vacuum which opens the valve and sucks sand or slurried cuttings into the tubing.

While drilling through consolidated formations, most boreholes are drilled as "open hole", *i.e.*, no casing is used during drilling operation. In such conditions, the cable tool bit is essentially a crusher. On the other hand, there is a danger of caving in while drilling through unconsolidated formations. For this reason, casing pipe must follow the drill bit closely to keep the borehole open in unconsolidated formations.

For the driving operation of the casing pipe, a drive head is fitted to the top of the casing. The drive head serves as an anvil and protects the top of the casing. Similarly, a drive shoe made of hardened and tempered steel is attached to the lower end of the casing pipe. The shoe prevents the damage to the bottom end of the casing pipe when it is being driven. Casing is driven down by means of drive clamps — constructed of heavy steel forgings made in halves — fastened to the top of the drill stem. Drive clamps act as the hammer face, and the up and down motion of tools provide the weight for striking the top of the casing pipe and, thus, driving it into the ground.

The procedure for drilling through unconsolidated formation consists of repeated driving, drilling and bailing operations. The casing pipe is initially driven for about 1 to 3 m in the ground. The material within the casing pipe is then mixed with water by the drill bit to form slurry. The slurry is bailed out and the casing pipe is driven again. Sometimes, the hole is drilled 1 to 2 m below the casing pipe; the casing is then driven down to the undisturbed

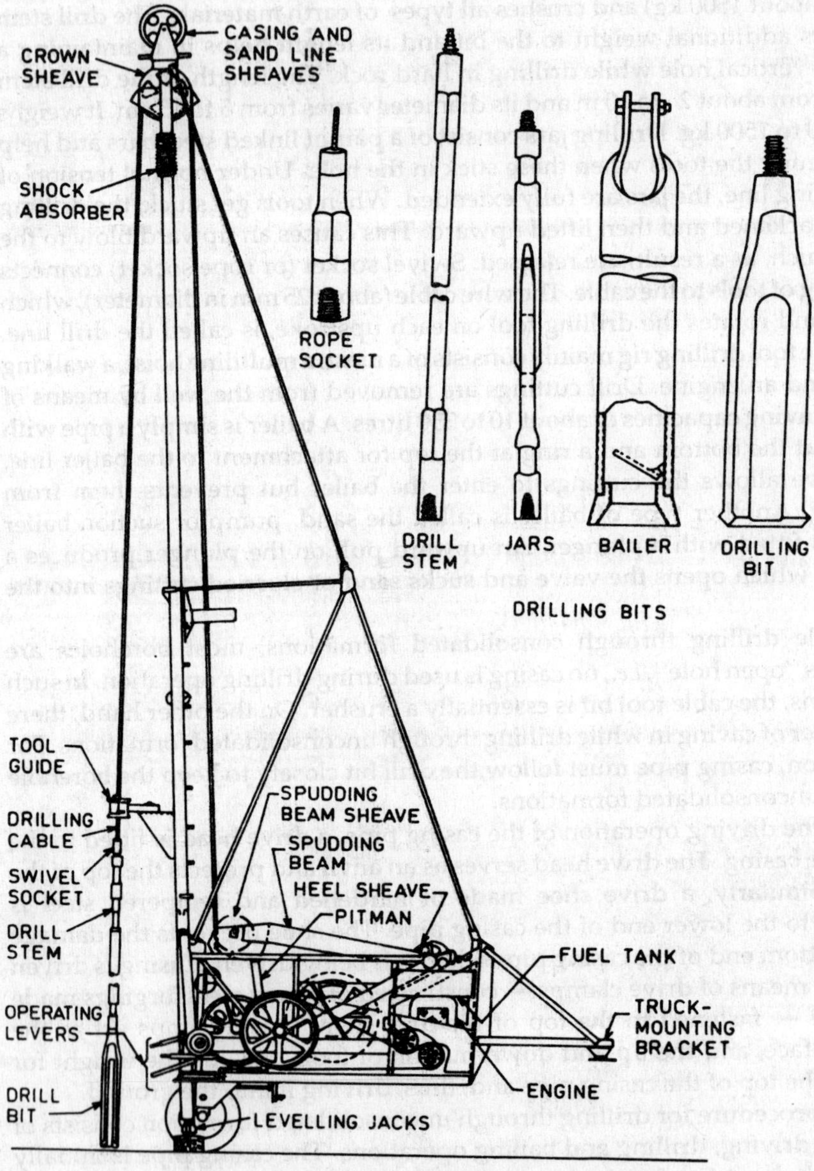

Fig. 4.6 Line diagram of cable tool drilling rig

material and drilling is resumed. The drilling tools make 40 to 60 strokes of about 40 to 100 cm length every minute. The drill line is rotated during drilling so that the borehole is round. The slurry formed by mixing of cuttings with added water (if not encountered in the ground) reduces the friction on the cutting bit and helps in bailing operations.

If the friction on the outside of the casing pipe increases so much that the casing pipe cannot be driven any more or further driving might damage the pipe, a string of smaller casing is inserted inside the first one. Drilling is, thus, continued. Sometimes, two or three such reductions may be required to reach the desired aquifer. The diameter of the well is reduced. If such situation is anticipated, casing in upper part should be of larger diameter.

The drilling process through consolidated formation, not requiring casing, would consist of repeated drilling and bailing operations only.

The cable tool method has survived mainly because of its suitability of a wide variety of geological conditions. It offers the following advantages.

i) Cable tool drilling rigs are relatively cheaper.
ii) The rigs are simpler and require little sophisticated maintenance.
iii) The machines have low power requirements.
iv) Borehole is stable during the entire drilling operation.
v) Recovery of reliable samples is possible at every depth.
vi) Wells can be drilled in water-scarce areas.
vii) Because of their size, the machines can be operated in more rugged, inaccessible terrains or in other areas where limited space is available.
viii) Wells can be drilled in formations where water is likely to be lost.

Slow drilling rate, higher cost of casing pipe and difficulty in pulling back long strings of casing pipe are the disadvantages of cable tool drilling.

4.5.6 Direct Rotary Drilling

The direct rotary drilling is the fastest method of drilling deep wells of diameter upto 45 cm (or more with the use of reamers) through unconsolidated formations. The drilling bit is attached to a heavy drill pipe which is screwed to the end of the kelly which is a drill pipe of square section (Fig. 4.7). The drill collar or stabiliser helps in maintaining straight hole in soft formations through its large wall contact.

The drill pipe is turned by a rotating table which fits closely around kelly and allows the drill rod to slide downward as the hole deepens. The drilling rig consists of a mast, a rotating table, a pump, a hoist and an engine. The borehole is drilled by rotating a hollow bit attached to the lower end of a string of a drill pipe. Cuttings are removed continuously by pumping drilling fluid (mixture of clay and water with some additives to make it viscous) down through the drill pipe and through the orifices in the bit. The drilling fluid, then, flows upward through the annular space between the drill pipe and the borehole, carrying the cuttings in suspension to the surface settling pits where the cuttings settle down in the pits. The clear drilling fluid is pumped back

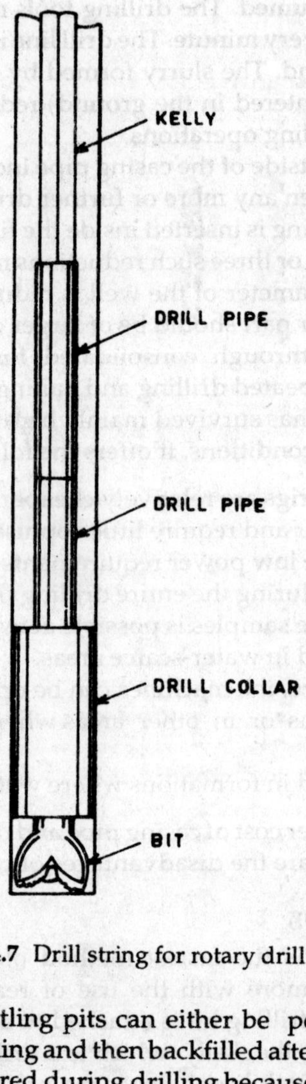

Fig. 4.7 Drill string for rotary drilling

into the borehole. The settling pits can either be portable or excavated for temporary use during drilling and then backfilled after completion of the well. Usually, no casing is required during drilling because the drilling mud forms a clay lining on the borehole walls which prevents caving in of the formation materials. After drilling, the casing pipe with perforated sections opposite aquifers is lowered into the borehole.

Drilling rotary method has become the most common method due to its following advantages:

i) Drilling rates are relatively high.
ii) Minimum casing is required during drilling.
iii) Rig mobilisation and demobilisation are fast.
iv) Well screens can be set easily as part of the casing installation.

Some major disadvantages of direct rotary method are as follows:

i) Drilling rigs are expensive.
ii) Maintenance of drilling rigs is costly.
iii) Mobility of rigs is restricted depending on the slope and wetness of the land surface.
iv) Collection of accurate samples requires special procedures.
v) Drilling fluid may cause plugging of some aquifer formations.

4.6.7 Reverse Rotary Drilling

Direct rotary drilling method is capable of drilling boreholes with maximum diameter of about 60 cm. High capacity wells, particularly those with filter pack, need to be much larger in size. Besides, the drilling rate becomes smaller with increase in borehole diameter in the case of direct rotary drilling. To overcome these limitations of direct rotary drilling, the reverse rotary drilling technique has been developed. This technique is capable of drilling boreholes of about 1.2 m diameter in unconsolidated formation. Recently, reverse rotary method has been used in soft consolidated rocks, such as sandstone and even in hard rocks using both water and air as the drilling fluid.

In reverse rotary drilling, the flow of the drilling fluid is reversed in comparison to that of direct rotary drilling. The reverse rotary drilling rig is similar to that of direct rotary drilling rig except that it requires larger-capacity centrifugal pumps, larger-diameter drill pipe and other components also of relatively larger size. The drilling fluid moves down the annular space between the borehole wall and the drill pipe, picks up the cuttings before entering the drill pipe through the ports of the drill bit. The drilling fluid alongwith its cuttings move upward inside the drill pipe which has been connected to the suction end of a centrifugal pump through kelly and swivel.

The mixture is brought to a settling pit where the cuttings settle at the bottom and the drilling fluid (*i.e.*, muddy water) moves down the borehole again. The drilling fluid is usually water mixed with fine-grained soil only. The hydrostatic pressure and the velocity head of the drilling fluid moving down the borehole supports the borehole wall. Therefore, to prevent caving of the hole, the fluid level must always be upto the ground surface even when drilling is suspended temporarily.

Advantages of the reverse rotary drilling method are as follows:

i) The formation near the borehole is relatively undisturbed compared to other methods.
ii) Large-diameter holes can be drilled rapidly and economically.
iii) No casing is required during the drilling operation.
iv) Well screens can be set easily while installing the casing.
v) The boreholes can be drilled through most geologic formations excepting igneous and metamorphic rocks.
vi) Because of low velocity of the drilling fluid, there is little possibility of its entering the formation.

Disadvantages of the reverse rotary drilling method are as follows:

i) Large quantity of water is needed.
ii) Reverse rotary drilling rig is costlier because of larger size of equipment.
iii) Large mud pits are required.
iv) Some drill sites may be inaccessible because of the larger size of the rig.

4.6 WELL COMPLETION

After drilling a well, well screen and filter pack (wherever necessary) are to be placed and the casing removed. If the formations are sufficiently strong and stable, ground water may directly enter into the uncased well. In unconsolidated formations, however, a casing with perforations (or a well screen) is needed to support the outside material and also to admit water freely into the well.

Installation of well screen and removal of casing is best done by pull-back method in which the casing is installed to the full depth of the well and the well screen (whose size is smaller than that of casing) is lowered inside the casing. Casing is, then, pulled back or lifted far enough to expose the screen to the water-bearing formation.

4.7 DEVELOPMENT OF WELLS

Drilling operations for well excavation change the hydraulic characteristics of the formation materials in the vicinity of the borehole. Very often, these changes result in the reduction of the hydraulic conductivity close to the borehole. When a well is drilled with cable tool rig equipped with casing driver, the repeated blows on the casing will rearrange the grains in the vicinity of the casing. In rotary drilling methods, the drilling fluids containing clay may flow into the aquifer for some distance and, thus, plug the pore spaces of the permeable formation. Before commissioning the well for use, it is, therefore, necessary to repair the damage done to the aquifer by the drilling operations. Besides, there is also a need to improve the basic physical characteristics of the aquifer in the vicinity of the well screen so that water can flow more freely into the well. A well is, therefore, 'developed' in order to attain these two objectives and, thus, maximise well yield. Well development involves applying some form of energy to the water-bearing formation in the vicinity of the well so as to remove fine materials (including drilling mud) from the aquifer and rearrange formation particles so that the well yields clear sand-free water in maximum quantity with minimum drawdown. Well development serves the following beneficial purposes:

i) It increases the permeability of the aquifer material surrounding the well and filter pack (if present) by
   a) reducing the compaction and intermixing of grains of different sizes during drilling by removing fine grains,

b) removing the filter cake or drilling fluid film that coats the borehole,
c) removing much or all of the drilling fluid which had entered the aquifer,
d) breaking sand-grain bridging across the screen openings, and
e) increasing the natural porosity of the previously undisturbed formation near the borehole by removing the finer fraction of the aquifer material.

ii) It creates a graded zone of aquifer material around the screen in a naturally developed well. This effect stabilises the formation so that the well will yield sand-free water.
iii) It reduces the head loss near the well screen.
iv) It increases the useful life of the well screen.
v) It brings the well to its maximum specific capacity, *i.e.*, the maximum yield at minimum drawdown.

The procedures usually adopted for well development are as follows:

i) Overpumping
ii) Backwashing
iii) Mechanical surging
iv) Air surging and pumping
v) High-velocity jetting
vi) High-velocity water jetting combined with simultaneous pumping.

There are several variations of most of these methods. Only the main features of these methods have been described in the following paragraphs.

4.7.1 Overpumping

In the overpumping method, the well is pumped at a discharge rate higher than the discharge rate of the well during its normal operation. The logic of the method is that any well which can be pumped sand-free at a high rate can be pumped sand-free at a lower rate. It is the simplest method of developing wells. However, the development by this method is not effective, and the developed well is seldom efficient. The aquifer material is also not fully stabilized. This incomplete development is due to the following reasons:

i) Water flows in one direction only and some sand grains may be left in a bridged condition. The formation is thus partially stabilized.
ii) Most of the development takes place in the most permeable zones of the aquifer which are usually closest to the top of the screen. Therefore, lesser development takes place in the lower layers of the aquifer.

Besides, this method usually uses the pump intended for regular use during the normal operation of the well. Pumping of silt-laden water at higher rates can reduce efficiency of the pump.

4.7.2 Backwashing

Reversal of flow through the screen openings will agitate the aquifer material, remove the finer fraction and rearrange the remaining aquifer particles. These effects will usually cause effective development of well. To minimise the chances of sand-locking the pump, the discharging rate of the pump should be gradually increased to the maximum capacity before stopping the pump. During this process, the well is occasionally pumped to waste to remove the sand brought to the well by surging action of this method of well development. As in the case of overpumping method, the surging action may be concentrated only in the upper layers of the aquifer. Besides, the surging effect is not vigorous enough to cause maximum benefits. When compared with other methods of well development, the overall effectiveness of backwashing as well as overpumping methods in case of high capacity wells is rather limited.

4.7.3 Mechanical Surging

In this method, a close-fitting surge plunger, moving up and down in the well casing, forces water to flow into and out of the well screen. The initial movements of the plunger should be relatively gentle so that the material blocking the screen may go into suspension and then move into the well. To minimise the problem of fine materials going back to the aquifer from the well, the fine material should be removed from the well as often as possible. Surging method is capable of breaking sand bridges and produces good results. However, it is not very effective in developing filter-packed wells because the water movement is confined upto the filterpack only and the aquifer remains unaffected by the surging action.

4.7.4 Air Surging and Pumping

This method requires two concentric pipes: the inner pipe is known as air line and the outer one is known as pumping pipe. The assembly of these pipes is lowered into the well. In air surging, compressed air is injected through air line into the well to force aerated water up through the annular space between the air line and the pumping pipe. As this aerated water reaches the top of the casing, the air supply is stopped so that aerated water column starts falling. Air-lift pumping is used to pump the well periodically to remove the sand brought into the well as a result of air surging. The compressed air produces powerful surging action. This method is used to develop wells in consolidated and unconsolidated formations.

4.7.5 High-Velocity Jetting

This method consists of shooting out high-velocity jets of water from a jetting tool to the aquifer through the screen openings. The equipment for this method consists of a jetting tool provided with two or more equally spaced nozzles, high-pressure pump, high-pressure hose and connections, and a water supply source. The forceful action of high-velocity jets loosens the drilling mud, and agitates and rearranges the sand and gravel particles around the well. The loosened material is removed by pumping. In this method of development, the entire surface of the screen can be subjected to vigorous jet action by slowly rotating and gradually raising and lowering the jetting tool.

This method has the following advantages:

i) The energy is concentrated over a small area with greater effectiveness.
ii) Every part of the screen can be developed selectively.
iii) The method is relatively simple.

The method of jetting is particularly successful in developing highly stratified and unconsolidated water-bearing formations.

4.7.6 High-Velocity Water Jetting Combined with Simultaneous Pumping

The method of high-velocity water jetting results in very effective development of wells. But maximum development efficiency can be obtained by combining high-velocity water jetting with simultaneous air-lift pumping or some other suitable pumping method. The method requires that the volume of water pumped from the well should always be more than the volume of water pumped into the well so that the water level in the well is always below the static level, and there is continuous movement of water from the aquifer to the well. This will help in removing some of the suspended material loosened by the jetting operation.

4.8 PUMPING EQUIPMENT FOR WATER WELLS

In most of the wells, static water level is below the ground surface and, hence, flowing wells are rare. The water has to be lifted from inside the well to the ground surface. Rope and bucket with or without windlass have been used and are still being used for shallow wells and for low discharges. For deeper wells and high yields of water, pumps have to be used.

The purpose of installing pumps in wells is to lift water from inside the well to the ground surface. The main factors which must be considered while selecting a pump for water well are the anticipated pumping conditions, specific installation and maintenance conditions, and the basic pump characteristics. As in well construction, the initial cost of the pump and its installation is relatively less important than the performance, reliability and operating costs during the life span of the pumping equipment.

Pumps can be broadly classified as shallow-well pumps and deep-well pumps depending upon the position of the pump and not the depth of the well. A shallow-well pump is installed on the ground and lifts water from the well by suction lift. A deep-well pump is installed within the well casing and its inlet is submerged below the pumping level. If the pumping level is lower than the limit of the suction lift (about 7.5 m), only the deep-well pump must be used.

Pumps are also classified on the basis of their design as positive displacement pumps and variable displacement pumps. Positive displacement pumps discharge almost the same volume of water irrespective of the head against which they operate. The input power, however, varies in direct proportion to the head. Such pumps are used extensively in ground water-monitoring wells, hand pump-equipped wells and wind-powered wells. They are rarely used for large-capacity water wells. Most common type of positive displacement pumps is the piston pump.

The variable displacement pumps are used for large-capacity wells. For these pumps, there is inverse relationship between the discharge and the working head. Maximum input power is required when the pump has to operate at low heads delivering large volumes of water. The major types of variable displacement pumps are as follows:

i) Centrifugal Pumps
   a) Suction lift pump
   b) Deep-well turbine pump
   c) Submersible turbine pump
ii) Jet pumps
iii) Air-lift pumps.

4.8.1 Centrifugal Pumps

Centrifugal pumps are the most popular pumps. They are capable of delivering large volumes of water against high as well as low heads with good efficiency. Besides, these pumps are relatively simple and compact. The basic principle of centrifugal pumping can be understood by considering the effect of swinging a bucket of water around in a circle at the end of a rope. The centrifugal force causes the water to press against the bottom of the bucket rather than spill out of the bucket. If a hole is cut in the bottom, water would discharge through the opening at a velocity which would depend on the centrifugal force. If an airtight cover was put on the bucket top, a partial vacuum would be created inside the bucket as water leaves through the opening in the bottom. If a water source is connected to the airtight cover through an intake pipe, the partial vacuum could draw additional water into the bucket as the water is being discharged through the bottom hole. The bucket and cover of this example correspond to the casing of a centrifugal pump; the discharge hole and the intake pipe correspond to the pump outlet and inlet respectively; the arm that swings the bucket correspond to the energy source and the rope performs the function of a pump impeller.

Suction-lift pumps create negative pressure at the pump intake. The atmospheric pressure at the free surface of water in the well forces the well water into and up the intake pipe. The maximum suction lift depends on the atmospheric pressure (10.4 m of water head), vapour pressure of water, head loss due to friction and the head requirements of the pump itself. Under field conditions, the average suction-lift capability of a suction-lift centrifugal pump is about 7.5 m.

Deep-well vertical turbine pump consists of one or more impellers housed in a single- or multi-stage unit called a bowl assembly. Each stage gives a certain amount of lift and sufficient number of stages (or bowl assemblies) are assembled to meet the total head requirement of the system.

Vertical turbine pumps in high capacity wells are highly reliable over long periods of time. The motors of these pumps are not susceptible to failure caused by fluctuations in electric supply. Motor repairs can be carried out easily because of their installation on the ground surface. These pumps, however, cannot be used in wells which are out of alignment. Besides, these pumps require highly skilled personnel for installation and service.

Submersible pumps have the bowl assemblies which are the same as those of vertical turbine pumps. But the motor of submersible pump is submerged and is directly connected to and located just beneath the bowl assembly. Water enters through an intake screen between the motor (at lower level) and the bowl assembly (at higher level), passes through various stages and is discharged directly through the pump column to the surface.

The motor of submersible pump is directly coupled to the impellers and is easily cooled because of complete submergence. Ground surface noise is also eliminated. The pump can be mounted in casings which are not entirely straight. Pump house is also not necessary. There are, however, electrical problems associated with submerged cables. These pumps cannot tolerate sand pumping and work less efficiently. The motor is less accessible for repairs and cannot tolerate voltage fluctuations.

4.8.2 Jet Pumps

Jet pump is a combination of a centrifugal pump and a nozzle-venturi arrangement, as shown in Fig. 4.8. The nozzle causes increased velocity and reduced pressure at point A. The lowered pressure at A draws additional water from the intake pipe, and this water is added to the total volume of water flowing beyond A. The venturi tube helps in recovery of pressure at B with minimum loss of head. Compared to the centrifugal pumps, the jet pumps are inefficient but have some advantageous features too. These are adaptable to small wells down to 5 cm inside diameter. All moving parts of the jet pump are accessible at the ground surface. Their design is simple which results in low equipment and maintenance costs.

4.8.3 Air-lift Pumps

Water can also be lifted from inside of a well by releasing compressed air into an air discharge pipe (air line) lowered into the well. Because of the reduced specific gravity,aerated water is lifted to the ground surface. Air-lift pumping is inefficient and requires cumbersome and expensive equipment and is, therefore, rarely used as a permanent pumping system.

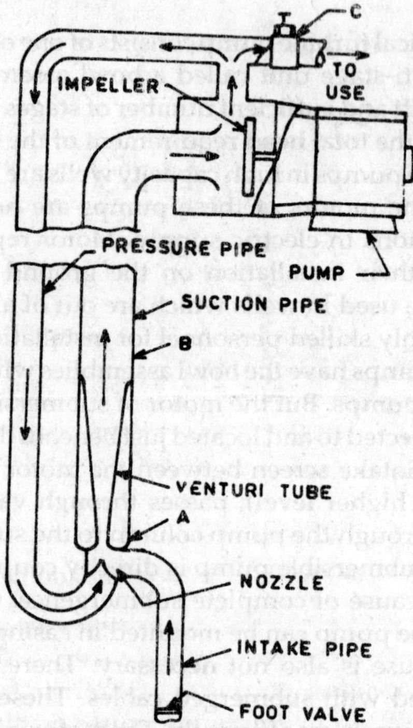

Fig. 4.8 Jet pump

EXERCISES

1. How is ground water better than surface water? Compare well irrigation with canal irrigation.
2. What is the meaning of conjunctive use? Why is it useful to consider it in water resources planning?
3. A 20 cm well completely penetrates an artesian aquifer. The length of the strainer is 16 m. What is the well yield for a drawdown of 3 m when the coefficient of permeability and the radius of influence are 30 m/day and 300 m, respectively?
4. A well with a radius of 0.5 m completely penetrates an unconfined aquifer with K = 32 m/day and the height of water table above the bottom of the aquifer as 45 m. The well is pumped so that the water level in the well remains at 35 m above the bottom of the well. Assuming that pumping has essentially no effect on water table at a distance of 300 m from the well, determine the steady-state well discharge.
5. Describe different methods of well drilling mentioning their merits and suitability for different field conditions.
6. What are the benefits of well development? Describe various methods of well development.
7. Constant head permeability test on a soil sample of 10 cm diameter and 15 cm length was carried out. If 100 c.c. of water was collected in 100 seconds under a constant head of 50 cm, determine the coefficient of permeability of the soil sample.

Chapter 5

Irrigation Canals

5.1 COMPONENTS OF FLOW IRRIGATION

Any flow irrigation system would comprise the following four subsystems:

i) The water supply subsystem which may be in the form of either a surface reservoir or diversion from a river.
ii) The water conveyance subsystem comprising of canal network in the command area and hydraulic structures on the canals.
iii) The water use (or application) subsystem which includes different methods of irrigation.
iv) The water removal subsystem *i.e.,* the drainage system.

In this chapter the water conveyance subsystem has been dealt with.

5.2 CANALS

A *canal* is defined as an artificial channel constructed on the ground to carry water from a river or another canal or a reservoir to the fields. Depending on their function, canals can be classified as:

i) irrigation canal,
ii) navigation canal,
iii) power canal,
iv) feeder canal, and
v) link canal.

An *irrigation canal* carries water from its source to agricultural fields. Canals used for transport of goods are known as *navigation canals. Power canals* are used to carry water for generation of hydroelectricity. A *feeder canal* feeds one or more canals. A *link canal* links the two canals so that, if required, water of one canal can be diverted to the other canal through the link canal. A given canal can serve more than one function.

Based on the nature of source of supply, a canal can be either a permanent or an inundation canal. A permanent canal has a continuous source of water supply. Such canals are also called perennial canals. An inundation canal (or non-perennial canal) draws its supply from a river only during the high stages of the river. Such canals do not have any headworks for diversion of river water to the canal, but are provided with a canal head regulator.

An irrigation canal system consists of canals of different sizes and capacities. Accordingly, the irrigation canals are further classified as:

i) main canal,
ii) branch canal,
iii) major distributary,
iv) minor distributary, and
v) watercourse (or field canal).

The *main canal* takes its supplies directly from the river through the head regulator and acts as a feeder canal supplying water to branch canals and major distributaries. Usually, direct irrigation is not carried out from the main canal.

Branch canal (also called 'branches') takes its supplies from the main canal. Branch canals generally carry a discarge higher than 5 m^3/s and act as feeder canals for major and minor distributaries. Large branches are rarely used for direct irrigation. However, outlets are provided on smaller branches for direct irrigation.

Major distributaries (also called distributaries or *rajbaha*) carry 0.25 to 5 m^3/s of discharge. These distributaries take their supplies generally from the branch canal and sometimes from the main canal. The major distributaries feed either watercourses through outlets or minor distributaries.

Minor distributaries (also called 'minors') are small canals which carry a discharge less than 0.25 m^3/s, and feed the watercourses for irrigation. They generally take their supplies from major distributaries or branch canals and rarely from the main canals.

A *watercourse* is a small canal which takes its supplies from an irrigation channel (generally distributaries) through an outlet, and carries water to different parts of the area to be irrigated through the outlet.

5.3 DESIGN OF STABLE IRRIGATION CANALS

Irrigation canals generally have alluvial boundaries and carry sediment-laden water. A hydraulic engineer is concerned with the design, construction, operation, maintenance and improvement of irrigation canals. Irrigation canals should be stable over a period of their life span. According to Lane, a stable channel (or canal) is an unlined earth channel

a) which carries water,
b) the bed and banks of which are not scoured objectionably by the flowing water, and
c) in which objectionable deposits of sediments do not occur. Sediment is a loose noncohesive material through which a river or channel flows. In other words, sediment is the fragmental material

transported by, suspened in, or deposited by water or accumulated in the bed of a river.

This means that silting and scouring in a stable channel should balance each other over a reasonable period so that the bed and banks of the channel remain unaltered. The cross-section of a stable alluvial channel would depend on the flow rate, sediment transport rate and the sediment size. Regime methods are commonly used for the design of alluvial channels carrying sediment-laden water.

5.4 REGIME METHODS

Regime methods for the design of stable channels were first developed by the British engineers working for canal irrigation in India in the 19th century. At that time, the problem of sediment deposition was one of the major problems of channel design in India. In order to find a solution for this problem, some of the British engineers studied the behaviour of such stretches of the existing canals where the bed was in a state of stable equilibrium. These stable reaches had not required any sediment clearance for several years of the canal operation. Such channels were called regime channels. These channels generally carried a sediment load, usually measured in terms of concentration defined as the ratio of weight (or volume) of solids and weight (or volume) of sediment-water mixture expressed either in percentage or parts per million (ppm), smaller than 500 ppm. Suitable relationships for the velocity of flow in regime channels were evolved. These relationships are now known as regime equations which find acceptance in other parts of the world as well. The regime relations do not account for the sediment load and, hence, should be considered valid when the sediment load is not large. Most commonly used regime methods are Kennedy's method and Lacey's method.

Kennedy's Method

Kennedy collected data from 22 channels of the Upper Bari Doab canal system in Punjab. His observations on this canal system led him to conclude that the sediment supporting power of a channel is proportional to its width (and not wetted perimeter).

On plotting the observed data, Kennedy obtained the relation, known as Kennedy's equation,

$$U_o = 0.55\, h^{0.64} \tag{5.1}$$

Kennedy termed U_o as the critical velocity (in m/s) (defined as the mean velocity which will not allow scour or silting) in a channel having depth of flow equal to h in metres. This critical velocity should be distinguished from the critical velocity of flow in open channels corresponding to Froude number equal to unity. Equation 5.1 is obviously applicable to such channels which have the same type of sediment as was presented in the Upper Bari Doab canal system. On recognising the effect of the sediment size on the critical velocity, Kennedy modified Eq. 5.1 to

$$U = 0.55 \, m \, h^{0.64} \tag{5.2}$$

in which m is the critical velocity ratio and is equal to U/U_o. Here, the velocity U is the critical velocity for all sizes of sediment, whereas U_o is the critical velocity for Upper Bari Doab sediment only. This means that the value of m is unity for sediment of the size of Upper Bari Doab sediment. For sediment coarser than Upper Bari Doab sediment, m is greater than 1, while for sediment finer than Upper Bari Doab sediment, m is less than 1. Kennedy did not try to establish any other relationship for the slope of regime channels in terms of either the critical velocity or the depth of flow. He suggested the use of the Kutter's equation alongwith the Manning's roughness coefficient. The final results do not differ much if one uses the Manning's equation instead of the Kutter's. Thus, the equations

$$U = 0.55 \, mh^{0.64} \tag{5.2}$$

$$Q = AU \tag{5.3}$$

$$\text{and } U = \frac{1}{n} R^{2/3} S^{1/2} \tag{5.4}$$

enable one to determine the unknowns B (*i.e.* bed width), h and U for given discharge Q, Manning's roughness coefficient n and m if the longitudinal slope S is specified. In Eqs. 5.3 and 5.4, A and R are, respectively, area of flow cross-section and hydraulic radius (*i.e.* A/P where P is the wetted perimeter). The longitudinal slope S is decided mainly on the basis of ground considerations. Such considerations limit the range of slope. However, within this range of slope, one can obtain different combinations of B and h satisfying Eqs. 5.2 to 5.4. The resulting channel sections can vary from very narrow to very wide. While all these channel sections would be able to carry the given discharge, not all of them would behave satisfactorily. Table 5.1 gives values of recommended width-depth ratio, *i.e.*, B/h for stable channels.

Table 5.1 Recommended Values of B/h for Stable Channels

Q, m^3/s	5.0	10.0	15.0	50.0	100.00	200.00	300.00
B/h	4.5	5.0	6.0	9.0	12.0	15.0	18.0

Several investigations carried out on similar lines indicated that the constant C′ and the exponent x in Kennedy's equation, $U = C'. \, mh^x$ are different for different canal systems. Table 5.2 gives the values of C′ and x in Kennedy's equation for some regions.

The design procedure based on Kennedy's theory involves trial. For known Q, n, m and S, assume a trial value of h and obtain the critical velocity U from Kennedy's equation, Eq. 5.2. From the continuity equation, Eq. 5.3, calculate area of cross-section A and, hence, the value of B for the assumed value of h and known channel geometr (trapezoidal section with side slope of 0.5H:1V), is known. Using these values of B and h, compute the mean velocity from the Manning's equation, Eq. 5.4. If this value of mean velocity matches with the value of the critical velocity obtained earlier, the assumed value of h and the computed value of B provide channel dimensions. If the two velocities do not match, assume another value of h and repeat the calculations.

Table 5.2 Values of C′ and x in Kennedy's equation for different regions

Region	C′	*x*
Egypt	0.25 to 0.31	0.64 to 0.73
Thailand	0.34	0.66
Rio Negro (Aregentina)	0.66	0.44
Krishna River (India)	0.61	0.52
Chenab River (India)	0.62	0.57
Pennar River (India)	0.60	0.64
Shwebo (Burma)	0.60	0.57
Imperial Valley (USA)	0.64 to 1.20	0.61 to 0.64

One can, alternatively, use Garrett's diagrams (Fig. 5.1), which are sort of nomograms. For this purpose draw a vertical line through the intersection of the relevant discharge curve and horizontal line representing the desired value of S. The vertical line would intersect several bed width curves. A horizontal line drawn through each of such points of intersection would enable determination of the depth of flow h and critical velocity U_o for the chosen width B corresponding to the selected point of intersection. Using the Manning's equation, Eq. 5.4, the velocity of flow U is estimated and U/U_o (= m) is thus determined. If this value of m matches with the given value of m, the selected value of B and the corresponding depth of flow h are acceptable. Otherwise, repeat the procedure after selecting another point of intersection of the vertical line and the bed width curves.

It should be noted that the Garrett's diagrams have been drawn for Manning's n = 0.0225. In case the value of Manning's n is different than 0.0225, then the vertical line (drawn through the intersection of the discharge curve and the slope-line) will be shifted towards either left (if $n < 0.0225$) or right (if $n > 0.0225$) by a small distance which is obtained from the small nomogram shown at the top of the Garrett's diagram. This distance is equal to the distance between the point marked with an arrow (and which corresponds to n = 0.0225) on the nomogram and the point on the same nomogram where the value of n equals the given value. Remaining procedure of determining B and h remains the same as explained earlier for n = 0.0225.

Example 5.1: Design a channel carrying a discharge of 30 m^3/s with critical velocity ratio and the Manning's n equal to 1.0 and 0.0225, respectively. Assume that the bed slope is equal to 1 in 5000.

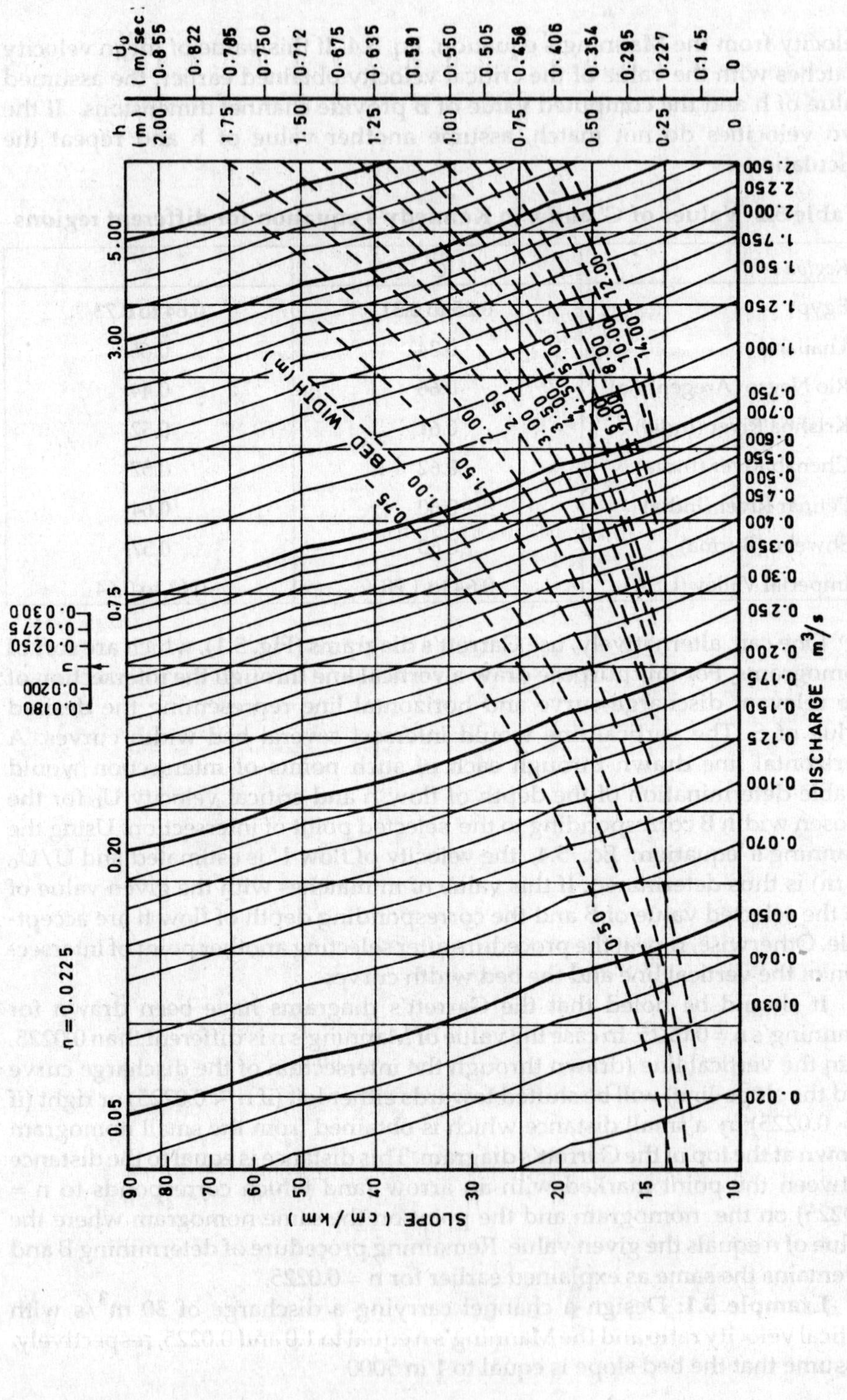

Fig. 5.1(a) Garett's diagrams

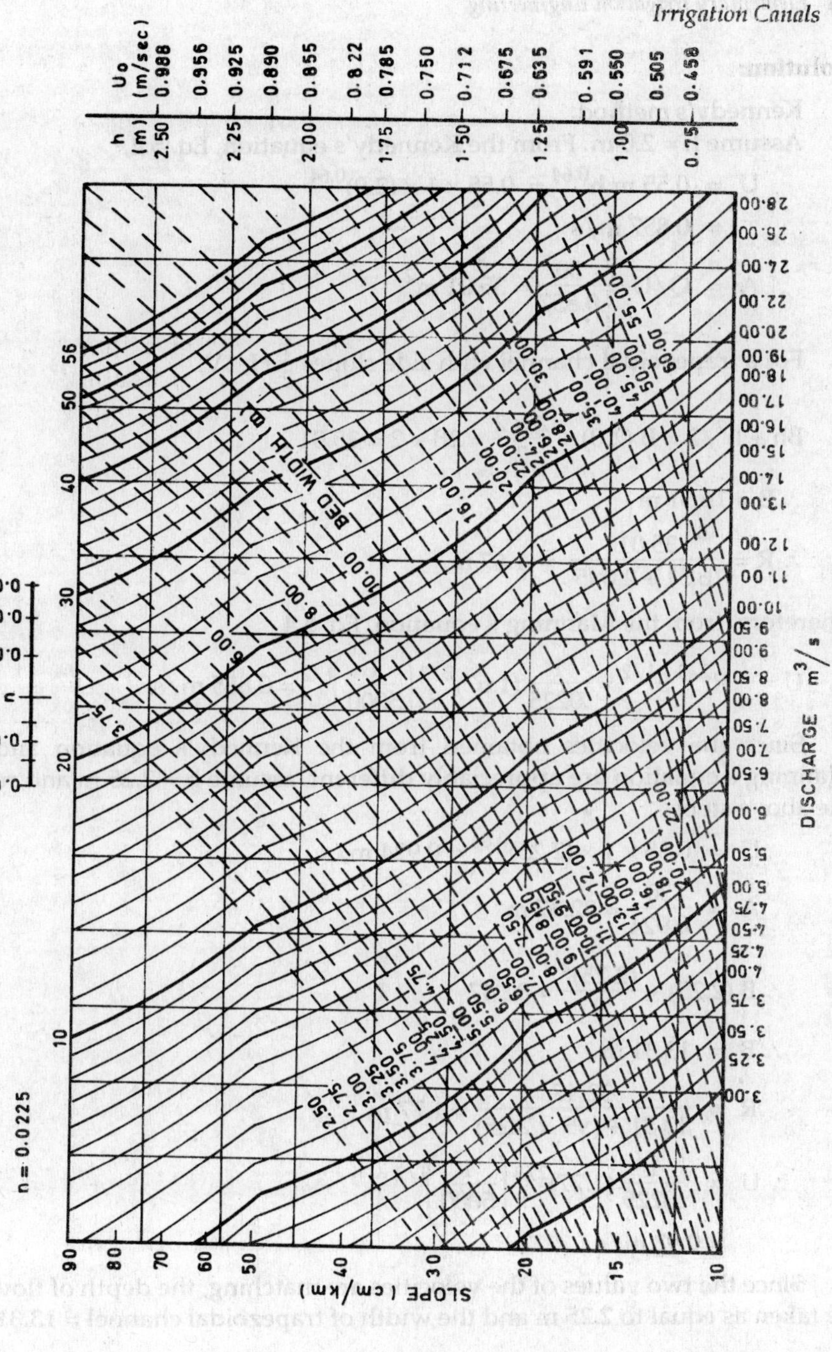

Fig. 5.1(b) Garett's diagrams

Solution:

Kennedy's method:

Assume h = 2.0 m. From the Kennedy's equation, Eq. 5.2,

$$U = 0.55\, m\, h^{0.64} = 0.55 \times 1 \times (2.0)^{0.64}$$

$$= 0.857 \text{ m/s}$$

$$\therefore A = Q/U = \frac{30}{0.857} = 35.01 \text{ m}^2.$$

For a trapezoidal channel with side slopes $\frac{1}{2}$ H: 1V,

$$Bh + h^2/2 = B\,(2.0) + \frac{2 \times 2}{2} = 2B + 2 = 35.01\,.$$

$$\therefore B = 16.51 \text{ m}$$

$$\therefore R = \frac{35.01}{16.51 + 2.0\sqrt{5}} = 1.67 \text{ m}$$

Therefore, from the Manning's equation, Eq. 5.4

$$U = \frac{1}{n} R^{2/3} S^{1/2} = \frac{1}{.0225} (1.67)^{2/3} \left(\frac{1}{5000}\right)^{1/2} = 0.885 \text{ m/s}.$$

Since the velocities obtained from the Kennedy's equation and the Manning's equation are appreciably different, assume h = 2.25 m and repeat the above steps.

$$U = 0.55 \times 1 \times (2.25)^{0.64} = 0.924 \text{ m/s}$$

$$A = \frac{30}{0.924} = 32.47 \text{ m}^2$$

$$\therefore B\,(2.25) + \frac{(2.25)^2}{2} = 32.47$$

$$\therefore B = 13.31 \text{ m}$$

$$R = \frac{32.47}{13.31 + (\sqrt{5} \times 2.25)} = 1.77 \text{ m}$$

$$\therefore U = \frac{1}{.0225} (1.77)^{2/3} \left(\frac{1}{5000}\right)^{1/2}$$

$$= 0.92 \text{ m/s}$$

Since the two values of the velocities are matching, the depth of flow can be taken as equal to 2.25 m and the width of trapezoidal channel = 13.31 m.

Lacey's Method

Lacey stated that the width, depth and slope of a regime channel to carry a given water discharge loaded with a given sediment discharge are all fixed by nature. According to him, the fundamental requirements for a channel to be in regime are as follows:

i) The channel flows uniformly in an incoherent alluvium. Incoherent alluvium is the loose granular material which can scour or deposit with the same ease. The material may range from very fine sand to gravel, pebbles and boulders of small size.
ii) The characteristics and the discharge of the sediment are constant.
iii) The water discharge in the channel is constant.

The perfect 'regime' conditions rarely exist. The channels which have lateral restraint (because of rigid banks) or imposed slope are not considered as regime channels. For example, an artificial channel, excavated with width and longitudinal slope smaller than the required, will tend to widen its width and steepen its slope if the banks and bed are of incoherent alluvium and non-rigid. In case of rigid banks, the width is not widened but the slope becomes steeper. Lacey termed this regime as *initial regime*. A channel in initial regime is narrower than what it would have been if the banks were not rigid. This channel has attained working stability. If the continued flow of water overcomes the resistance to bank erosion so that the channel now has freedom to adjust its perimeter, slope and depth in accordance with the discharge, the channel is likely to attain what Lacey termed as the *final regime*.

The river bed material may not be active at low stages of the river, particularly if the bed is composed of coarse sand and boulders. However, at higher stages, the bed material becomes active, *i.e.*, it starts moving. As such, it is only during the high stages that the river may achieve regime conditions. This fact is utilised in solving problems related to floods in river channels.

Based on the analysis of data Lacey finally gave the following regime relations which can be used to obtain channel dimensions, channel slope S and the flow velocity U for given discharge Q and sediment size d in an alluvial channel carrying sediment-laden water :

$$U = 10.8\, R^{2/3} S^{1/3} \quad (5.5)$$

$$P = 4.75\sqrt{Q} \quad (5.6)$$

$$q = 0.212 Q^{1/2} \quad (5.7)$$

$$f_1 = 1.76\sqrt{d} \quad (5.8)$$

$$R = 0.48\left(\frac{Q}{f_1}\right)^{1/3} \quad (5.9)$$

$$R = 1.35\left(\frac{q^2}{f_1}\right)^{1/3} \quad (5.10)$$

$$S = 0.0003\frac{f_1^{5/3}}{Q^{1/6}} \quad (5.11)$$

$$S = 0.000178\frac{f_1^{5/3}}{q^{1/3}} \quad (5.12)$$

Here,

f_1 = the silt factor,

d = the sediment size in mm, and

q = the discharge per unit width of channel.

Equations 5.5 to 5.12 are all dimensional equations in which units of metre and second have been used for length and time dimensions except in case of d which is in mm.

Lacey's regime equation, Eq. 5.5 is of considerable use in estimating mean velocity of flood flow and hence, flood discharge in an alluvial stream. Equation 5.6 is very useful in fixing clear waterways for structures such as bridges and weirs.

Equation 5.7 relates the discharge per unit width of a regime channel with the total discharge flowing in the channel. For wide channels, the hydraulic radius is almost equal to the depth of flow h. Hence, Eq. 5.9 reduces to

$$h = 0.48\left(\frac{Q}{f_1}\right)^{1/3} = 1.35\left(\frac{q^2}{f_1}\right)^{1/3} \qquad (5.13)$$

which can be utilised to estimate the depth of flow in a river during flood. Equation 5.13, therefore, gives the depth of scour below high flood level. This helps in estimating the levels of foundations, vertical cutoffs and lengths of launching aprons of a structure constructed across a river. Compared to Kennedy's equations, Lacey's equations yield explicit solution for the design of stable channels. Nevertheless, Lacey's regime diagrams, Fig. 5.2, are also available to obtain the design perameters graphically. The use of these charts involves obtaining the intersection of the relevant f_1 curve with the relevant discharge curve and then read the values of the bed width B and depth of flow h from the abscissa and ordinate. Figure 5.2 also enables determination of the slope S for known Q and f.

The regime equations are purely empirical relations lacking any sound theoretical basis. These equations consider only sediment size to be important and do not take into account the sediment load. Nevertheless, the regime equations are generally used on the plea that structures designed using regime concepts have stood the test of time and worked satisfactorily.

It should be noted that the regime charts (*i.e.*, Garrett's and Lacey's diagrams) were very useful in times when calculators and computers were not available. However, in the present times, one would prefer to compute the design parameters directly from Lacey's equation using calculators rather than use the Lacey's diagrams. Similarly, one can prepare a computer programme for Kennedy's method and obtain design parameters and thus avoid the cumbersome task of mannual trial or making interpolation errors in reading the Garrett's diagrams.

Example 5.2: Design a stable channel for carrying a discharge of 30 m^3/s using Lacey's method assuming silt factor equal to 1.0.

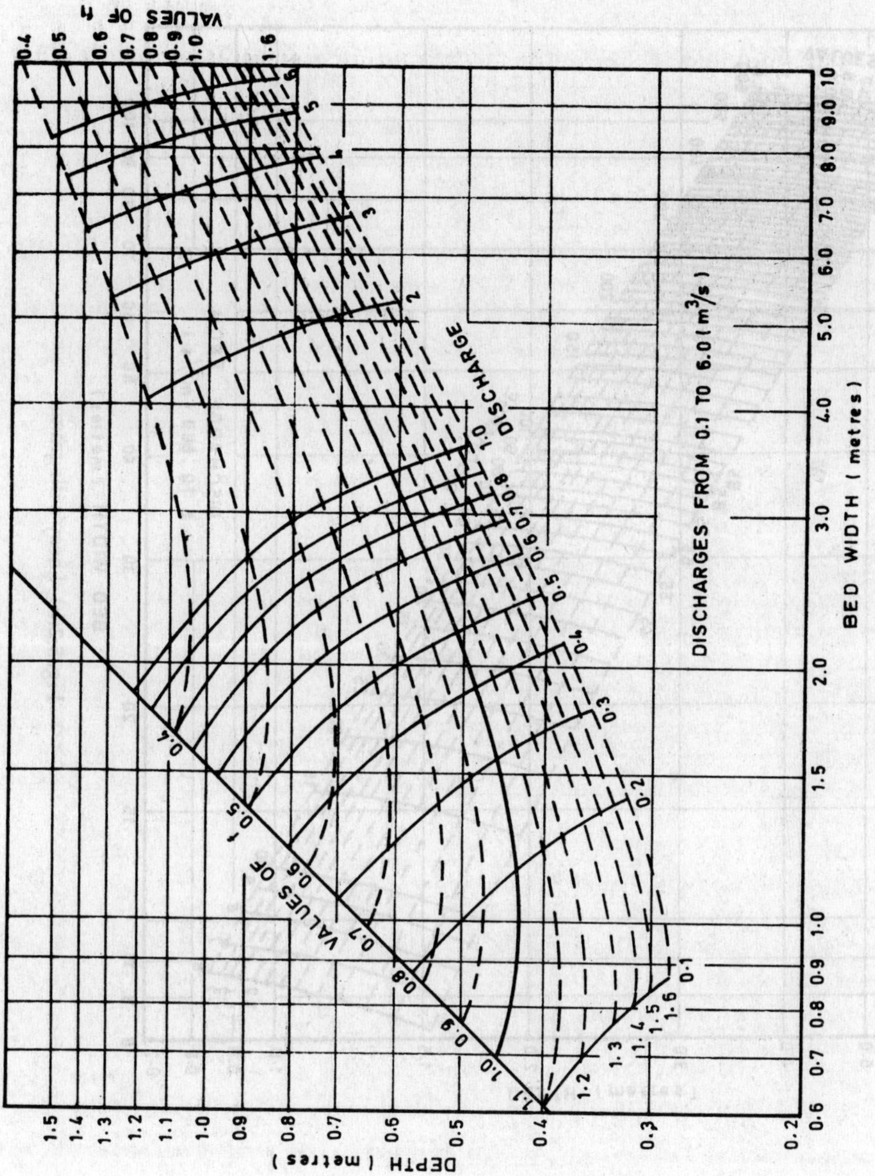

Fig. 5.2(a) Lacey's diagrams

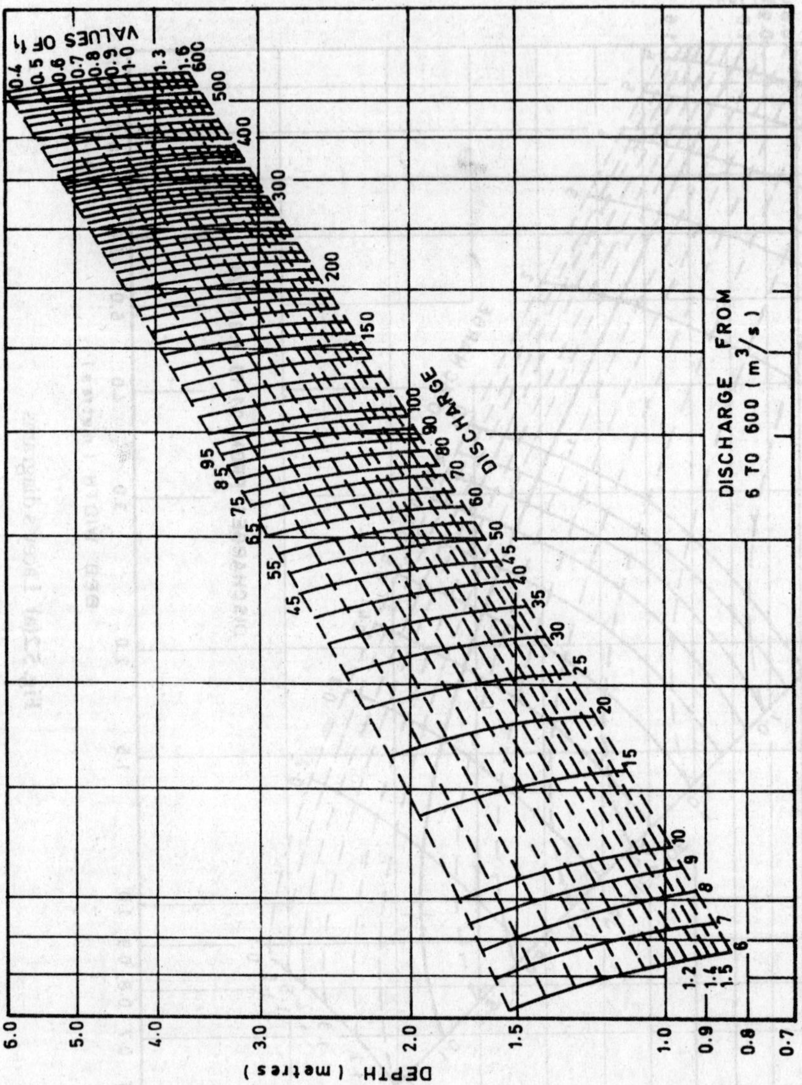

Fig. 5.2(b) Lacey's diagrams

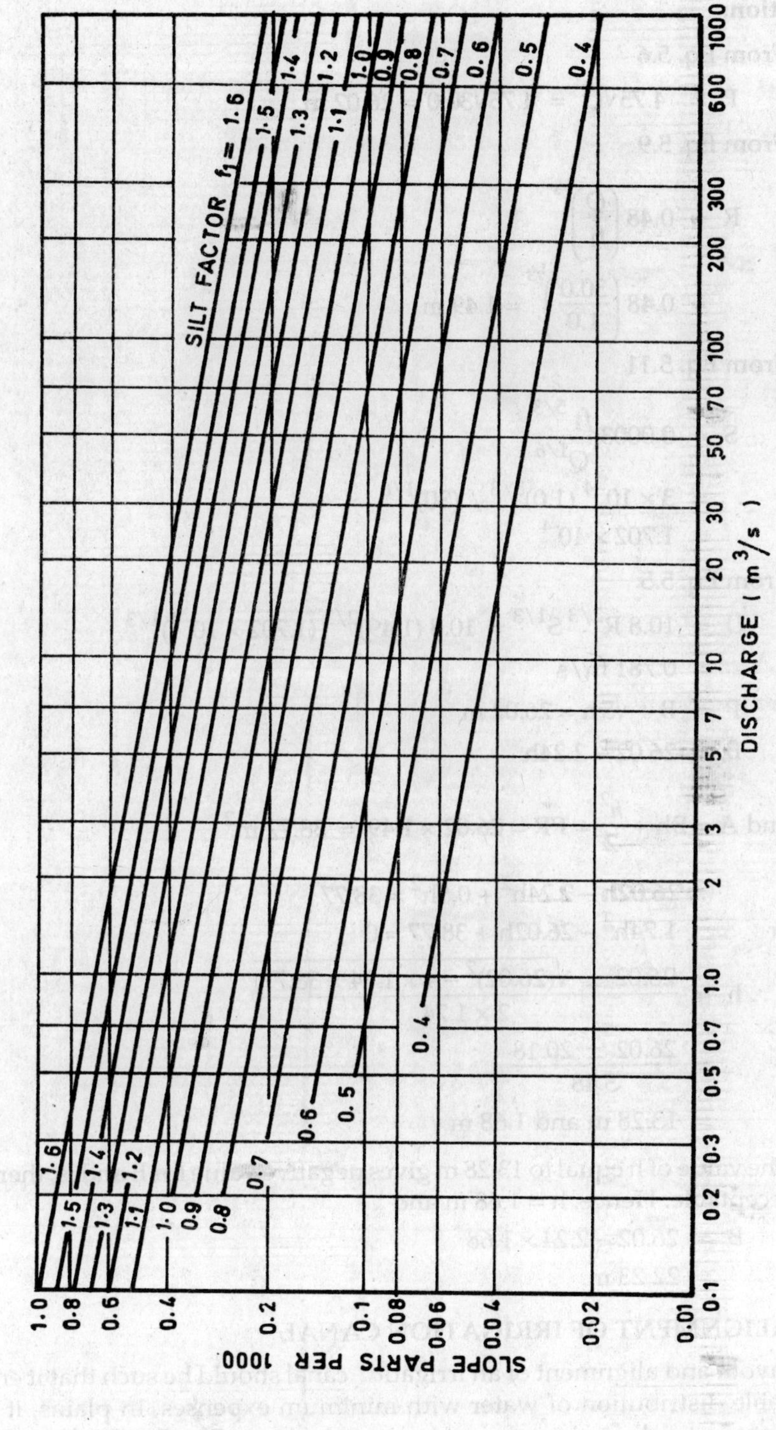

Fig. 5.2(c) Lacey's diagrams

Solution:

From Eq. 5.6

$$P = 4.75\sqrt{Q} = 4.75\sqrt{30.0} = 26.02 \text{ m}$$

From Eq. 5.9

$$R = 0.48\left(\frac{Q}{f_1}\right)^{1/3}$$

$$= 0.48\left(\frac{30.0}{1.0}\right)^{1/3} = 1.49 \text{ m}$$

From Eq. 5.11

$$S = 0.0003\frac{f_1^{\;5/3}}{Q^{1/6}}$$

$$= 3\times10^{-4}\,(1.0)^{5/3} / (30)^{1/6}$$

$$= 1.702\times10^{-4}$$

From Eq. 5.5

$$U = 10.8\,R^{2/3}\,S^{1/3} = 10.8\,(1.49)^{2/3}\,(1.702\times10^{-4})^{1/3}$$

$$= 0.781 \text{ m/s}$$

$$P = B + \sqrt{5}h = 26.02 \text{ m}$$

$$B = 26.02 - 2.24h$$

and $A = Bh + \dfrac{h^2}{2} = PR = 26.02\times1.49 = 38.77 \text{ m}^2$

$$\therefore 26.02h - 2.24h^2 + 0.5h^2 = 38.77$$

or $\quad 1.74h^2 - 26.02h + 38.77 = 0$

$$\therefore h = \frac{26.02 \pm \sqrt{(26.02)^2 - 4\times1.74\times38.77}}{2\times1.74}$$

$$= \frac{26.02 \pm 20.18}{3.48}$$

$$= 13.28 \text{ m and } 1.68 \text{ m.}$$

The value of h equal to 13.28 m gives negative value for B and is, therefore, not acceptable. Hence, h = 1.68 m and

$$B = 26.02 - 2.24\times1.68$$

$$= 22.23 \text{ m.}$$

5.5 ALIGNMENT OF IRRIGATION CANAL

The layout and alignment of an irrigatic canal should be such that it ensures equitable distribution of water with minimum expenses. In plains, it is advantageous to align a canal on the watershed; see Fig. 5.3. *Watershed* is the

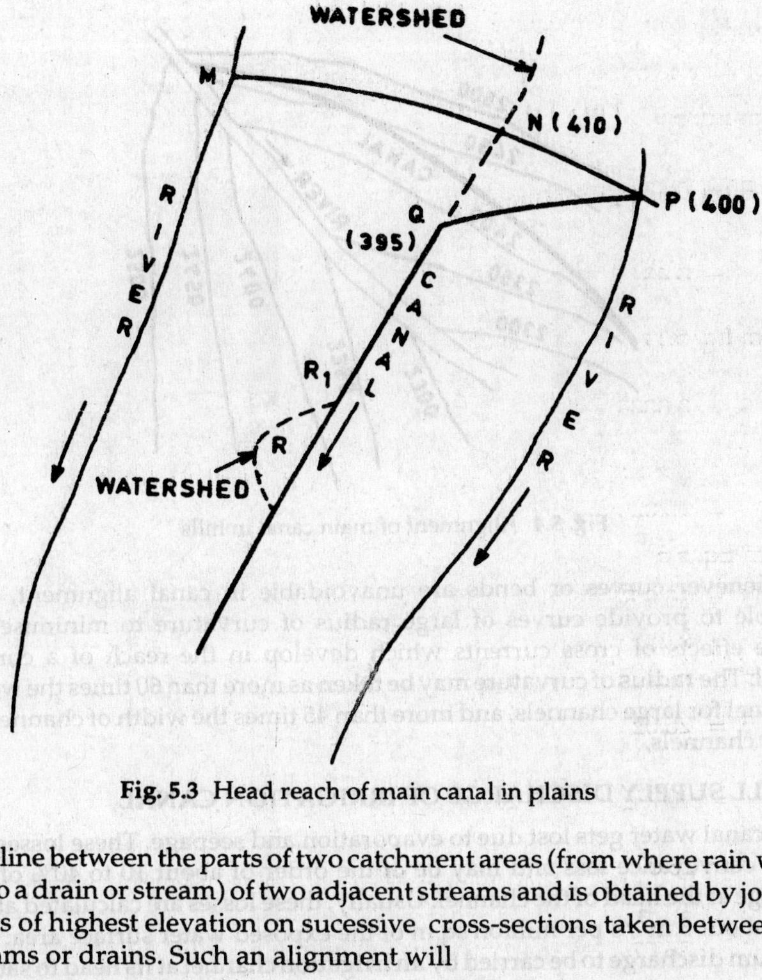

Fig. 5.3 Head reach of main canal in plains

dividing line between the parts of two catchment areas (from where rain water flows into a drain or stream) of two adjacent streams and is obtained by joining the points of highest elevation on sucessive cross-sections taken between the two streams or drains. Such an alignment will

i) ensure gravity flow irrigation on either side of the channel, and also
ii) minimise the expenses on cross-drainage structures.

Since the main canal takes off its water from a river (which is at the lowest point in the cross-section), the main canal necessarily crosses some streams before it mounts the watershed. Once the canal mounts the watershed, it is always kept aligned along the watershed as far as possible. Sometimes the canal has, however, to leave watershed in order to either keep its alignment straight (such as at R in Fig. 5.3) or bypass a township or for some such reasons.

In hilly areas, however, contour alignment (Fig. 5.4) is followed. After taking off from a river in a valley, a channel follows contours maintaining its required slope. As river slopes are much steeper than the required channel bed slope, the channel encompasses more and more area between itself and the river.

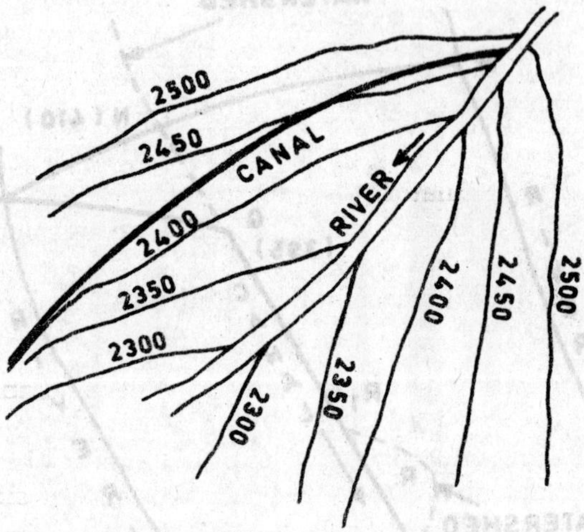

Fig. 5.4 Alignment of main canal in hills

Whenever curves or bends are unavoidable in canal alignment, it is advisable to provide curves of large radius of curvature to minimise the adverse effects of cross currents which develop in the reach of a curved channel. The radius of curvature may be taken as more than 60 times the width of channel for large channels, and more than 45 times the width of channel for smaller channels.

5.6 FULL SUPPLY DISCHARGE OF IRRIGATION CANAL

Part of canal water gets lost due to evaporation and seepage. These losses are termed conveyance loss and may be of the order of about 10 to 40% of the discharge at the head of the channel. Usually, these losses are calculated at the rate of about 3 m^3/s per million sq m of the exposed water surface area. The maximum discharge to be carried by an irrigation channel at its head to satisfy the irrigation requirements for its command area under the worst conditions during any part of a year is said to be the designed full supply discharge (or capacity) of the channel. The water level in the channel when it is carrying its full supply discharge is termed full supply level (FSL), and the corresponding depth of flow is called full supply depth.

5.7 LONGITUDINAL SECTION OF IRRIGATION CANAL

The full supply level of a canal aligned on the watershed need to be only about 10-30 cm higher than the adjacent ground level to ensure gravity flow irrigation in its command area. Too high an FSL would result in

i) uneconomical canal cross-section of higher banks,
ii) increased seepage loss (and, therefore, increased chances of waterlogging) due to higher head, and

iii) wasteful use of water by the farmers.

The FSL of an offtaking canal at its head should always be kept at least 15 cm lower than the water level of the parent (*i.e.*, supply) channel so as to account for

i) the loss in the regulator;
ii) the possibility of the off-taking canal bed getting silted up in its head reaches, and
iii) the possibility of increase in the withdrawal discharge sometime in future.

If the designed slope of a canal is steeper than the available ground slope, the canal is laid at a slope equal to the ground slope, and adequate measures are taken at the head regulator to prevent or minimise the entry of coarse sediment into the canal so that there would not occur any silting problem in the canal due to its flatter slope. On the other hand, if the designed slope of a canal is flatter than the available ground slope, the canal is laid at the designed slope. Such a canal would soon have its entire section above the ground surface and its FSL would also be at too high level above the ground. Therefore, vertical falls (or drops) are provided at intervals in the canal. For economic reasons, a fall can be combined with a regulator or a bridge. Such falls can also be used for generation of power. One may provide either a larger number of smaller falls (*i.e.*, falls with smaller drop in the channel bed elevation) or smaller number of larger falls. Relative economy of these alternatives will decide the location of falls which also depends on other considerations such as balanced earthwork and existence of another offtaking channel. If the offtaking channel is located immediately upstream of a fall, it may not be able to withdraw its designed supply on account of lowered water surface due to drawdown effects of the fall.

Payment of earthwork for canal construction is made on the basis of either the excavation or the filling in embankments, whichever is more. Therefore, it will be economical to keep excavation and filling reasonably balanced which requires that the amount of the excavated soil is fully utilized in fillings. If the amount of earth required for filling exceeds the amount of the excavated earth, this excess requirement of filling is met by digging earth material from suitable places known as borrow pits. These borrow pits can be made in the bed of the channel; Fig. 5.5. Such borrow pits will get silted up in due course of time when the canal carries sediment-laden water. If still more material is need for filling, the borrow pits can be located about 5 to 10 m away from the toe of the canal bank. These should not be deeper than 0.3 m, and should always be connected to a drain. Surplus excavated earth material can be utilized

i) to widen or raise canal banks, and
ii) fill up local depressions in the vicinity. Remaining surplus excavated earth has to be deposited in spoil banks (Fig. 5.5) on one or both sides of the canal. The spoil banks should be discontinuous to allow cross drainage between them.

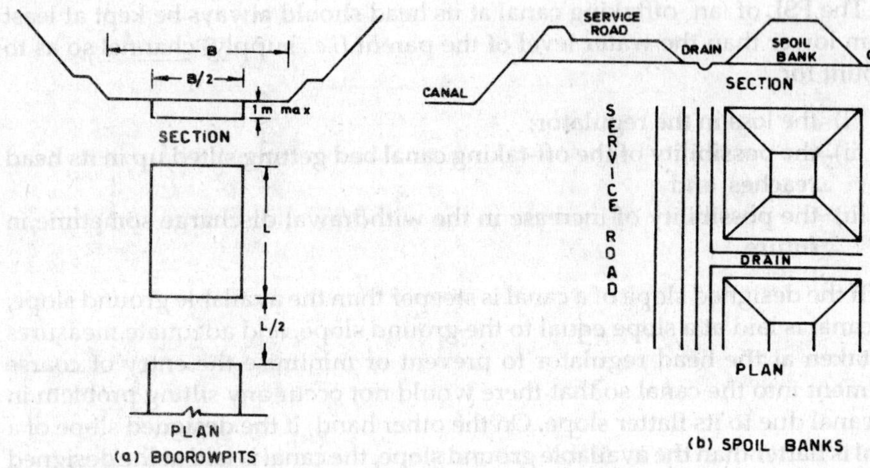

Fig. 5.5 Borrow pits and spoil banks

5.8 FREEBOARD

Freeboard is the vertical distance from the full supply level to the top of the canal bank. It provides the margin of safety against overtopping of the banks due to sudden rise in the water surface of the canal on account of

i) improper operation of gates at the head regulator,
ii) accidents in operations,
iii) wave action,
iv) land slides, and
v) inflow during heavy rainfall.

Freeboard in unlined canals may vary from 0.3 m in small canals to about 2 m in large canals. Freeboard can also be estimated by adding 0.3 m to one quarter of the flow depth in metres.

5.9 CROSS-SECTION OF IRRIGATION CANAL

When the full supply level of an irrigation canal is lower than the surrounding ground level (Fig. 5.6 (a)), the canal is said to be in cutting. If the canal bed is at or higher than the surrounding ground level the canal is in filling. When the surrounding ground level is in between the full supply level and the bed level of the canal (Fig. 5.6 (c)), the canal is partly in cutting and partly in filling and such a canal, usually, results in balanced earthwork.

For the purpose of proper inspection and maintenance of irrigation canals, service roads are provided on one or both sides of the canal. These service roads can be part of the bank embankment as shown in Fig. 5.6. These service roads are about 6 m wide and may or may not be metalled. If these service roads are likely to meet the communication needs of the local people, they will

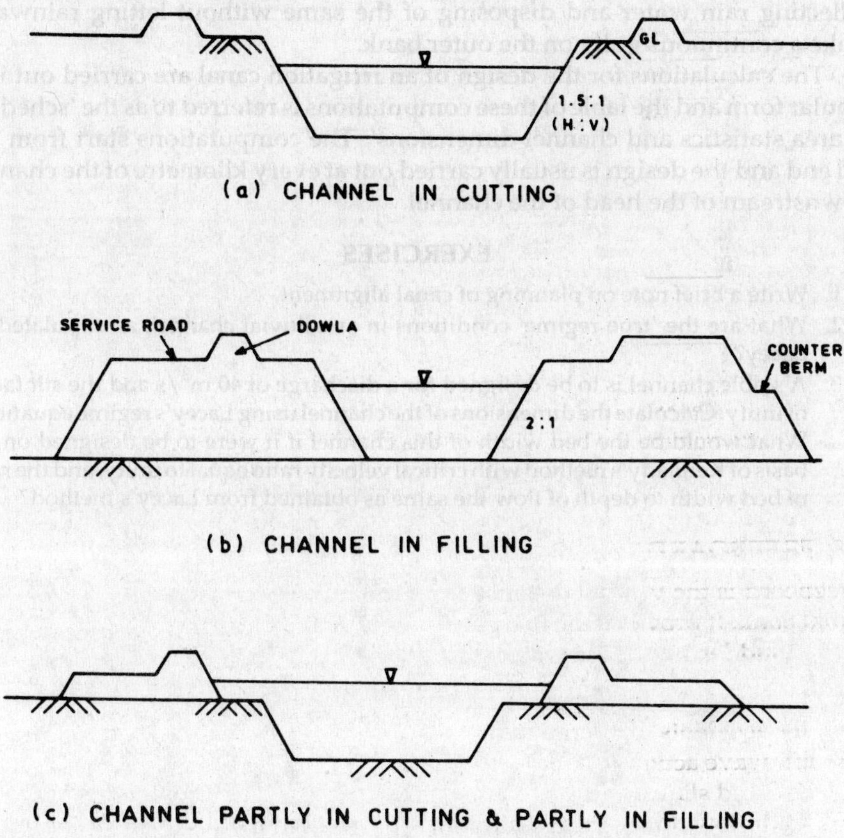

Fig. 5.6 Cross-section of irrigation canals

be much wider and also metalled. Between the canal road and the canal, a 'dowla' of height 0.5 m and top width 0.5 m is also provided.

To prevent sloughing of inner surface and canal banks, a narrow horizontal strip is provided on the inner sloping surface of the bank. This strip is known as berm. For stability of banks, side slopes of an unlined channel should, obviously, be flatter than the angle of repose of the saturated bank soil. Generally, it varies from 1 : 1 to about 2(H) : 1(V). Further, the bank dimensions should be such that there is a minimum cover of 0.5 m above the saturation line which, for small embankments, may be approximated by a straight line drawn at a slope ranging from 4H : 1V (for relatively impermeable material) to 10H : 1V (for porous sand and gravel) from the point where full supply level meets the bank. Cover over saturation line can be increased by providing a horizontal strip similar to berm on the outer slope of bank in which case this strips is known as counter berm (Fig. 5.6(b)). It also helps in collecting rain water and disposing of the same without letting rainwater make a continuous gully on the outer bank.

The calculations for the design of an irrigation canal are carried out in a tabular form and the table of these computations is referred to as the 'schedule of area statistics and channel dimensions'. The computations start from the tail end and the design is usually carried out at every kilometre of the channel downstream of the head of the channel.

EXERCISES

1. Write a brief note on planning of canal alignment.
2. What are the 'true regime' conditions in an alluvial channel, as stipulated by Lacey?
3. A stable channel is to be designed for a discharge of 40 m^3/s and the silt factor of unity. Calculate the dimensions of the channel using Lacey's regime equations. What would be the bed width of this channel if it were to be designed on the basis of Kennedy's method with critical velocity ratio equal to unity, and the ratio of bed width to depth of flow the same as obtained from Lacey's method?

Chapter 6

Waterlogging and Lining of Irrigation Canal

6.1 WATERLOGGING

A land is said to be waterlogged when the soil pores within the root zone of the plants get saturated, and the normal growth of the plant is adversely affected due to insufficient air circulation. The waterlogged land results in reduction of agricultural production. The problem of waterlogging is a world wide phenomenon which occurs mainly due to the rise of ground water table beyond permissible limits. The problem of waterlogging has already affected about 6 million hectares of culturable land in India.

6.1.1 Causes of Waterlogging

The main causes of waterlogging can be grouped into two categories:

i) natural, and
ii) artificial.

Topography, geological features and rainfall characteristics of an area can be the natural causes of waterlogging.

Introduction of surface water irrigation facilities disturbs the balance between natural outflow and inflow of a ground water reservoir. This forms the artificial cause of waterlogging. Besides, defective methods of cultivation, defective irrigation practices and blocking of natural drainages are also included in the artificial causes of waterlogging.

6.1.2 Effects of Waterlogging

Following are the adverse effects of waterlogging:

i) Absence of soil aeration
ii) Difficulty in cultivation operations
iii) Weed growth
iv) Accumulation of salts.

In addition, the increased dampness of the waterlogged area adversely affects the health of the persons living in that area.

i) Absence of Soil Aeration

In waterlogged lands, the soil pores within the root zone of crops are saturated and air circulation is cutoff. Waterlogging, therefore, prevents free circulation of air in the root zone. Thus, waterlogging adversely affects the chemical processes and the bacterial activities which are essential for the proper growth of a plant. As a result, the yield of the crop is reduced considerably.

ii) Difficulty in Cultivation

For optimum results in crop production, the land has to be prepared. The preparation of land (*i.e.*, carrying out operations such as tillage, etc.) in wet condition is difficult and expensive. As a result, cultivation may be delayed and the crop yield adversely affected. The delayed arrival of the crop in the market brings less returns to the farmer.

iii) Weed Growth

There are certain types of plants and grasses which grow rapidly in marshy lands. In waterlogged lands, these plants compete with the desired useful crop. Thus, the yield of the desired useful crop is adversely affected.

iv) Accumulation of Salts

As a result of high watertable in waterlogged areas, there is an upward capillary flow of water to the land surface where water gets evaporated. The upward moving water brings with it soluble salts from salty soil layers well below the surface. These soluble salts carried by the upward moving water are left behind in the root zone when this water evaporates. The accumulation of these salts in the root zone of the soil may affect the crop yield considerably.

6.1.3 Remedial Measures of Waterlogging

The main cause of waterlogging in an area is the introduction of canal irrigation in the area. It is, therefore, better to plan an irrigation scheme in such a way that the land is prevented from getting waterlogged. Measures, such as

i) limiting the intensity of irrigation,
ii) provision of intercepting drains,
iii) keeping the full supply level of channels as low as possible,
iv) encouraging economical use of water,
v) removing obstructions in natural drainage,
vi) rotation of crops,

vii) running of canals by rotation, *etc.*

can help considerably in preventing the area from getting waterlogged.

Combined use of surface and subsurface water resources of a given area in a judicious manner is called conjunctive use of water. During dry periods, the use of ground water is increased which results in lowering of the water table. The use of surface water is increased during wet season. Because of the lowered water table, ground water reservoir receives rainfall supplies through increased percolation. Utilisation of water resources in this manner results neither in excessive lowering of the water table nor in its excessive rising. Conjunctive use of surface and subsurface water serves as a precautionary measure against waterlogging. It helps in greater water conservation and lesser evapotranspiration losses, and brings larger area under irrigation.

6.2 LINING OF IRRIGATION CANALS

The most effective method of preventing waterlogging in a canal irrigated area, however, is to eliminate or reduce the seepage of canal water into the ground. This can be achieved by the lining of irrigation canals (including watercourses, if feasible).

Most of the irrigation canals in India today are earth channels. The major advantage of an earth channel is its low initial cost. The disadvantages of an earth channel are: (i) the low velocity of flow maintained to prevent erosion necessitates larger cross-section of channels, (ii) excessive seepage loss which may result in water-logging and related problems, such as salinity of soils, expensive road maintenance, drainage activities, safety of foundation structures *etc.*, (iii) favourable conditions for weed growth which further retards the velocity, and (iv) breaching of banks due to erosion and burrowing of animals. These problems of earth channels can be got rid of by lining the channel.

A lined canal decreases the seepage loss and, thus, reduces the chances of waterlogging. It also saves water which can be utilised for additional irrigation. A lined canal provides safety against breaches and prevents weed growth thereby reducing the annual maintenance cost of the canal. Because of relatively smooth surface of lining, a lined canal requires a flatter slope. This results in the increase of command area of the canal. The increase in the useful head is advantageous in case of power channels also. Lining of watercourses in the area irrigated by tubewells assumes special significance as the pumped water supply is more costly.

The cost of lining a canal is, however, the only factor against lining. A detailed cost analysis is essential for determining the economic feasibility of lining a canal. The true cost of lining is its annual cost rather than the initial cost. The cost of lining is compared with the direct and indirect benefits of lining to determine the economic feasibility of lining of a canal. Besides economic factors, there might be intangible factors, such as high population density, aesthetics etc. which may influence the final decision in lining of a canal.

6.3 TYPES OF LINING

Types of lining are generally classified according to the materials used for the construction of lining. Concrete, rock masonry, brick masonry, bentonite-earth mixtures, natural clays of low permeability and different rubble, plastic and asphaltic compounds are the commonly used materials for canal lining. The suitability of the lining material is decided by (i) economy, (ii) structural stability, (iii) durability, (iv) repairability, (v) impermeability, (vi) hydraulic efficiency, and (vii) resistance to erosion. The principal types of lining are as follows:

i) Concrete lining
ii) Shotcrete lining
iii) Precast concrete lining
iv) Lime concrete lining
v) Stone masonry lining
vi) Brick lining
vii) Boulder lining
viii) Asphaltic lining
ix) Earth lining

i) Concrete Lining

Concrete lining is probably the best type of lining. It fulfills practically all the requirements of lining. It is durable, impervious and requires least maintenance. The smooth surface of the lining increases the conveyance of the channel. Properly constructed concrete lining can easily last about 40 years. Concrete linings are suitable for all sizes of canals, and for both high and low velocities. The lining cost is, however, high but can be reduced by using mechanised methods.

Thickness of concrete lining depends on canal size, bank stability, amount of reinforcement and climatic conditions. Small channels in warm climates require lesser thickness of lining. Channel banks are kept at self-supporting slope (1.5H: 1V to 1.25 H: 1V) so that the lining is not required to bear earth pressures and its thickness does not increase. Concrete lining is laid without form work and, hence, the workability of the concrete should be good. Besides, experienced workmen are required for laying the concrete lining.

Reinforcement in concrete linings usually varies from 0.1 to 0.4 % of the area in the longitudinal direction and 0.1 to 0.2 % of the area in the transverse direction. The reinforcement in concrete linings prevents serious cracking of the concrete to reduce leakage, and ties adjacent sections of the lining together to provide increased strength against settlement damage due to unstable subgrade soils or other factors.

The reinforcement in concrete linings does not prevent the development of small shrinkage cracks which tend to close when canals are operated and linings are watersoaked. The damage due to shrinkage and temperature changes is avoided/reduced by the use of special construction joints. Reinforced concrete linings may result in increased water tightness of the lining. However, well-constructed unreinforced concrete linings may be almost equally watertight.

Earlier practice of reinforced concrete lining is now being replaced with well-constructed unreinforced concrete lining. However, reinforcement must be provided in (a) large canals which are to be operated throughout the year, (b) sections where the unreinforced lining may not be safe, and (c) canals in which the flow velocities are likely to be very high.

Proper preparation of subgrade is essential for the success of concrete lining which may, otherwise, develop cracks due to settlement. Natural earth is generally satisfactory for this purpose and, hence, subgrade preparation is the least for channels in excavation. Thorough compaction of subgrade for channels in filling is essential for avoiding cracks in lining due to settlement.

Some cracks usually develop in concrete lining. These can be sealed with asphaltic compounds. The lining may be damaged when flow in the canal is suddenly stopped and the surrounding water table is higher than the canal bed. This damage occurs in the excavated channels and can be prevented by providing weep holes in the lining or installing drains with outlets in the canal section.

Minimum thickness of concrete lining based on canal capacity have been specified, as given in Table 6.1.

Table 6.1 Thickness of Concrete Lining

Canal Capacity m^3/s	*Thickness of M-150 concrete lining, cm*		*Thickness of M-100 concrete, cm*	
	Controlled	Ordinary	Controlled	Ordinary
0 to less than 5	5.0	6.5	7.5	7.5
5 to less than 15	6.5	6.5	7.5	7.5
15 to less than 50	8.0	9.0	10.0	10.0
50 to less than 100	9.0	10.0	12.5	12.5
100 and above	10.0	10.0	12.5	15.0

Concrete lining has been used in Nangal Hydel canal, Amaravathi, Krishnagiri Reservoir project and several other projects. The use of concrete lining in India is, however, limited because of relatively small cost of water and higher cost of lining. The Bureau of Indian Standards does not specify use of reinforcement for cement concrete lining.

ii) Shotcrete Lining

Shotcrete lining is constructed by applying cement mortar pneumatically to the canal surface. Cement mortar does not contain coarse aggregates and, therefore, proportion of cement is higher in shotcrete mix than in concrete lining. The shotcrete mix is forced under pressure through a nozzle of small diameter and, hence, size of sand particles in the mix should not exceed 0.5 cm. Equipment needed for laying shotcrete lining is light, portable and of smaller size, compared to the equipment for concrete lining. Thickness of shotcrete lining may vary from 2.5 to 7.5 cm. The preferred thickness is from 4 to 5 cm.

Shotcrete lining is suitable for (a) lining small sections, (b) placing linings on irregular surfaces without any need to prepare the subgrade, (c) placing linings around curves or structures, and (d) repairing badly cracked and leaky old concrete lining.

Shotcrete linings are subject to cracking and may be reinforced or unreinforced. Earlier shotcrete lining was usually reinforced. Larger thickness of shotcrete lining was preferred for convenient placing of reinforcement. The reinforcement was in the form of a wire mesh. In order to reduce the cost of lining, shotcrete linings are not reinforced these days particularly on relatively small jobs.

iii) Precast Concrete Lining

Precast concrete slabs, laid properly on carefully prepared subgrades and the joints effectively sealed, constitute a serviceable type of lining. The precast slabs are about 5 to 8 cm thick with suitable width and length to suit channel dimensions, and to result in weights which can be conveniently handled. Such slabs may or may not be reinforced. This type of lining is best suited for repair works as these can be placed rapidly without long interruptions in canal operation. Side slopes of Tungbhadra project canals have been lined with precast concrete slabs.

iv) Lime Concrete Lining

The use of this type of lining is limited to small and medium size irrigation channels with capacities upto 200 m^3/s and in which the velocity of water does not exceed 2 m/s. The materials required for this type of lining are lime, sand, coarse aggregate and water. Lime concrete mix should be such that it gives minimum compressive strength of about 5.00 kN/m^2 after 28 days of moist curing. Usually, lime concrete is prepared with 1:1.5:3 of kankar lime: kankar grit or sand: kankar (or stone or brick ballast) aggregate. The thickness of lining may vary from 10 to 15 cm for discharge upto 200 m^3/s. Lime concrete lining has been used in the Bikaner canal taking off from the left bank of Sutlej.

v) Stone Masonry Lining

Stone masonry linings are laid on the canal surface with cement mortar or lime mortar. The thickness of stone masonry is about 30 cm. The surface of the stone masonry may be smooth plastered to increase the hydraulic efficiency of the canal. Stone masonry linings are stable, durable, erosion resistant, and very effective in reducing seepage losses. Such lining is very suitable where only unskilled labour is available and suitable quarried rock is available at low price. This lining has been used in Tungbhadra project.

vi) Brick Lining

Bricks are laid in layers of two with about 1.25 cm of 1:3 cement mortar sandwiched in between. Good quality bricks should be used and these should be well soaked in water before laying on the moistened canal surface.

Brick lining is suitable when concrete is expensive and skilled labour is not available. Brick lining is favoured where conditions of low wages, absence of mechanisations, shortage of cement and inadequate means of transportation exist. Brick linings have been extensively used in north India. The Sarda power channel has been lined with bricks. The thickness of the brick lining remains fixed even if the subgrade is uneven. Brick lining can be easily laid in rounded sections without form work. Rigid control in brick masonry is not necessary. Sometimes reinforced brick linings are also used.

vii) Boulder Lining

Boulder lining of canals, if economically feasible, is useful for preventing erosion and where the ground water level is above the bed of the canal and there is possibility of occurrence of damaging back pressures. The stones used for boulder lining should be sound, hard and durable which can sustain weathering and water action. Rounded or sub-angular river cobbles or blasted rock pieces with sufficient base area are recommended types of stone for boulder lining. Dimensions of stones and thickness of lining are as given in Table 6.2.

Table 6.2 Dimensions of Stones and Thickness of Boulder Lining

Canal capacity m^3/s	*Thickness of lining mm*	*Average dimension along the longest axis mm*	*Minimum dimension at any section mm*
0 to less than 50	150	150	75
50 to less than 100	225	225	110
100 and above	300	300	150

Wherever required, a 15 cm thick layer of filter material is to be provided. For laying of boulders, the subgrade (both bed and side slope) of the canal is divided into compartments by stone masonry or concrete ribs. These compartments will not have dimensions more than 15 m along and across the centre line of the canal.

vii) Asphaltic Lining

Material for asphaltic lining is asphalt-based cement and sand mixture which is mixed in hot condition. The most commonly used asphaltic linings are

(a) asphaltic concrete, and (b) buried asphaltic membrane. Asphaltic linings are relatively cheaper, flexible and can be rapidly laid during any part of the year. Because of their flexibility, minor movements of the subgrade are not of serious concern. However, asphaltic linings have short life and are unable to permit high velocity of flow. They have low resistance to weed growth and, hence, it is advisable to sterilise the subgrade to prevent the weed growth.

Asphaltic concrete is a mixture of asphalt cement, sand and gravel mixed at a temperature of about 110°C, and is placed either by manual labour or with laying equipment. Experienced and trained workmen are required for this purpose. Lining is compacted with heavy iron plates while hot.

A properly constructed asphaltic concrete lining is the best asphaltic lining. Asphaltic concrete lining is smooth, flexible and is erosion resistant. Since asphaltic concrete lining becomes distorted at higher temperatures, it is unsuitable for warmer climatic regions. It is preferred in comparison to concrete lining in situations where aggregate is likely to react with the alkali constituents of portland cement.

Buried asphaltic membrane can be of two types:

a) Hot-sprayed asphaltic membrane, and
b) Pre-fabricated asphaltic membrane

- Hot-sprayed asphaltic membrane is constructed by spraying hot asphalt on the subgrade to result in a layer of about 6 mm thickness. This layer, after cooling, is covered with about 30 cm thick layer of earth material. Asphalt temperature is around 200°C and the spraying pressure is about 3×10^5 N/m^2. For this type of lining, the channel section has to be overexcavated. The lining is flexible and easily adopts to the subgrade surface. Skilled workmen are required for the construction of this type of lining.

Pre-fabricated asphaltic membrane is prepared by coating rolls of heavy paper with a 5 mm layer of asphalt or 3 mm of glass fibre-reinforced asphalt. These rolls of pre-fabricated asphaltic membrane are laid on the subgrade, and then covered with earth material. These linings can be constructed by commonly available labour.

Materials used for covering the asphaltic membrane determine the permissible velocities which are generally lower than the velocities in unlined canals. Maintenance cost of such linings is high. Cleaning operations should be carried out carefully so as not to damage the membrane.

ix) Earth Linings

Different types of earth linings have been used in irrigation canals. They are inexpensive, but require high maintenance expenditure. The main types of earth linings are: (a) stabilized earth linings, (b) loose earth blankets; (c) compacted earth linings, (d) buried bentonite membranes, and (e) soil-cement linings.

a) Stabilised earth linings: Stabilised earth linings are constructed by stabilising the subgrade. This can be done either physically or chemically. Physically stabilised linings are constructed by adding corrective materials (such as clay for granular subgrade) to the subgrade, mixing and then compacting. If corrective materials are not required, subgrade can be stabilised by scarifying, adding moisture and then compacting. Chemically stabilised linings use chemicals which may tighten the soil. Such use of chemicals, however, has not developed much.

b) Loose earth blankets: This type of lining is constructed by dumping fine-grained soils, such as clay, on the subgrade and spreading it so as to form a 15 to 30 cm thick layer. Such lining reduced seepage only temporarily and are soon removed by erosion unless covered with gravel. Better results can be obtained by saturating the clay and then pugging it before dumping on the subgrade. The layer of pugged clay is protected by a cover of about 30 cm silt. This type of lining requires flatter side slopes.

c) Compacted earth linings: These linings are constructed by placing graded soils on the subgrade and then compacting it. The graded soil should contain about 15% of clay. The compacted earth linings may be either thin-compacted or thick compacted. In thin-compacted lining, the layer thickness of about 15 to 30 cm along the entire perimeter is used. Thick-compacted linings have about 60 cm thick layer on the channel bed, and 90 cm thick layer on the sides. If properly constructed, both types are reasonably satisfactory. However, thick type of lining has been generally preferred.

Compacted earth linings are feasible when excavated materials are suitable or when suitable materials are available nearby. Compaction operations along the side slopes are more difficult (particularly in thin-compacted lining) than along the channel bed. The lining material should be tested in the laboratory for densities, permeability and optimum moisture contents. The material must be compacted in the field so as to obtain the desired characteristics.

d) Buried bentonite membranes: Pure bentonite is a hydrous silicate of alumina. Natural deposits of bentonite are special types of clay soil which swell considerably when wetted. The impurities of these soils affect the swelling and, hence, the suitability of these as canal lining material. Buried bentonite linings are constructed by spreading soil-bentonite mixture over the subgrade and covering it with about 15 to 30 cm of gravel or compacted earth. Sandy soil mixed with about 5 to 25 per cent of fine-grained bentonite and compacted to a thickness of 5 to 7.5 cm results in a membrane which is reasonably tough and suitable for lining.

e) Soil-cement linings: These linings are constructed using portland cement (15 to 20 % by volume) and sandy soil (not containing more than about 35 % of silt and clay particles). Cement and sandy soil can be mixed in place and compacted at optimum moisture content. This method of construction is known as dry-mixed soil-cement method. Alternatively, soil-cement lining can be constructed by machine mixing the cement and soil with water and placing it on the subgrade in a suitable manner. This method is called plastic soil-cement method and is preferable. In both these methods, the lining should be kept moist for about seven days to permit adequate curing.

The construction cost of soil-cement lining is relatively high. But these resist weed growth and erosion, and also permit velocities slightly higher than in unlined earth channels. The use of soil-cement lining for irrigation canals is restricted to small irrigation canals with capacities upto 10 m^3/s and in which the velocity of water does not exceed 1 m/s.

6.4 FAILURE OF LINING

The main cause of failure of lining is the water pressure that builds up behind the lining material due to high water table, saturation of embankments by canal water, sudden lowering of water levels in the channel and saturation of embankment sustained by continuous rainfall. Embankment of relatively pervious soil does not need drainage measures behind lining. In all situations requiring drainage measures to relieve pore pressures behind lining, a series of longitudinal and transverse drains satisfying filter criteria are provided. A typical arrangement of longitudinal filter drain is as shown in Fig. 6.1.

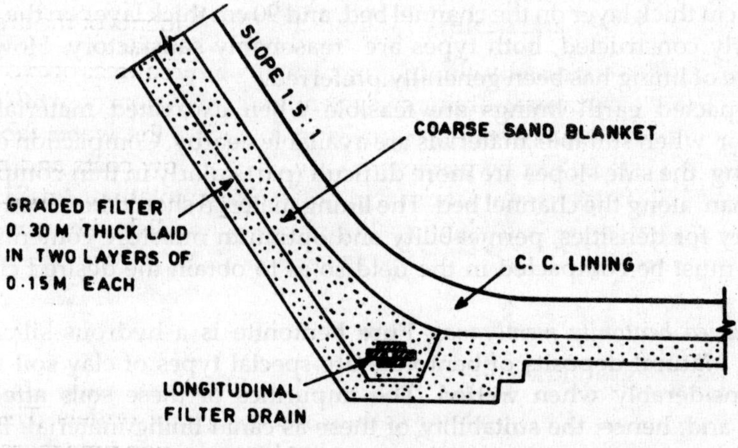

Fig. 6.1 Longitudinal filter drain

Growth of weeds on canal banks and other aquatic plants in channels may not result in failure of lining but affect the conveyance of channels which may be lined or unlined. Weeds and aquatic plants consume water for their growth and thus consumptive use of irrigation water increases. The weed growth increases the channel roughness and, hence, reduces the flow velocity thereby increasing evaporation losses. Cleaning of channels having excessive weed growth is, therefore, a vital maintenance problem. Cleaning operations can be carried out manually or by mechanical devices such as dragline excavation and tractor-drawn cranes. Commonly used methods for cleaning of channals are pasturing, moving, burning and applying chemical weed killers.

6.5 DRAINAGE OF IRRIGATED LANDS

Irrigation and drainage are complementary to each other. In humid area, drainage attains much greater importance than in arid regions. Irrigated lands require adequate drainage to remain capable of producing crops. Adequate drainage of fertile lands require lowering of shallow water table and this forms the first and basic step in reclamation of waterlogged, saline and alkali soils. The drainage of farm lands

i) improves soil structure and increases the soil productivity,
ii) facilitates early ploughing and planting,
iii) increases the depth of root zone thereby increasing the available soil moisture and plant food,
iv) increases soil ventilation,
v) increases water infiltration into the ground thereby decreasing soil erosion on the surface,
vi) creates favourable conditions for growth of soil bacteria,
vii) leaches excess salts from soil,
viii) maintains favourable soil temperature, and
ix) improves sanitary and health conditions for the residents of the area.

Water table can be lowered by eliminating or controlling sources of excess water. Improvement in natural drainage system and provision of artificial drainage system will be of considerable help in lowering the water table. Natural drainage systems can be properly maintained at low costs and are feasible means to protect irrigated lands from excessive percolation. Artificial drainage also aims at lowering of water table and is accomplished by any of the following methods:

i) Open drains
ii) Closed drains
iii) Pumping of ground water

Open drains are used to convey excess water to distant outlets. These accelerate removal of storm water and thus reduce the detention time thereby decreasing the percolation of water into the ground. Open drains can be either shallow surface drains or deep open drains. Shallow surface drains do not affect subsurface drainage. Deep open drains act as outlet drains for a closed drain system and collect surface drainage too.

The alignment of open drains follows the paths of natural drainage and low contours. The drains are not aligned across a pond or marshy land. Every drain has an outlet the elevation of which decides the bed and water surface elevations of the drain at maximum flow. The longitudinal slope of drain should be as large as possible and is decided on the basis of non-scouring velocities. The bed slope ranges from 0.0005 to 0.0015. The depths of about 1.5 to 3.5 m are generally adopted for open drains. The side slopes depend largely on the type of embankment soil and may vary from 1/2 H: 1V (in very stiff and compact clays) to 3H: 1V (in loose, sandy formations).

The open drains should be designed to carry part of storm runoff also. The cross-section of an open drain is decided using the general principles of channel design. The channel will be in cutting and the height of banks will be small. If the drain has to receive both seepage and storm water, it may be desirable to have a small drain in the bed of larger open drain. This will keep the bed of the drain dry for most part of the year and maintenance problems will be considerably less. Only the central deeper section would require maintenance.

Flow of clear water at low velocities permit considerable weed growth on the channel surface. The open drains have, therefore, to be cleaned frequently. Besides manual cleaning, chemical weed killers are also used. But, at times the drain water is being used for cattles and the weed poison may be harmful to the cattles. Aquatic life is also adversely affected by the chemical weed killers.

Closed drains are usually made of porous earthenware. These are laid below the ground surface and are covered by the earth. These do not occupy land surface and, hence, are useful when land value is high. If such drains are to be placed in impervious soil, the drains should be surrounded by filter of a coarser material to increase the permeability and also prevent migration of soil particles and blocking of drains. Vertical relief wells tapping water from confined stratum and connected to the closed drain system form a very effective drainage system. The drains are placed at about 1.8 to 2.0 m below the ground level so that the water table can be lowered to about 1.5 m below the ground surface.

The major drawback of the gravity drainage system is that it is not capable of lowering the water table to large depths. Pumping ground water is more effective drainage method of lowering water table to relatively large depths. Pumping methods consist of withdrawing water from wells drilled or already existing in the waterlogged area.

EXERCISES

1. What is waterlogging ? Discuss its causes, effects and remedial measures.
2. Describe in brief different types of canal lining.
3. In what ways drainage of an irrigated land is beneficial? How is it achieved?

Chapter 7

Canal Regulation Structures

7.1 GENERAL

Regulation structures are hydraulic structures which are constructed to regulate the discharge, the flow velocity or the supply level in an irrigation channel. These are necessary for efficient working as well as for the safety of an irrigation channel. Regulation structures can be of the following types:

i) Canal fall: Canal fall (or simply 'fall' or 'drop') regulates the supply level in a canal by negotiating the change in its bed elevation necessitated by the difference in ground slope and canal slope.
ii) Distributary head regulator: This controls the supply to an offtaking channel from the parent channel.
iii) Cross regulator: This structure controls the water level of a channel and the discharge downstream of another hydraulic structure.
iv) Canal escape: Canal escape disposes of extra supplies when the safety of a canal is endangered due to heavy rains or closure of outlets by farmers.
v) Canal outlets: A canal outlet is a masonry structure through which water is admitted from the distributary into a watercourse.

7.2 CANAL FALLS

A canal fall is a hydraulic structure constructed across a canal to lower down its water level. This is achieved by negotiating the change in bed elevation of the canal necessitated by difference in ground slope and canal slope. The necessity of a fall arises when the available ground slope exceeds the design bed slope of the canal and which condition is rather usual. Thus, an irrigation channel which is in cutting in its head reach soon meets a condition when it has to be entirely in filling. An irrigation channel in embankment i.e., in filling has the disadvantages of : (i) higher construction and maintenance cost,

(ii) higher seepage and percolation losses; (iii) adjacent area being flooded due to any possible breach in the embankment, and (iv) difficulties in irrigation operations. Hence, an irrigation channel should not be located in high embankments. Falls are, therefore, introduced at appropriate places to lower the supply level of an irrigation channel.

The canal water immediately downstream of the fall structure possesses excessive kinetic energy which, if not destroyed, may scour the bed and banks of the canal downstream of the fall. This would also endanger the safety of the fall structure. Therefore, a canal fall is always provided with measures to dissipate surplus energy which, in fact, is the consequence of constructing the fall.

The location of a fall is primarily influenced by the topography of the area and the desirability of combining a fall with other masonry structures, such as bridge, regulator, *etc.* In case of main canals, economy in the cost of excavation is to be considered. Besides, relative economy of providing large number of smaller falls (achieving balanced earth work and ease in construction) compared to that of smaller number of larger falls (resulting in reduced construction cost and increased power production) is also worked out. In case of channels which irrigate the command area directly, a fall should be provided before the bed of the channel comes into filling. The full supply level of a channel can be kept below the ground level for a distance upto about 500 metres downstream of the fall as the command area in this reach can be irrigated by the channels offtaking from upstream of the fall.

7.2.1 Types of Canal Falls

Canal falls are generally one of the following types:

i) Notch Falls

The shape of the notch in a notch fall is either trapezoidal or rectangular. The rectangular notch or low weir is economical and more suitable for discharge measurement. In trapezoidal notch fall, a number of trapezoidal notches are made in a high breast wall across the channel. This arrangement provides an opening for flow right upto the bed level and, thus, eliminates silting in the channel upstream of the fall.

When the subsidiary channels upstream of the fall have to be fed with minimum supply level in the parent channel, the fall should be capable of controlling the upstream water level. Such falls consist of rectangular notches combined with one of the following three types of regulators:

a) Sluice gates—Raising or lowering the gate helps in controlling the upstream level.
b) Horizontal stop logs inserted into grooves—Their removal or insertion causes the required change in the upstream level.
c) Vertical strips (or needles)—These change the effective width (*i.e.,* the width of opening) of the channel and do not cause silting.

ii) High-crested Falls

These falls nearly maintain a fixed water surface level in the upstream channel. This is useful when either a subsidiary channel takes off upstream of the fall, or the fall is combined with a hydroelectric plant, and it becomes desirable that the water surface in the parent channel is maintained at a fixed level as far as possible.

High-crested falls are usually not flumed so as to keep the discharge per metre length of fall, q small. Smaller discharge intensity, q requires smaller head and, hence, the water level upstream of the fall can be maintained at a relatively fixed level to a considerable extent. Smaller value of q also makes energy dissipation easier. Such falls are, therefore, relatively cheaper. Generally, the length of a fall is limited to the width of the channel, but can be increased by providing an expansion followed by contraction in the channel. However, this type of provision would increase the construction cost of the fall. Depending upon the type of the weir crest, *viz.*, broad or narrow, and the flow condition, *viz.*, free or submerged, one can use these falls as metering devices after suitable calibration.

A raised crest fall with vertical impact was first used on the Sarda canal system in U.P. and is known as Sarda fall (Fig. 7.1.) Sarda fall may have either a rectangular crest (for canal discharge less than 14 m^3/s) or a trapezoidal crest (for canal discharge more than 14 m^3/s). The amount of the drop at any fall in this canal system does not exceed 1.80 m. Large number of smaller falls were necessitated on this system because of the stratum of pure sand lying below the thin stratum of clay sand. As such, the depth of excavation for channel construction had to be kept low so as to keep the seepage losses to the minimum.

Another type of raised-crest fall can be a glacis fall (Fig. 7.2). In case of glacis fall, the energy is dissipated through the hydraulic jump which forms at the toe of the glacis.

Canal falls can, alternatively, be divided on the basis of their capability to measure discharge. Accordingly, they may be either meter falls or non-meter falls.

7.2.2 Cistern Element

As a result of the flow passing over a fall, the potential energy of the flow gets converted into kinetic energy. This excess kinetic energy, if not destroyed properly, will result in undesirable scour of the bed and sides of the downstream channel. Hence, provision of suitable means to dissipate the surplus kinetic energy is essential in all types of canal falls, and it is provided in a portion of the canal fall which is known as cistern element.

The cistern element or simply cistern located at the downstream of the crest of a fall structure forms an important part of any canal fall. The cistern element, is defined as that portion of the fall structure in which the surplus energy of the water leaving the crest is destroyed and the subsequent turmoil stilled, before the water passes into the lower level channel. The cistern

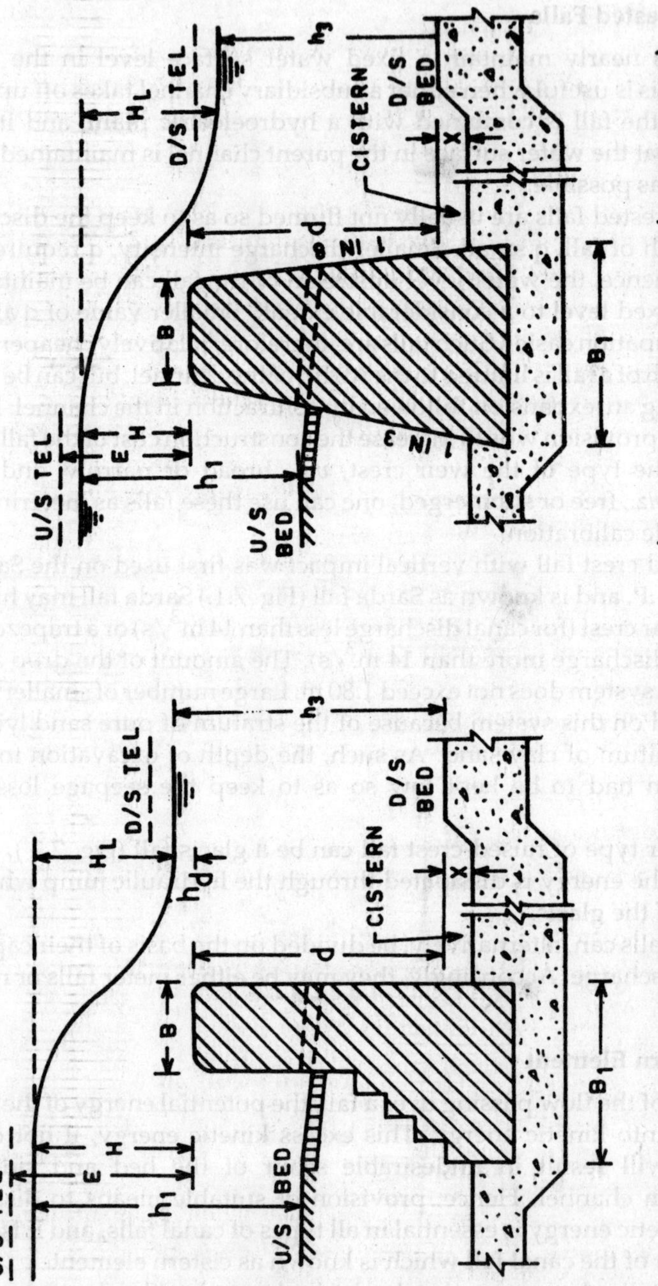

(a) RECTANGULAR CREST (DROWNED FLOW)

(b) TRAPEZOIDAL CREST (FREE FLOW)

Fig. 7.1 Sarda fall

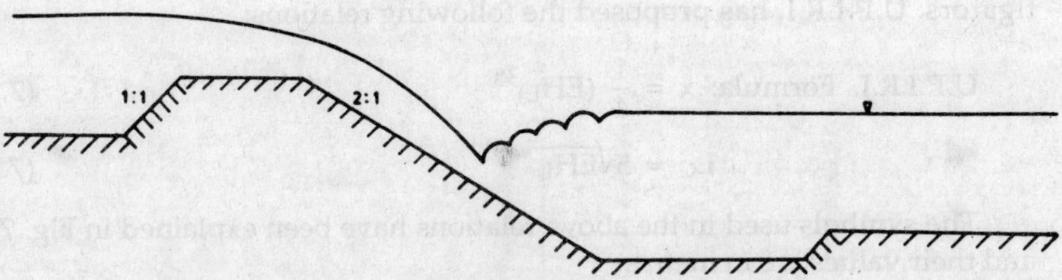

Fig. 7.2 Glacis fall

element includes glacis, if any, devices for ensuring the formation of hydraulic jump and deflecting the residual high velocity jets, the roughening devices and the pool of water in which hydraulic impact takes place. In other words, the cistern element includes the complete structure from the downstream end of the crest to the upstream end of the lower channel.

Most of the cisterns employ hydraulic impact of the supercritical stream of the falling water with the subcritical stream of the lower channel for the dissipation of surplus energy. Depending upon the type of impact, the cisterns are divided into the following four categories:

i) Vertical Impact Cisterns

In these cisterns (Fig. 7.3), there is impact of a stream of water falling freely. The path of such a stream is, obviously, parabolic. This type of cistern is very efficient for the dissipation of surplus energy when the drop is sufficient so that the falling stream becomes almost vertical. The dimensions of the cistern should be such that it serves the purposes of stilling and combing out the residual eddies and disturbances. The length L_C and the depth, x of the cistern

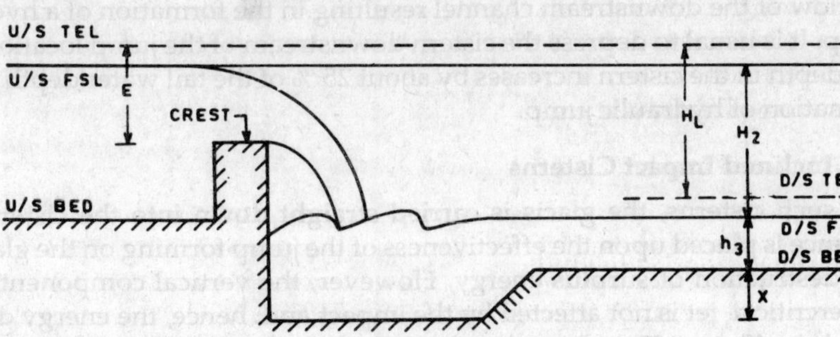

Fig. 7.3 Vertical impact cistern

can be determined only by empirical expressions given by different investigators. U.P.I.R.I. has proposed the following relations:

$$\text{U.P.I.R.I. Formula: } x = \frac{1}{4}(EH_L)^{2/3} \quad (7.1)$$

$$L_C = 5\sqrt{EH_L} \quad (7.2)$$

The symbols used in the above relations have been explained in Fig. 7.3 and their values are in metres.

In most of the vertical impact cisterns, roughening is not provided. Instead, a short length of cistern is provided for stilling, and such a provision has been found to be satisfactory. To prevent the falling nappe from adhering to the masonry face of the fall, aeration of nappe is necessary and is provided by aeration pipes embedded in the wing walls just downstream of the crest. The exit from the cistern should be smooth so that the flow is streamlined before it enters the downstream channel.

ii) Horizontal Impact Cisterns

For this type of cistern (Fig. 7.4), water, after passing over the crest, flows on a glacis whose reverse curve at the downstream end turns the inclined

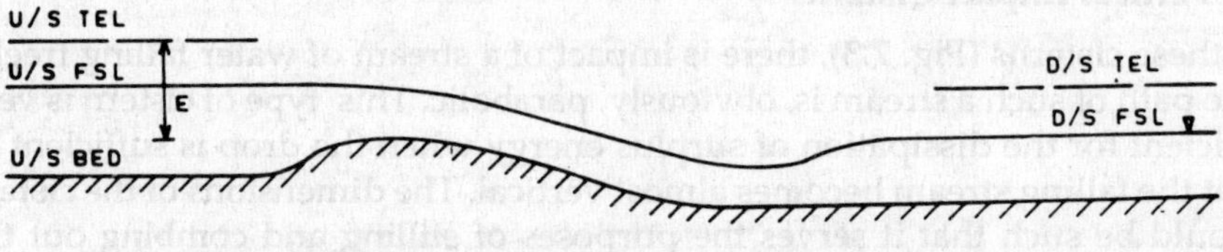

Fig. 7.4 Horizontal impact cistern

supercritical flow to horizontal supercritical flow before it strikes the subcritical flow of the downstream channel resulting in the formation of a hydraulic jump. It is usual to depress the cistern downstream of the jump location until the depth in the cistern increases by about 25 % of the tail water depth for the formation of hydraulic jump.

iii) Inclined Impact Cisterns

For such cisterns, the glacis is carried straight down into the cistern, and reliance is placed upon the effectiveness of the jump forming on the glacis for the destruction of surplus energy. However, the vertical component of the supercritical jet is not affected by the impact and, hence, the energy dissipation is inefficient. Therefore, the cistern has to accommodate the roughening devices and, hence, the cistern length for this class of cisterns is more than that for the preceding classes of cisterns.

iv) No Impact Cisterns

Hydraulic impact is possible only when a supercritical flow meets a subcritical flow. In low falls and falls with large submergence, hydraulic impact may not be possible. Hence, other means of energy dissipation are adopted. A properly designed baffle wall alongwith suitable roughening devices are useful means of energy dissipation for such cases.

7.2.3 ROUGHENING MEASURES FOR ENERGY DISSIPATION

Hydraulic impact is the best means of energy dissipation in case of most of the hydraulic structures including canal falls. Out of the three possible types of impact cisterns *viz.*, vertical impact, horizontal impact and inclined impact cisterns—the vertical impact cistern is the most effective, while the inclined impact cistern is the least effective. However, even in the case of efficient vertical impact cistern, the high turbulence persists downstream of the cistern and means for dissipating the residual energy are essential. In case of cisterns with no hydraulic impact, the roughening devices (provided on the cistern floor) are the only means to destroy the surplus kinetic energy. Artificial roughness increases the actual wetted area which, in turn, increases the boundary friction. Besides, if correctly shaped and placed, the roughness increases the internal friction by increasing the interaction between high speed layers of the stream. Projections from the bed and sides of the channel are the most effective means of energy dissipation. Following roughening devices are generally used.

i) Friction Blocks

Rectangular concrete blocks properly anchored into the cistern floor and projecting upto one fourth the full supply depth are simple, effective and commonly used devices for dissipating surplus kinetic energy in hydraulic structures. The spacing between the blocks in a row is kept about twice the height of the blocks. Depending upon the need, two or more staggered rows of these friction blocks may be provided (Fig. 7.5).

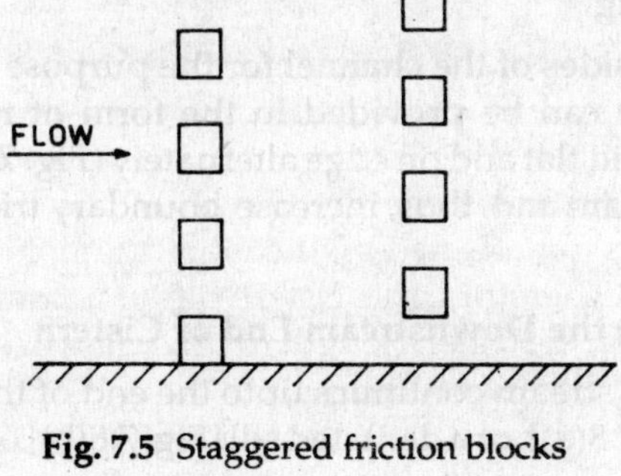

Fig. 7.5 Staggered friction blocks

The 'arrows' are specially shaped friction blocks (Fig. 7.6). The plan form of these arrows is approximately an equilateral triangle with rounded corners. The back face of the arrows is vertical. The top of arrows is sloped from the front rounded corner to the back edge to give an upward deflection to stream filaments.

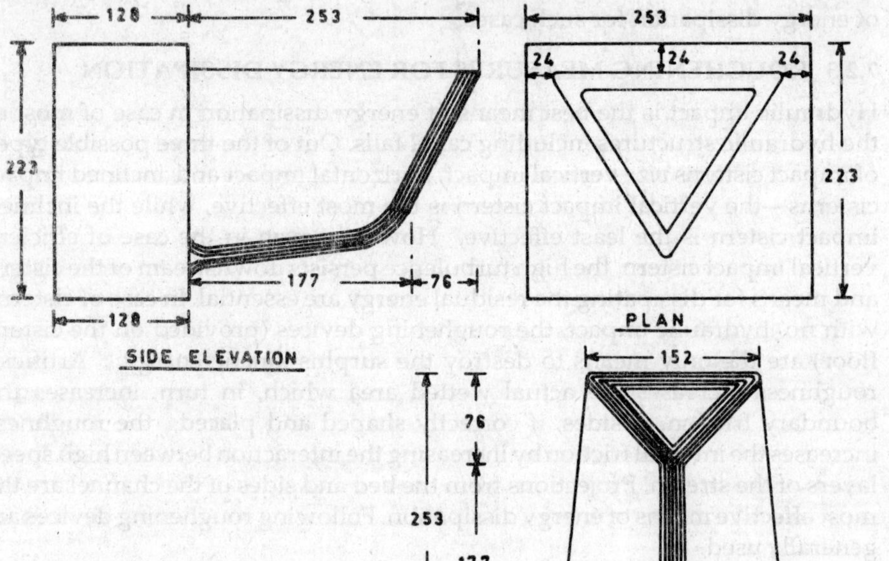

Fig. 7.6 Arrows (all dimensions in mm)

ii) Ribbed Pitching

Projections on the sides of the channel for the purpose of dissipating surplus energy of the flow can be provided in the form of ribbed pitching which consists of bricks laid flat and on edge alternately (Fig. 7.7). Bricks laid on edge project into the stream and, thus, increase boundary friction and dissipate the surplus energy.

7.2.4 Provisions at the Downstream End of Cistern

If the high velocity stream continues upto the end of the cistern, a baffle wall or a deflector [Fig. 7.8(a)], or a dentated sill [Fig. 7.8(b)] or a biff wall [Fig. 7.8(c)]

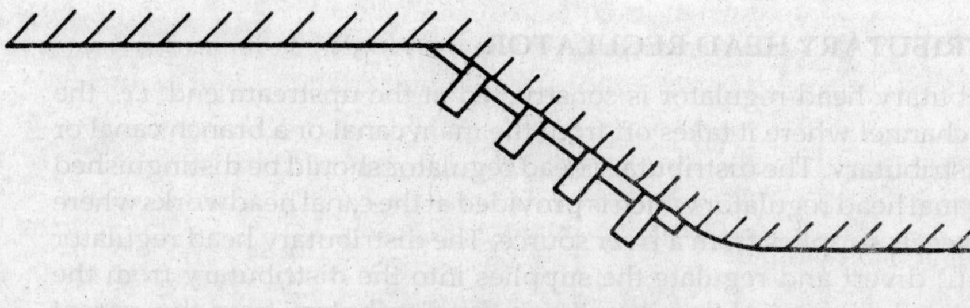

Fig. 7.7 Ribbed pitching

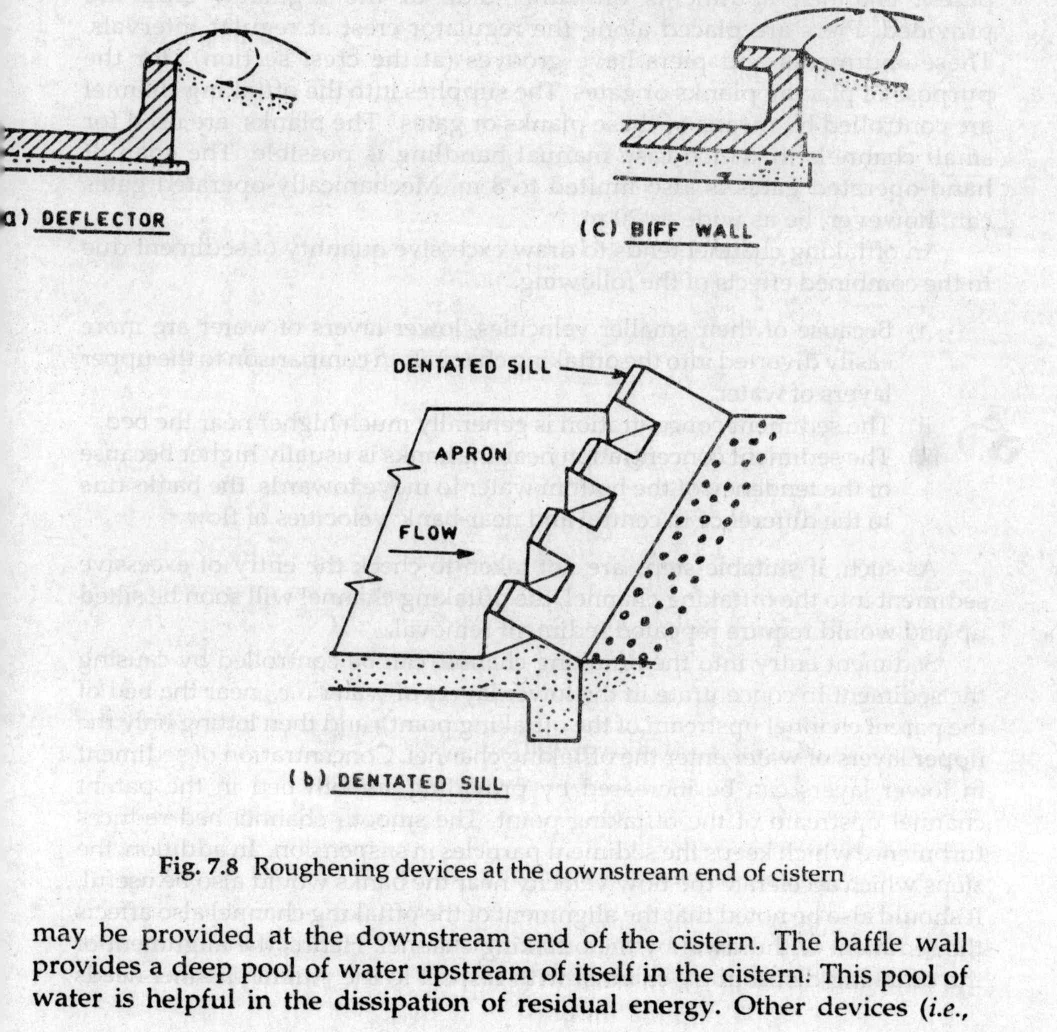

Fig. 7.8 Roughening devices at the downstream end of cistern

may be provided at the downstream end of the cistern. The baffle wall provides a deep pool of water upstream of itself in the cistern. This pool of water is helpful in the dissipation of residual energy. Other devices (*i.e.,* deflector, dentated sill, biff wall) produce a reverse roller which results in a limited scour away from the toe and piles up material against the toe of the structure. A dentated sill, in addition, breaks up the stream jet.

7.3 DISTRIBUTARY HEAD REGULATOR

The distributary head regulator is constructed at the upstream end, *i.e.*, the head of a channel where it takes off from the main canal or a branch canal or a major distributary. The distributary head regulator should be distinguished from the canal head regulator which is provided at the canal headworks where a canal takes its supplies from a river source. The distributary head regulator serves to (i) divert and regulate the supplies into the distributary from the parent channel, (ii) control the silt entering the distributary from the parent channel, and (iii) measure the discharge entering the distributary.

For regulating the supplies entering the offtaking channel from the parent channel, abutments on either side of the regulator crest are provided. Piers are placed along the regulator crest at regular intervals. These abutments and piers have grooves (at the crest section) for the purpose of placing planks or gates. The supplies into the offtaking channel are controlled by means of these planks or gates. The planks are used for small channels in which case manual handling is possible. The span of hand-operated gates is also limited to 8 m. Mechanically-operated gates can, however, be as wide as 20 m.

An offtaking channel tends to draw excessive quantity of sediment due to the combined effects of the following:

i) Because of their smaller velocities, lower layers of water are more easily diverted into the offtaking channels in comparison to the upper layers of water.
ii) The sediment concentration is generally much higher near the bed.
iii) The sediment concentration near the banks is usually higher because of the tendency of the bottom water to move towards the banks due to the difference in central and near-bank velocities of flow.

As such, if suitable steps are not taken to check the entry of excessive sediment into the offtaking channel, the offtaking channel will soon be silted up and would require repeated sediment removal.

Sediment entry into the offtaking channel can be controlled by causing the sediment to concentrate in the lower layers of water (*i.e.*, near the bed of the parent channel upstream of the offtaking point), and then letting only the upper layers of water enter the offtaking channel. Concentration of sediment in lower layers can be increased by providing smooth bed in the parent channel upstream of the offtaking point. The smooth channel bed reduces turbulence which keeps the sediment particles in suspension. In addition, the steps which accelerate the flow velocity near the banks would also be useful. It should also be noted that the alignment of the offtaking channel also affects the sediment withdrawal by the offtaking channel. Hence, the alignment of the offtaking distributary channel with respect to the parent channel needs careful consideration. The angle of offtake may be kept between 60° and 80° to prevent excessive sediment withdrawal by the offtaking channel. For all important works, the alignment of offtaking channels should be fixed on the basis of model studies.

For the purpose of regulating the discharge in the distributary, it is essential to measure the discharge for which one can use the gauge-discharge relationship of the distributary. However, this relationship is likely to change with the change in the channel regime. Hence, it is advantageous to use the head regulator as a metering structure too.

7.4 CROSS REGULATOR

Cross regulator is a structure constructed across a canal to regulate the water level in the canal upstream of itself and the discharge passing downstream of it for one or more of the following purposes:

i) To feed offtaking canals located upstream of the cross regulator.
ii) To escape water from canals in conjunction with escapes.
iii) To control water surface slopes in conjunction with falls for bringing the canals to regime slope and section.
iv) To control discharge at an outfall of canal into another canal or lake.

A cross regulator is generally provided downstream of an offtaking channel so that the water level upstream of the regulator can be raised, whenever necessary, to enable the offtaking channel draw its required supply even if the main channel is carrying low supply. The need of a cross regulator is essential for all irrigation systems which supply water to distributaries and field channels by rotation and, therefore, require to provide full supplies to the distributaries even if the parent channel is carrying low supplies.

Cross regulators may be combined with bridges and falls for economic and other special considerations.

7.5 CANAL ESCAPE

Canal escape is a structure to dispose of surplus or excess water from a canal. A canal escape essentially serves as a safety valve for the canal system. It provides protection of the canal against possible damage due to excess supplies which may be on account of either a mistake in releasing water at headworks, or a heavy rainfall due to which there may be sudden reduction in demand and the cultivators, therefore, close their outlets. The excess supply makes the canal banks vulnerable to breaches or dangerous leaks and, hence, provision for disposing of excess supply in the form of canal escapes at suitable intervals along the canal is desirable. Besides, emptying of canal for repairs and maintenance and removing a part of sediment deposited in the canal can also be carried out with the help of the canal escapes. The escapes are usually of the following types:

i) Weir or surface escape: These are weirs or flush escapes constructed either in masonry or concrete with or without crest shutters which are capable of disposing of surplus water from the canal.

ii) Sluice escapes: Sluices are also used as surplus escapes. These sluices can empty the canal for repairs and maintenance and, in some cases, act as scouring sluices to facilitate removal of sediment.

Location of escape depends on the availability of suitable drains, depressions or rivers with their bed level at or below the canal bed level for disposing surplus water through the escapes, directly or through an escape channel.

7.6 CANAL OUTLETS

When the canal water has reached near the fields to be irrigated, it has to be transferred to the watercourses. At the junction of the watercourse and the distributary, an outlet is provided. An *outlet* is a masonry structure through which water is admitted from the distributary into a watercourse. It also acts as a water-measuring device. The discharge though an outlet is usually less than 0.085 m^3/s. It plays a vital role in the warabandi system of distributing water. Thus, an outlet is like a head regulator for the field channel.

The main objective of providing an outlet is to provide ample supply of water to the fields, whenever needed. If the total available supply is insufficient, the outlets must be such that equitable distribution can be ensured. The efficiency of irrigation system depends on the proper functioning of canal outlets which should satisfy the following requirements:

i) The outlets must be strong and simple with no moving parts which would require periodic attention and maintenance.

ii) The outlets should be tamper-proof, and in case there is any interference in the functioning of the outlet, it should be easily detectable.

iii) The cost of outlets should be less since a large number of outlets have to be installed in an irrigation network.

iv) The outlet should be able to draw sediment in proportion to the amount of water withdrawn so that there is no silting problem in the distributary downstream of the outlet.

v) The outlets should be able to function efficiently even at low heads.

Choice of type of an outlet and its design are governed by factors, such as water distribution policy, water distribution method, method of water assessment, source of supply and the working of the distributary channel.

Water may be distributed on the basis of either the actual area irrigated in the previous year or the actual culturable commanded area. The discharge from the outlet should be capable of being varied in the first case, but can remain fixed in the second. The method of water distribution may be such that each cultivator successively receives water for a duration in proportion to his area. Or, alternatively, all the cultivators share the outlet discharge simultaneously. The first system is better as it results in less loss of water. The outlet capacity is decided keeping in view the method of water distribution.

If the assessment is by volume, the outlet discharge should remain constant and not change with variation in the water levels of the distributary and the watercourse. On the other hand, if water charges are decided on area basis, the variation in the outlet capacity with water levels of the distributary and the watercourse is relatively immaterial.

With a reservoir as supply source, the cultivators can be provided water whenever needed and, hence, the outlets should be capable of being opened or closed. The outlets would generally remain open if the supply source is a canal without storage so that water is diverted to the field when the canal is running.

At times, the amount of water in the main canal may not be sufficient to feed all the channels simultaneously to their full capacity. As such, either all the channels may run with low discharge or groups of channels may be supplied their full capacity by rotation. In the first case, the outlets must be able to take their proportionate share even with large variations in the discharge of the distributary channel. In the second case, the outlets must be such that the required amount of water is available for all the channels being fed with their full capacity.

It should be noted that whereas the cultivator prefers to have outlets capable of supplying constant discharge, the canal management would prefer that the outlets supply variable discharge depending upon the discharge in the distributary channel so that the tail end of the channel is neither flooded nor dried. Obviously, both these requirements cannot be fulfilled simultaneously.

7.6.1 Types of Outlets

Canal outlets are of the following three types:

i) Non-modular outlets
ii) Semi-modular outlets
iii) Modular outlets

i) Non-modular Outlets

In *non-modular outlets,* discharge capacity depends on the difference of water levels in the distributary and the watercourse. The discharge through non-modular outlets fluctuates over a wide range with variations in the water levels of either the distributary or the watercourse. The non-modular outlet is controlled by a shutter at its upstream end. Loss of head in non-modular outlet is less than that in a modular outlet. Hence, non-modular outlets are very suitable for low head conditions. However, in non-modular outlets, the discharge may vary even when the water level in the distributary remains constant. Hence, it is very difficult to ensure equitable distribution of water at all outlets at times of keen demand of water.

The non-modular outlet is usually in the form of a submerged pipe outlet or a masonry sluice which is fixed in the canal bank at right angle to the direction of flow in the distributary. The diameter of the pipe varies from

10 to 30 cm. The pipe is laid on a light concrete foundation to avoid uneven settlement of the pipe and consequent leakage problems. The pipe inlet is generally kept about 25 cm below the water level in the distributary. When considerable fluctuation in the distributary water level is anticipated, the inlet is so fixed that it is below the minimum water level in the distributary. Figure 7.9 shows a pipe outlet.

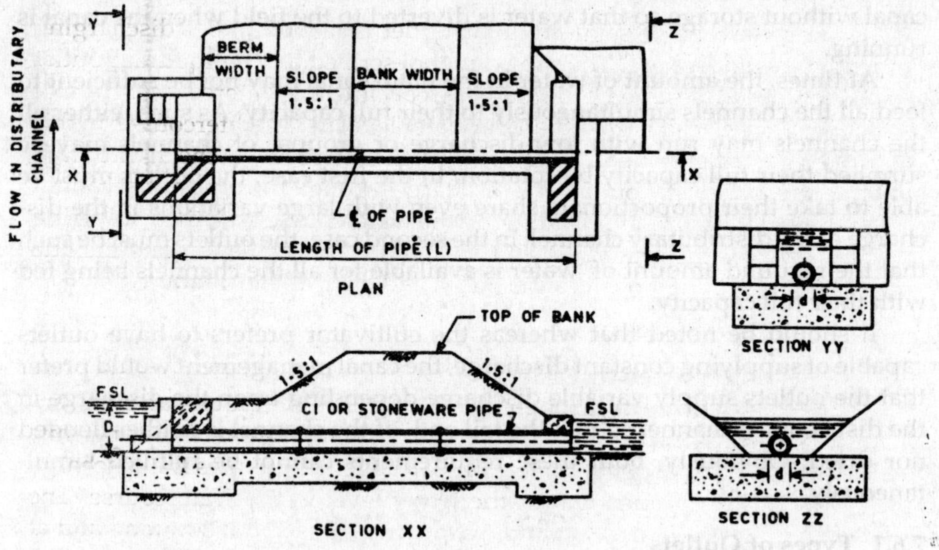

Fig. 7.9 Pipe outlet

Obviously, the discharge through non-modular outlets varies with water levels in the distributary and the watercourse. In case of fields located at high elevations, the watercourse level is high and, hence, the discharge is relatively small. But in case of fields located at low elevations, the discharge is relatively larger due to lower water course levels. Further, depending upon the amount of withdrawal of water in the head reaches, the tail reach may be completely dry or get flooded. The discharge through pipe outlets can be increased by deepening the watercourse and thereby lowering the water level in it. The discharge varies from outlet to outlet because of flow conditions and also at different times on the same outlet due to sediment discharge in the distributary channel. As such, proper and equitable distribution of water is very difficult. These are serious drawbacks of pipe outlets. The non-modular outlets can, however, work well for low heads too and this is their chief merit. Pipe outlets are adopted in the initial stages of distribution or for additional irrigation in a season when excess supply is available.

ii) Semi-modular Outlets

The discharge through a *semi-modular outlet* (or semi-module or flexible outlet) depends only on the water level in the distributary, and is unaffected by the water level in the watercourse provided a minimum working head required for its working is available. A semi-module is more suitable for achieving equitable distribution of water at all outlets of a distributary. The only disadvantage of a semi-modular outlet is that it involves comparatively greater loss of head.

The simplest type of semi-modular outlet is a pipe outlet discharging freely into the atmosphere. The pipe outlet described as non-modular outlet works as semi-module when it discharges freely into the watercourse. The exit end of the pipe is placed higher than the water level in the watercourse. In this case, working head H is the difference between water level in the distributary and the centre of the pipe outlet. The discharge through the pipe outlet cannot be increased by the cultivator by digging the watercourse and, thus, lowering the water level of the watercourse. Other types of flexible outlets include Kennedy's gauge outlet, open flume outlet and orifice semi-modules.

Kennedy's Gauge Outlet

This outlet was developed by R.G. Kennedy in 1906. It mainly consists of an orifice with bellmouth entry, a long-expanding delivery pipe and an intervening vertical air column above the throat (Fig. 7.10). The air vent pipe permits free circulation of air around the jet. This arrangement makes the discharge through the outlet independent of the water level in the watercourse. The water jet enters the cast iron expanding pipe which is about 3 m long and at the end of which a cement concrete pipe extension is generally provided. Water is then discharged to the watercourse.

This outlet can be easily tampered with by the cultivator who blocks the air vent pipe to increase the discharge through the outlet. Because of this drawback and its high cost, Kennedy's gauge outlet is generally not used.

Open Flume Outlet

An open flume outlet is a weir with sufficiently constricted throat to ensure supercritical flow, and long enough to ensure that the controlling section remains within the throat at all discharges upto the maximum. A gradual expansion is provided downstream of the throat. The entire structure is built in brick masonry, but the controlling section is generally provided with cast iron or steel bed and check plates. This arrangement ensures the formation of hydraulic jump and hence the outlet discharge remains independent of the water level in the watercourse. Figure 7.11 shows an open flume outlet which is commonly used in Punjab. The discharge through the outlet is proportional to $H^{3/2}$.

Orifice Semi-Modules

An orifice semi-module consists of an orifice followed by a gradually expanding flume on the downstream side (Fig. 7.12). Supercritical flow through the

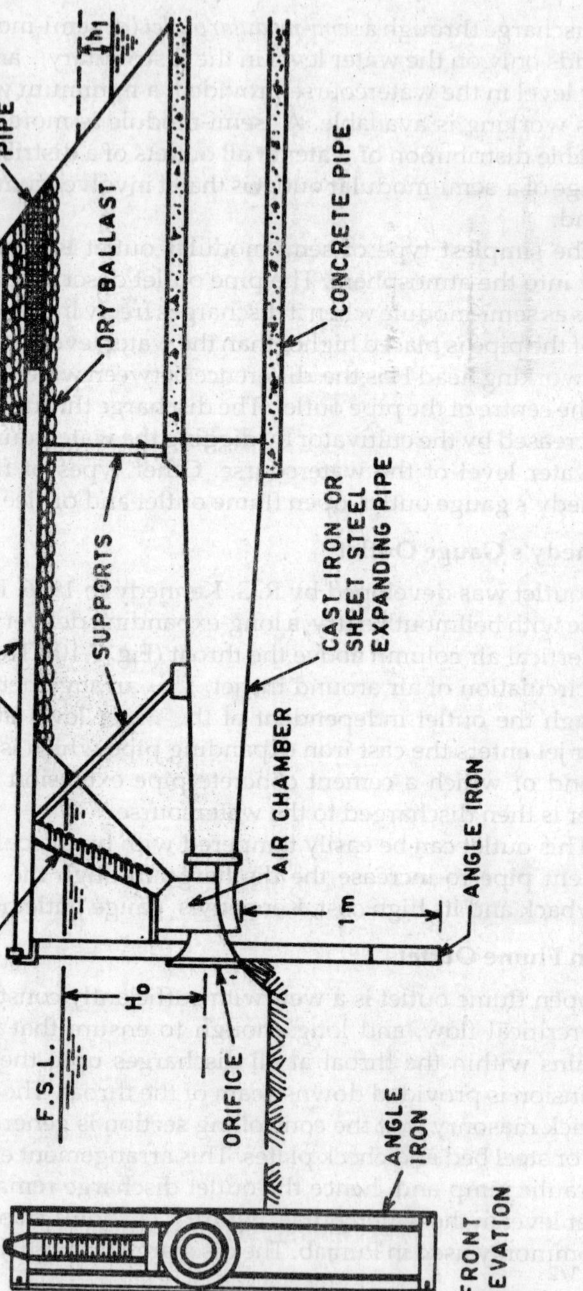

Fig. 7.10 Kennedy's gauge outlet

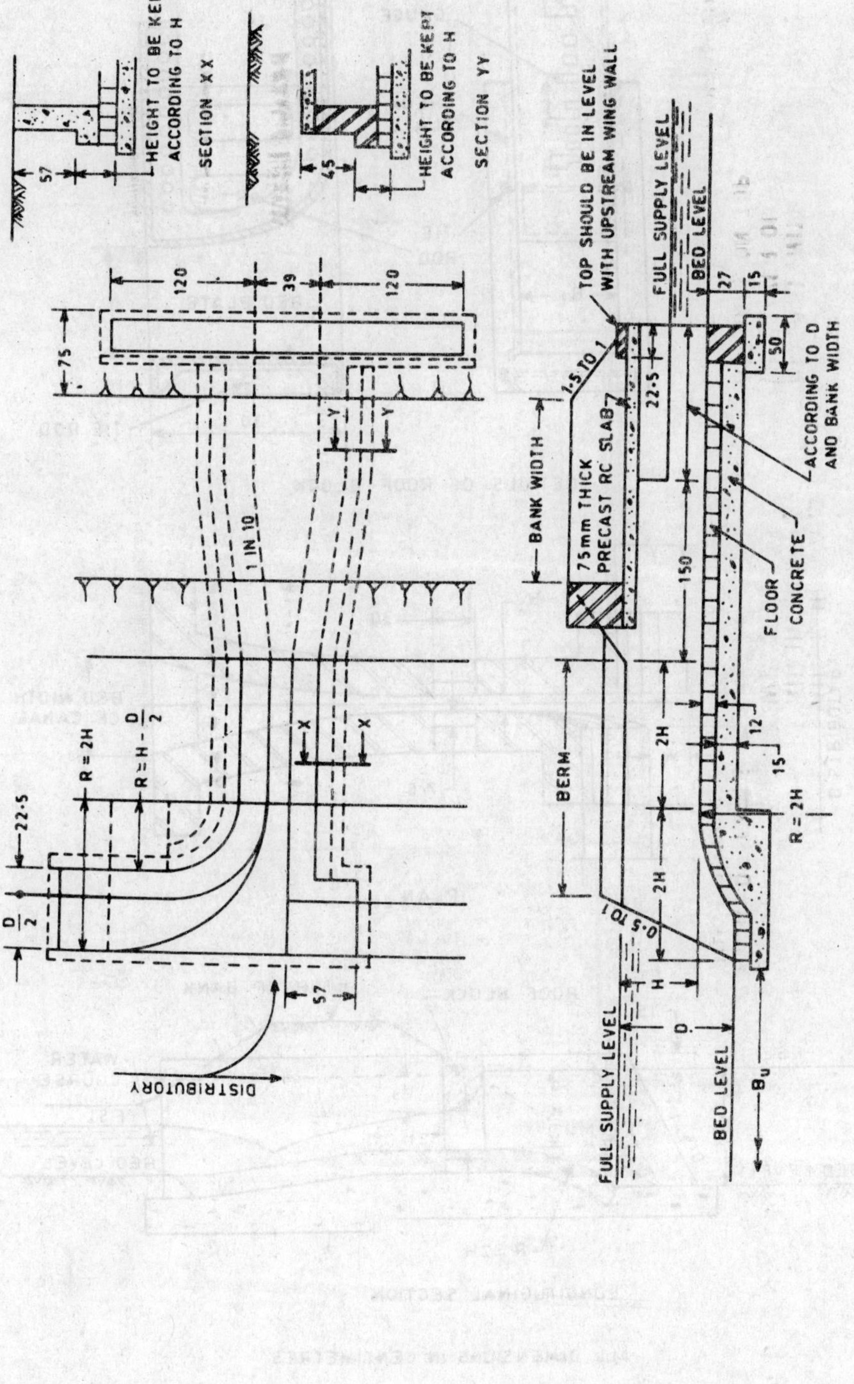

ALL DIMENSIONS IN CENTIMETRES

Fig. 7.11 Open flume outlet

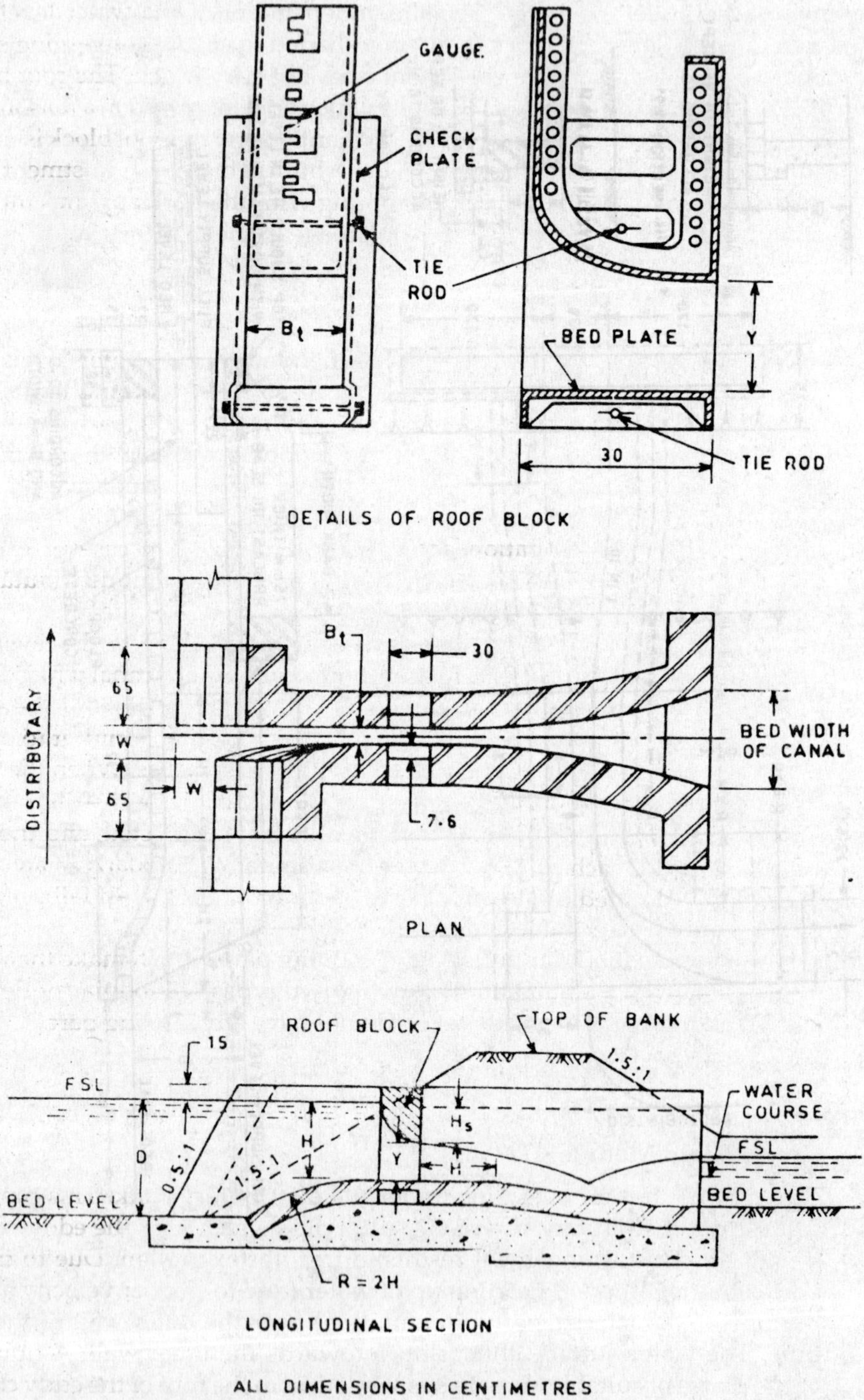

Fig. 7.12 Orifice semi-module

orifice causes the formation of hydraulic jump in the expanding flume and, hence, the outlet discharge remains independent of the water level in the watercourse. The roof block is suitably shaped to ensure converging streamlines so that the discharge coefficient does not vary much. The roof block is fixed in its place by means of two bolts which are embedded in a masonry key. For adjustment, this masonry can be dismantled and the roof block is suitably adjusted. After this, the masonry key is rebuilt. Thus, the adjustment can be made at a small cost. However, tampering with the outlet by the cultivators would be easily noticed through the damage to the masonry key. This is the chief merit of this outlet.

iii) Modular Outlets

In *modular outlets*, the discharge is independent of the water levels in the distributary and the watercourse, within reasonable working limits. These outlets may have moving parts or may be without moving parts. In the latter case, these are called rigid modules. The modular outlets with moving parts are not simple to design and construct and are, hence, expensive.

A modular outlet supplies fixed discharge and, therefore, enables the farmer to plan his irrigation accordingly. However, in case of excess or deficient supplies in the distributary, the tail-end reach of the distributary may either get flooded or be deprived of water. This is due to the reason that the modular outlet would not adjust its discharge according to the level in the distributary. But, if an outlet is to be provided in a branch canal which is likely to run with large fluctuations in discharge, a modular outlet would be an ideal choice. The outlet would be set at a level low enough to permit it to draw its due share when the branch is running with low supplies. When the branch has to carry excess supplies to meet the demands of the distributaries, the discharge through the modular outlet would not be affected, and the excess supplies would reach upto the desired distributaries. Similarly, if an outlet is desired to be located upstream of a regulator or a raised crest fall, a modular outlet would be a suitable choice.

Most of the modular outlets have moving parts which make them costly to install as well as maintain. Following two types of modular outlets (also known as rigid modules), however, do not have any moving part.

i) Gibb's rigid module
ii) Khanna's rigid module

Gibb's Rigid Module

This module has an inlet pipe under the distributary bank. This pipe takes water from distributary to a rising spiral pipe which joins the eddy chamber (Fig. 7.13). This arrangement results in free vortex motion. Due to this free vortex motion, there is heading up of water (due to smaller velocity at larger radius—a characteristic of vortex motion) near the outer wall of the rising pipe. The water surface, thus, slopes towards the inner wall. A number of baffle plates of suitable size are suspended from the roof of the eddy chamber

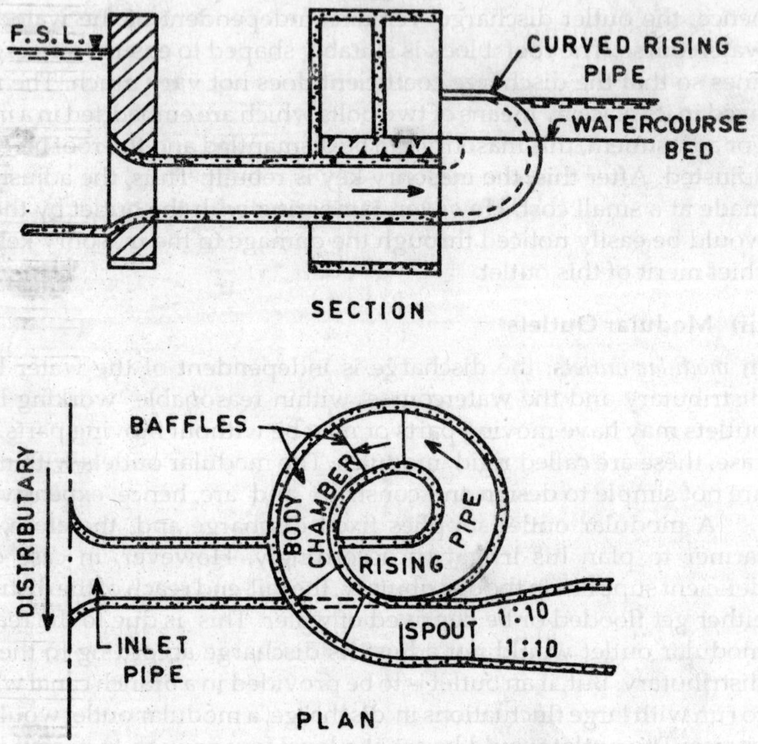

Fig. 7.13 Gibb's rigid module

such that the lower ends of these plates slope against the flow direction. With the increase in head, the water banks up at the outer wall of the eddy chamber and impinges against the baffles and spins round in the compartment between two successive baffle plates. This causes dissipation of excess energy and results in constant discharge. The outlet is relatively more costly and its sediment withdrawal is also not good.

Khanna's Rigid Orifice Module

This outlet is similar to an orifice semi-module. But it has, in addition, sloping shoots fixed in the roof block (Fig. 7.14). These shoots cause back flow and, thus, keep the outlet discharge constant. If the water level in the distributary is at or below its normal level, the outlet behaves like an orifice semi-module. But when the water level in the parent channel is above its normal level, water level rises in chamber A and enters the first sloping shoot. This causes back flow and dissipates additional energy. This results in maintaining a constant discharge. The number of sloping shoots and their height above the normal level can vary to suit local requirements. The shoots are housed in a chamber so that these cannot be tampered with. If the shoots are blocked, the outlet continues to function as a semi-module.

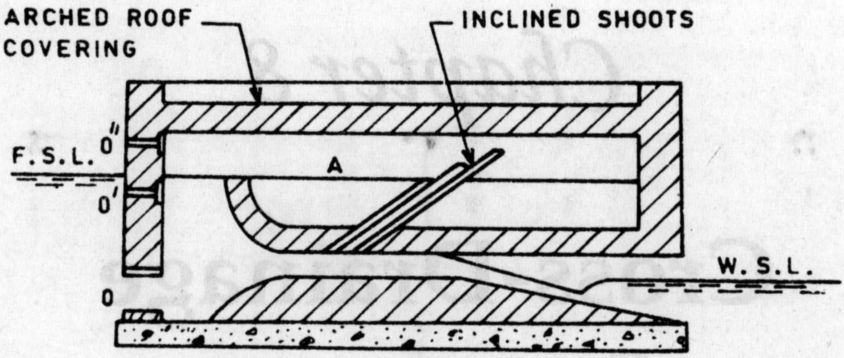

Fig. 7.14 Khanna's rigid module

EXERCISES

1. Why does the need of a canal fall arise? Describe different types of fall.
2. What are the functions of a distributary head regulator and a cross regulator?
3. Describe different types of outlets mentioning their suitability for different sets of field conditions.

Chapter 8

Cross-Drainage Structures

8.1 GENERAL

Aligning a canal on the watershed of an area is necessary so that water from the canal can flow by gravity to fields on both sides of the canal. However, a canal taking off from a river at A (Fig. 8.1) has to necessarily cross some streams or drainages (such as at a, b, c and d in the figure) before it can mount the watershed of the area at B. In order to carry the canal across the streams, major cross-drainage structures have to be constructed. Once the canal is on

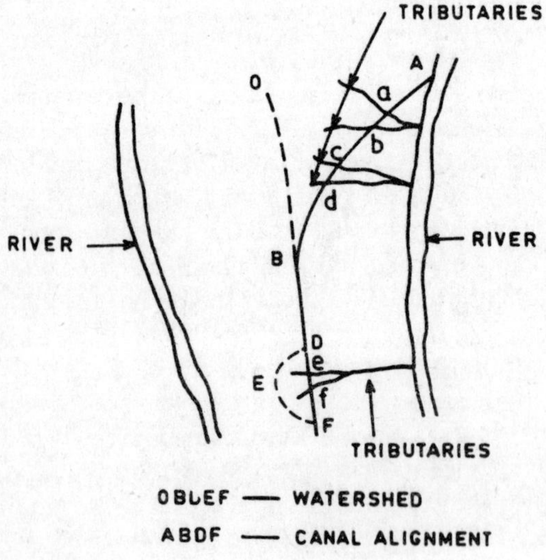

Fig. 8.1 Canal alignment between the offtake and watershed

the watershed at B, usually no cross-drainage structure is required except in situations when the canal has to leave a looping watershed (such as, DEF in Fig. 8.1) for a short distance between D and F and may cross tributaries (as at e and f). The *cross-drainage structures* are constructed to negotiate a channel over, below or at the same level of a stream.

8.2 TYPES OF CROSS-DRAINAGE STRUCTURES

Such structures can be classified under three broad categories depending on whether the structure is built to negotiate a carrier channel over, below or at the same level as the stream channel.

8.2.1 Structures for a Carrier Channel over a Natural Stream

The structures falling under this category are aqueducts and siphon aqueducts. Maintenance of such structures is relatively easy as these are above ground and can be easily inspected.

When the full supply level (F.S.L.) of a canal is much higher than the high flood level (H.F.L.) of stream, the canal is carried over the stream by means of a bridge-like structure which is called *aqueduct*. The stream water passes through the space below the canal such that the H.F.L. is lower than the underside of the canal trough (Fig. 8.2).

Siphon aqueducts (Fig. 8.3) are the aqueducts in which the bed of the stream is depressed when it passes under the canal trough, and the stream water flows under pressure below the canal. In siphon aqueducts, the stream bed is usually provided with a concrete or masonry floor.

Aqueducts and siphon aqueducts are further classified into the following three types:

Type I: In this type of structure, the earthen canal banks are carried as such and, hence, the culvert length (*i.e.*, the length of barrels through which the stream water is passed under the canal) has to be long enough to support the water section as well as the earthen banks of the canal [Fig. 8.4 (a)]. In this type of structure, the canal section is not flumed and remains unaltered. Hence, the width (across the canal) of the structure is maximum. This type of structure, obviously, saves on canal wings and bank connections, and is justified only for small streams so that the length (along the canal) of the structure is small. An extreme example of such a structure would be to carry the stream by means of a pipe laid under the bed of the canal.

Type II: This type of structure is similar to the Type I with a provision of retaining walls to retain the outer slopes of the earthen canal banks [Fig. 8.4 (b)]. This reduces the length of the culvert. This type of construction can be considered suitable for streams of intermediate size.

Type III: In this type of structure, the earthen canal banks are discontinued through the aqueduct, and the canal water is carried in a trough which may be of masonry or concrete, Fig. 8.4 (c). The earthen canal banks are connected to the respective trough walls on their sides by means of wing walls. The width of the canal is also reduced over the crossing. In this type of structure, the width of the structure is minimum and, hence, the structure is

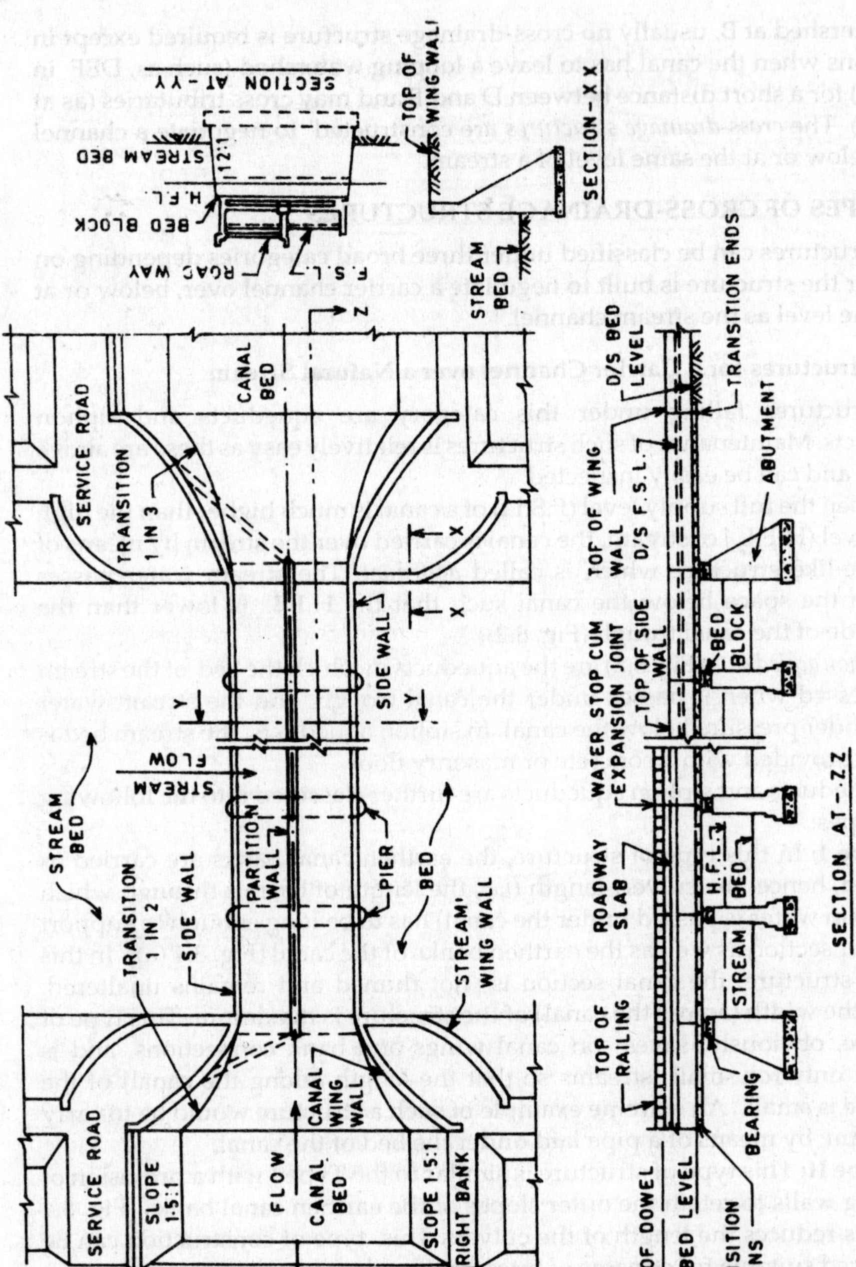

Fig. 8.2 Typical plan and section of an aqueduct

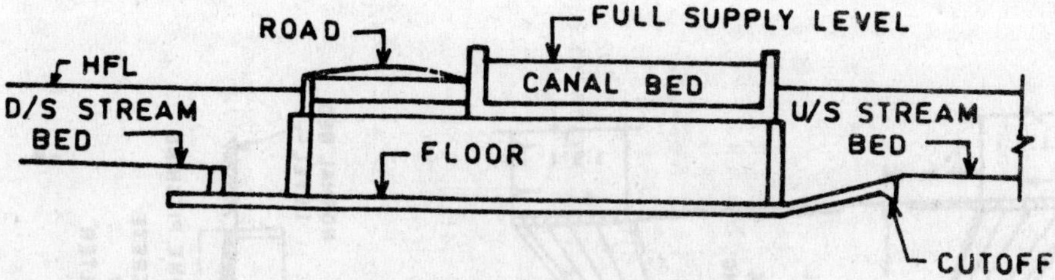

Fig. 8.3 Siphon aqueduct

suitable for large streams requiring considerable length of aqueduct between the abutments.

8.2.2 Structures for a Carrier Channel Underneath a Natural Stream

The structures falling under this category are superpassages and siphons. The maintenance of such structures is relatively difficult as these are not easily accessible.

Superpassage (Fig. 8.5) is like an aqueduct, but carries the stream over the canal. The canal F.S.L. is lower than the underside of the stream trough and, hence, canal flows with a free surface.

Siphon (Fig. 8.6) carries the canal water under pressure through barrels below the stream trough. For siphoning small discharges, precast RCC pipes will be economical.

For siphoning higher discharges, horse-shoe shaped, rectangular or circular barrels, single or multiple, are adopted. Roof of rectangular barrels are, at times, arch-shaped for economy. For discharges under high pressures, circular or horse-shoe shaped barrels are more suitable.

8.2.3 Structures for Carrier Channel Crossing a Natural Stream at the same Level

Structures falling under this category are level crossings and inlets. Inlets are, at times, combined with escapes. When the canal and the stream meet each other at practically the same level, a level crossing (Fig. 8.7) is provided. The level crossings involve intermixing of the canal and the stream waters. These are usually provided when a large-sized canal crosses a large stream which carries a large discharge during high floods and when siphoning of either of the two is prohibitive on consideration of economy or non-permissibility of head loss through siphon barrels. Across the stream and at the upstream end of the junction with the canal is constructed a barrier with its top at the canal F.S.L. The regulators are provided across the stream and the canal at the downstream junctions of the level crossing. These regulators control the flow into the canal and the stream downstream of the crossing. This type of arrangement is also useful in augmenting the canal supplies with the stream discharge.

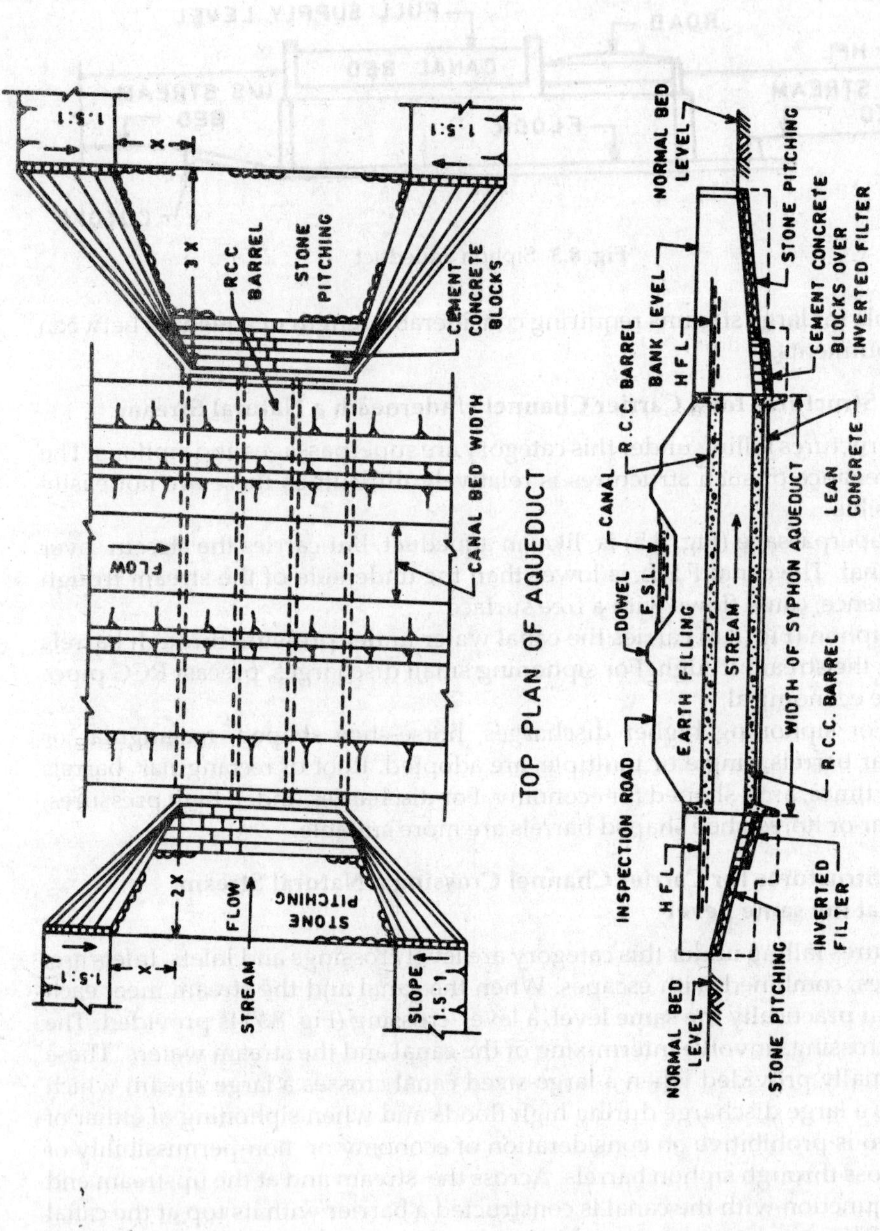

Fig. 8.4(a) Typical plan and section of siphon Aqueduct (Type I)

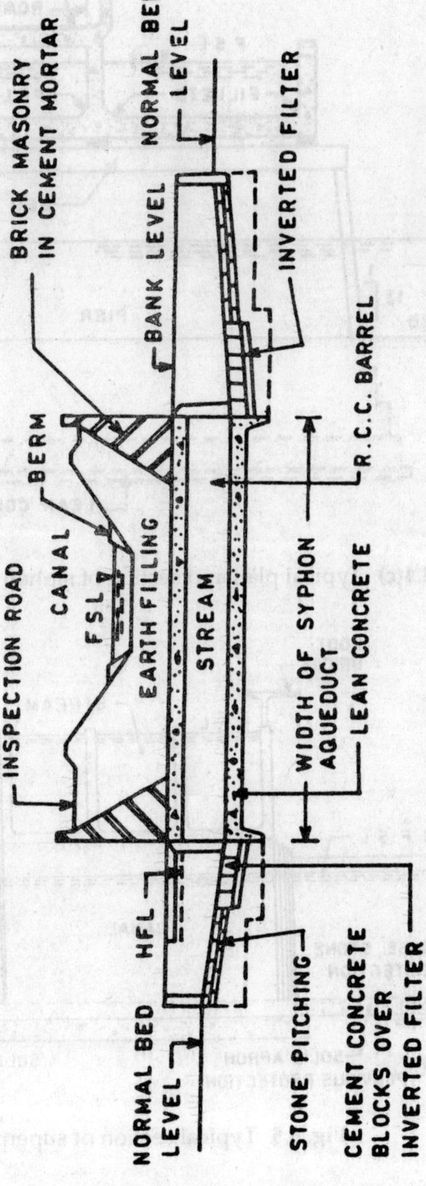

Fig. 8.4(b) Typical section of siphon Aqueduct (Type II)

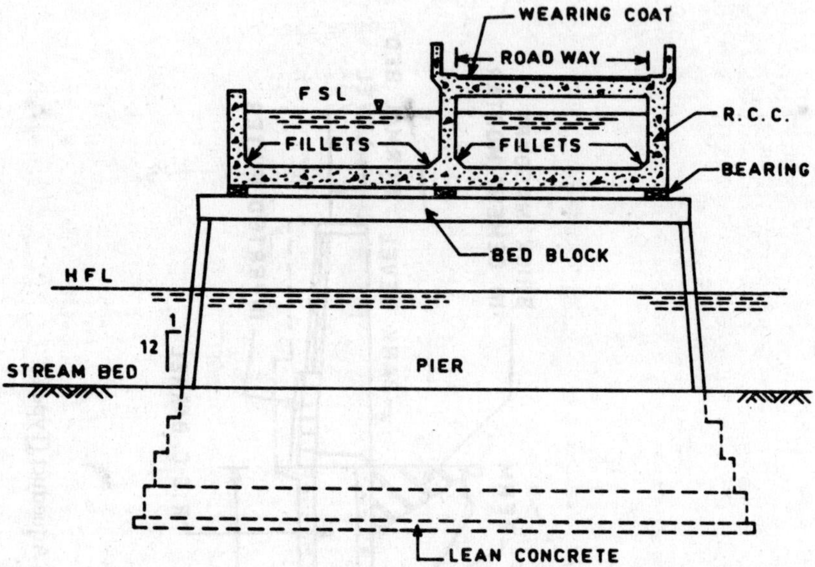

Fig. 8.4(c) Typical plan and section of siphon Aqueduct (Type III)

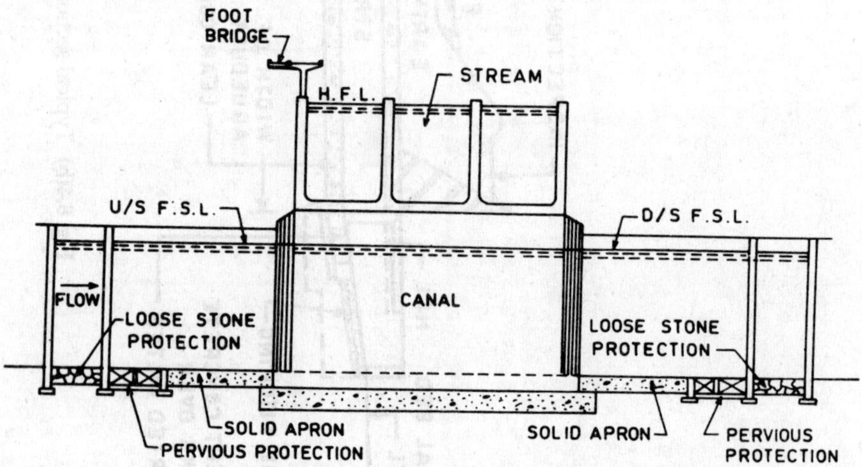

Fig. 8.5 Typical section of superpassage

When the stream is dry, the stream regulator is kept closed and the canal regulator is opened so that the canal water flows in the canal itself without interruption. When the stream is bringing water, it mixes with the canal water,

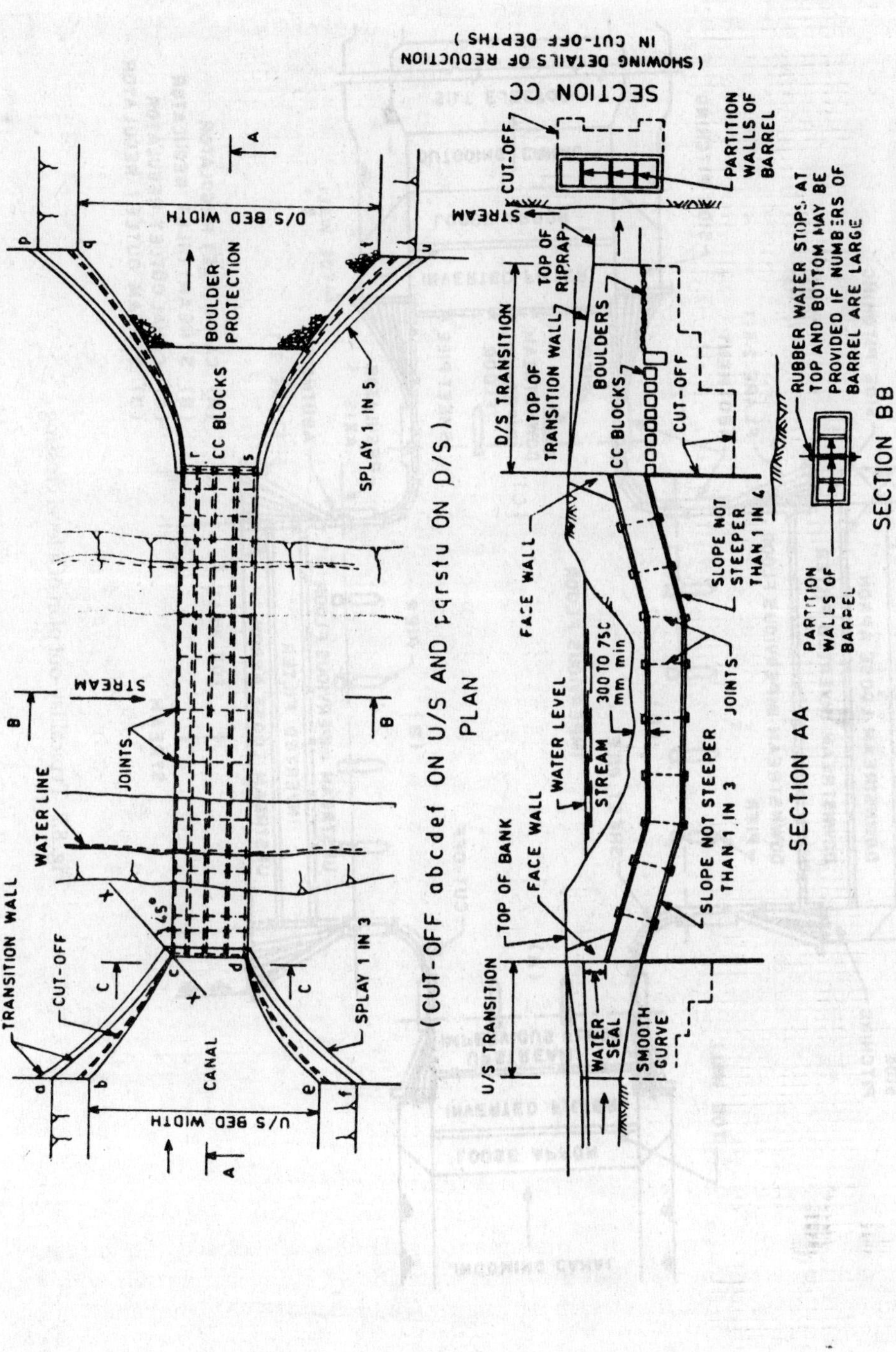

Fig. 8.6 Typical plan and section of a canal siphon

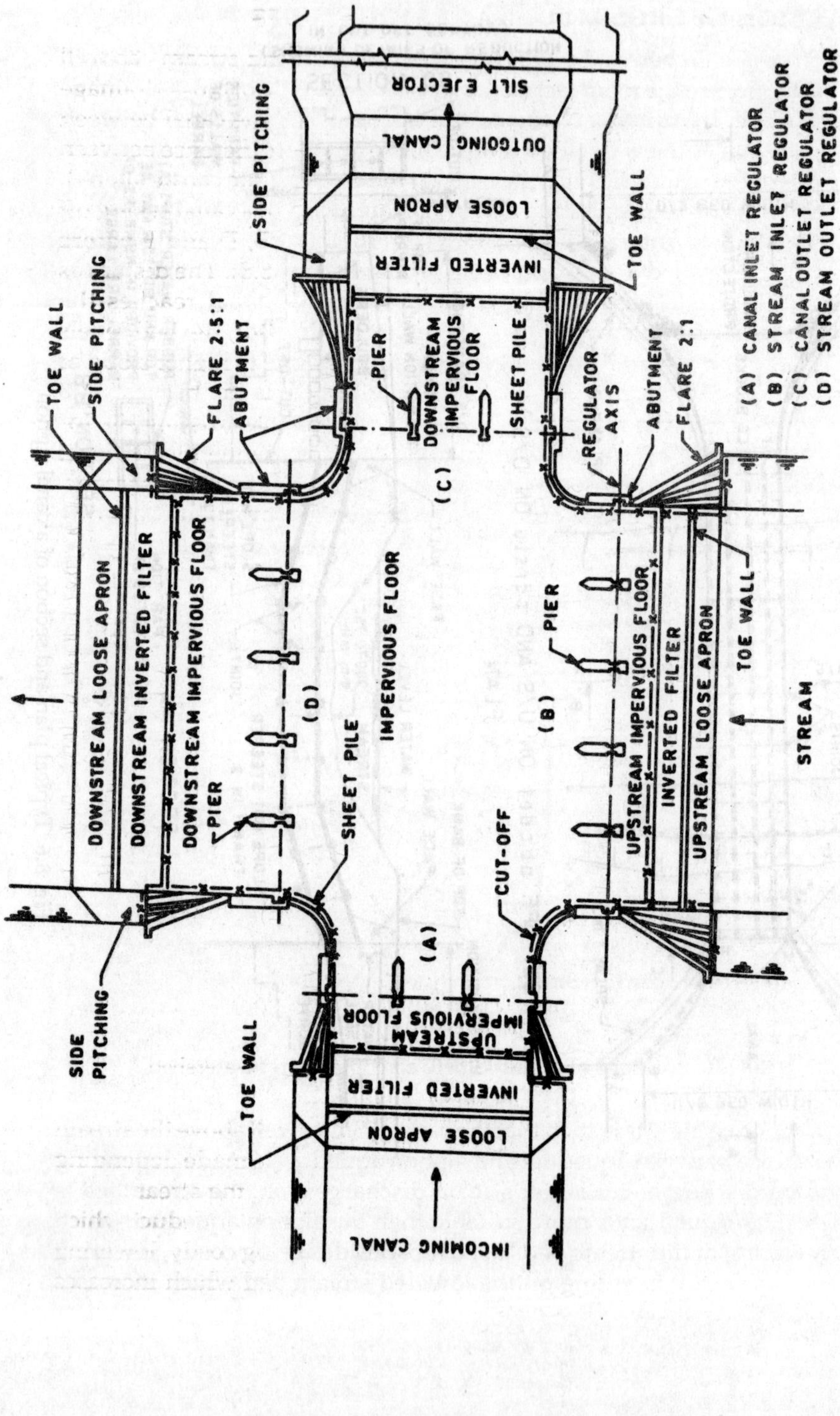

Fig. 8.7 Typical lay-out plan of a level crossing

and the stream regulator is used to dispose of that part of stream water which is not used to augment the canal supply.

8.3 SELECTION OF CROSS-DRAINAGE STRUCTURES

Relative difference in bed and water levels of the canal and stream as well as their discharges are the main factors for deciding the type of cross-drainage structure at a site. By suitably changing the alignment of the canal between offtaking point A and the watershed (Fig. 8.8), the relative difference between the bed levels of the tributaries and the canal at the crossing site can be altered. Consider three possible alignments ABC, ADE and AFG of a canal taking off from a river at A and intersecting a tributary HBDFI at B, D and F before mounting the watershed at C, E and G, respectively (Fig. 8.8). The distances AB, AD and AF are almost the same and, hence, the canal reaches the crossing site with its bed more or less at the same level. But, the bed levels of the tributary at B, D and F are significantly different due to higher slope of the tributary. Obviously, the bed level of the tributary is the highest at B and the lowest at F in the reach BDF. Thus, if F is a suitable crossing site for aqueduct, site D may necessitate construction of siphon aqueduct or level crossing, and site B may require construction of a siphon or a superpassage. Thus, the type of cross-drainage structure can be changed by suitably altering the crossing site.

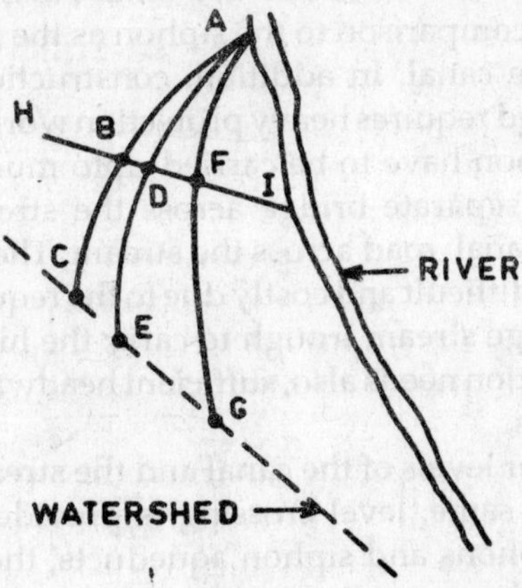

Fig. 8.8 Different canal alignments between offtake and watershed

When the crossing site is such that the canal F.S.L. is well above the stream H.F.L. the choice between aqueduct and siphon aqueduct is made depending on the stream discharge. For larger stream discharges (*i.e.*, the streambed is much wider), an aqueduct is more suitable than the siphon aqueduct which requires lowering of the stream bed by a drop. Besides being costly, lowering of the bed may result in silting on the lowered stream bed which increases the risk of failure. However, an aqueduct necessitates heavy canal embankments towards the crossing (Fig. 8.9). This is due to the wide flood cross-section of streams in plains and the requirements that the canal must be well above the H.F.L. and the aqueduct has to be constructed in a smaller part of the cross-section of the stream.

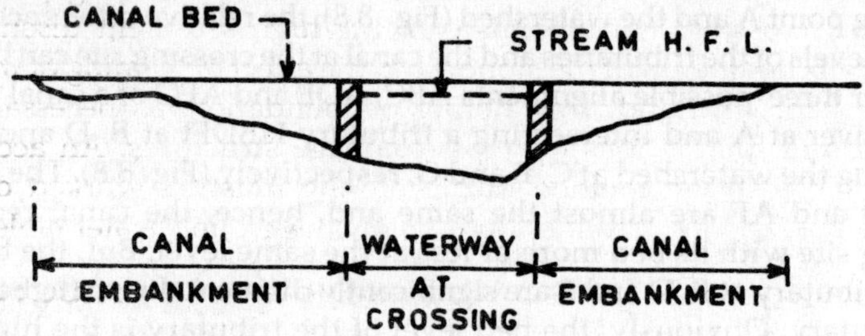

Fig. 8.9 Canal embankment near crossing site

Siphon aqueducts are more suitable when the stream size is small compared to the canal size. In case of siphon aqueducts, the relative difference of water and bed levels of the canal and stream is small and, hence, embankments of only small height are required.

If the stream H.F.L. is well above the canal F.S.L., the superpassage is generally preferred in comparison to the siphon as the latter involves considerable head loss in the canal. In addition, construction of siphon under a stream with erodible bed requires heavy protection works. Foundation of both superpassage and siphon have to be carried upto much below the erodible bed of the stream. A separate bridge across the stream trough has to be provided to carry the canal road across the stream. The construction of these structures is relatively difficult and costly due to the requirements of extensive training works and large stream trough to carry the high flood discharge. If the canal serves navigation needs also, sufficient headway should be provided for the passage of boats.

If the bed and water levels of the canal and the stream at the crossing site are approximately the same, level crossing is provided. Sometimes due to prohibitive costs of siphons and siphon aqueducts, the canal alignment between the offtake and the watershed is suitably altered so that level crossing can be provided at the crossing site. The initial cost of a level crossing is generally much smaller than the cost of other cross-drainage structures. Also, the perennial discharge of the stream can be diverted to the canal to provide additional irrigation. However, the level crossings require permanent staff for continuous watch, maintenance and operation of gates. Also, when the stream is passing the high flood discharge, the canal may have to be closed down to prevent the sediment load of the stream from entering the canal and silting it. Further, if the canal F.S.L. is higher than the general ground level, the H.F.L. of the stream would increase on the upstream side of the crossing site, and submerge the land. To prevent such submergence of the land, marginal banks are provided.

Besides the above factors, the topography of the terrain, foundation conditions, regime of the stream, and dewatering requirements would also affect the choice of the type of cross-drainage structures. Detailed examination of the terrain topography and the foundation is necessary to locate a stable reach of the stream with good foundations and permitting preferably a right-angled crossing. For streams carrying high sediment discharge, the possibility of choking up of the siphon and the effect of fluming of the stream should be kept in mind. Dewatering of foundations is necessary in the construction of foundations for cross-drainage structures. An accurate estimate of the cost and method of dewatering must be worked out when designs involve laying of foundations below the ground water table.

8.4 SOME REQUIREMENTS OF CROSS-DRAINAGE STRUCTURES

Any cross-drainage structure should preferably be located in a straight reach of the stream crossing the canal at right angles as far as possible. Alignment of the canal should also be such that it results in minimum lengths of embankments (for aqueduct and siphon aqueduct structures). If required, the site of the structure may even be shifted away from the existing stream channel, when it is possible to divert the channel and also keep it there by reasonable training works. One obvious advantage of such an alternative would be that the construction will be carried out in dry conditions.

The type of foundation for cross-drainage strucures will depend primarily on the depth of scour, calculated from Lacey's equation (Eqs. 5.9 or 5.10), and the bearing capacity of the soil. The depth of scour around piers is taken as twice the depth of scour calculated from Lacey's equation. In alluvial streams, well foundation is usually provided where deep foundation is required. With the provision of an impervious floor (necessary for siphon and siphon aqueduct) alongwith cutoff walls, the depth of foundation may be reduced. The floor itself may be designed as either a gravity floor or a raft. The floor is designed to resist the total uplift pressure caused by subsoil water and the water seeping from the canal. The uplift pressure is counterbalanced by the dead weight of the gravity floor. The worst condition occurs when there is no water in the barrel and, hence, the weight of water in the barrel is not included. At times, it may be economical to design the floor as a raft so that the uplift is counterbalanced by the entire weight of the superstructure.

The spacing of the piers (*i.e.*, the span) depends on structural and economic considerations. Fewer piers (*i.e.*, longer span) are preferable at sites which require costly foundation.

In case of siphon aqueducts and siphons, the drop at the upstream end of the culvert may be vertical (generally economical) or sloping. But, at the downstream end of the culvert, the rise should always be at a slope flatter than 1 in 4 so that the bed load can be moved out of the siphon barrel. The culvert floor should extend upstream of the barrel inlet by a distance equal to the difference between the H.F.L. and the culvert floor level. Barrel inlet should be bell-mouthed to reduce the head losses.

Suitable arrangement has to be provided to pass the service road across the stream. This requirement does not pose much problem in structures of type I and II in which earthen embankments are continued. In structures of type III, the simplest arrangement is to carry the road on either side (or only on one side for economic reasons) by providing slabs and arches on either side (or on one side) of the canal trough. The piers are suitably raised to keep the road and bank slabs at a level higher than the canal bed so that the flood water may find clear entry and exit (if roads on both sides of canal trough are provided) conditions at the siphon barrels. Also, the quantity of masonry is reduced.

The sides of the canal trough are generally designed as beams in reinforced concrete structures. The bottom slab is suspended from these beams. Additional beams, if required, are projected into the canal to divide the canal trough into number of parallel channels. For wider troughs having intermediate beams, the service road may be provided on one of the compartments. Canal troughs of the smaller width can be constructed as a hollow box girder and the service road can be provided on the top slab.

Wing walls of stream are suitably connected to high ground. The stream should be guided towards the structure by means of suitable river training works. Similarly, the canal banks, adjacent to the crossing, should be protected by measures, such as pitching, launching apron, *etc.*, wherever necessary.

EXERCISES

1. What is the purpose of providing a cross-drainage structure? In which reach of a canal, does the need of such structures arise, and why?
2. Explain how the type of a cross-drainage structure may change with the shift in the site of the structure along the stream.

Chapter 9

River Training Methods

9.1 RIVERS

Rivers have always played an important role in shaping civilisation. Besides supplying water, rivers also provide means of transportation, recreation, hydropower generation and waste disposal. However, rivers have also generally caused problems of flooding, change of course resulting in migration of people, loss of properties, *etc.*

Rivers can be classified in the following ways:

i) Based on the variation of discharge in a river, it may be either
   a) perennial river, if it obtains its water from melting snow for the larger part of the year and, therefore, carries significant flow throughout the year, or
   b) non-perennial river which gets its supplies only during the monsoon season as a result of rains in its catchment areas and may get completely dried up during summer season.

ii) Based on the stability of a river, it may be either
   a) stable river in which case its slope and regime show little variation from year to year, or
   b) non-stable river, if it has a tendency to either aggrade or degrade. Rivers aggrade when sediment load entering a river reach is more than its sediment-carrying capacity. Therefore, part of the sediment load gets deposited in that reach. Such a river is known as aggrading river in that reach. On the other hand, when sediment load being carried by river is less than its capacity and the river bed is erodible under the river flow conditions, the river flow picks up the material from the river bed. Such a river is called degrading river.

iii) Based on the plan-form of a river, it can be

a) straight,
b) meandering, and
c) braided.

Straight reaches of an alluvial river for a large length are rare. Alluvial rivers have a tendency to vary their plan-forms into bends which eventually result in a meandering pattern (Fig. 9.1). When a river flows in two or more channels around alluvial islands, it is called a braided river.

iv) Based on the location of the reach under consideration, a river may be called

a) mountainous river, if the reach is in the mountains and hills,
b) flood plain river, if the river is in flood plains, and
c) tidal river when the river reach is located just upstream of the sea.

9.2 RIVER TRAINING

Whenever the equilibrium of a river is disturbed by man-made structures or natural causes, the river tends to attain a new equilibrium condition by scouring the bed or by depositing the sediment on the bed or by changing its own plan-form. River training includes all such measures as are taken for controlling and regulating river flow and river configuration.

9.2.1 Objectives of River Training

River-training measures aim at achieving one or more of the following objectives:

i) **Flood Protection**

Floods cause enormous damage to life and property almost every year. River training for flood protection (also known as 'high water training' or 'training for discharge') can be achieved by one or more of the following methods:

a) By constructing levees or embankments to confine water in a narrower channel.
b) By increasing the discharge capacity of natural channels by some suitable methods such as straightening, widening or deepening.
c) By constructing reservoirs.
d) By providing escapes or diversion from rivers.

ii) **Navigation**

The measures to achieve adequate depth of flow in a river for navigation (also known as 'low water training' or 'training for depth') include dredging the shallow reaches of rivers and using spurs to contract the river channel and, thus, increase its depth. Canalisation makes a non-navigable river navigable and is accomplished by building a serie of dams (or weirs) and locks.

iii) **Sediment Control**

River training for sediment control (also known as 'mean water training' or 'training for sediment') aims at attaining efficient

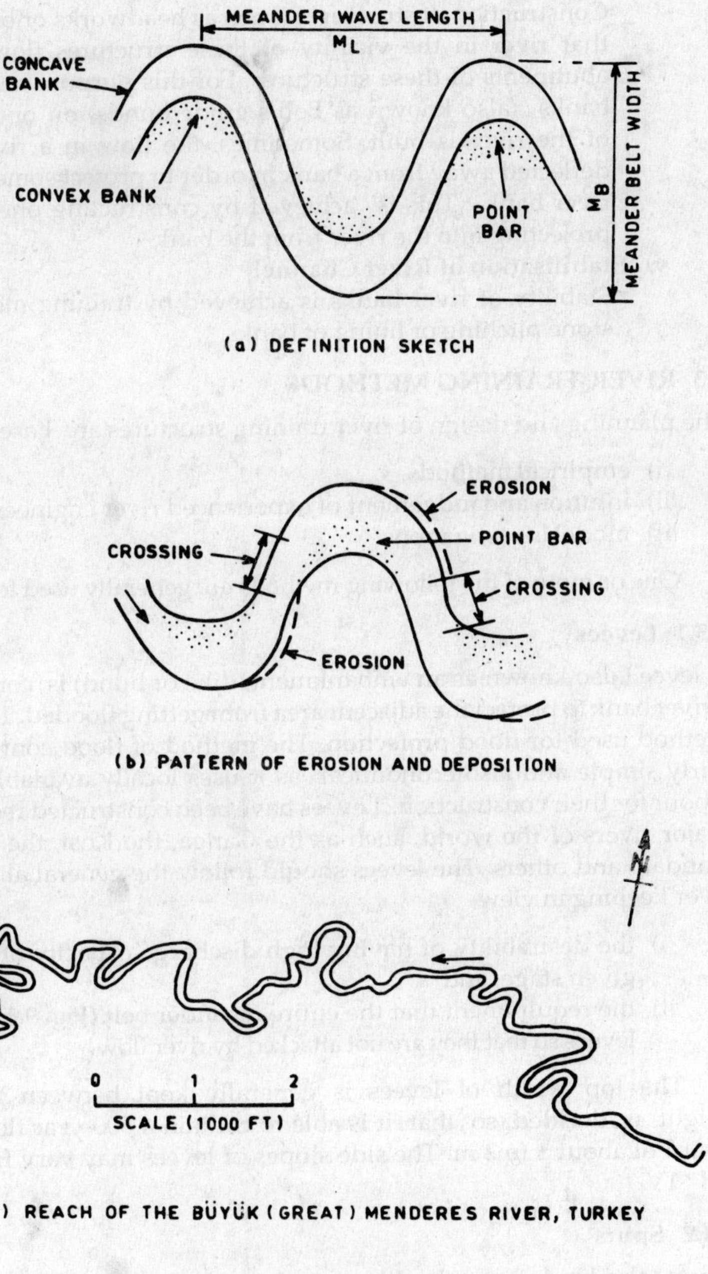

Fig. 9.1 Meandering river

movement of sediment load for keeping the river channel in a state of equilibrium. Spurs and pitched islands are normally used for training the river for sediment.

iv) **Guiding the Flow in River**

Construction of structures (such as headworks or bridges) requires that river in the vicinity of these structures flows between the abutments of these structures. For this purpose a system of guide banks (also known as Bell's guide bunds) on one or both banks of the river is built. Sometimes, the flow in a river needs to be deflected away from a bank in order to protect some portions of the river bank. This is achieved by constructing one or more spurs projecting into the river from the bank.

v) **Stabilisation of River Channel**

Stability of river banks is achieved by training methods, such as stone pitching or lining of banks.

9.3 RIVER TRAINING METHODS

The planning and design of river training structures are based on

i) empirical methods,
ii) intution and judgement of experienced river engineers, and
iii) model investigations.

One or more of the following methods are generally used for river training.

9.3.1 Levees

A levee (also known as an embankment, dike or bund) is constructed along a river bank to protect the adjacent area from getting flooded. This is the oldest method used for flood protection. The method of flood control by levees is fairly simple and also economical as it uses locally available material and labour for their construction. Levees have been constructed recently on many major rivers of the world, such as the Ganga, the Kosi, the Mahanadi, the Gandak and others. The levees should follow the general alignment of the river keeping in view

i) the desirability of having high discharge capacity of the river for a given stage, and
ii) the requirement that the entire meander belt (Fig. 9.1) be within the levees so that they are not attacked by river flow.

The top width of levees is generally kept between 3 to 8 m and its height is decided so that it is able to contain a 500-year flood with a free board of about 1 to 2 m. The side slopes of levees may vary from 2H : 1V to 6H : 1V.

9.3.2 Spurs

Spurs (also known as spur dikes, groynes or transverse dikes) are generally made of locally available earth material in the form of an embankment constructed transverse to the flow extending from one of the river banks into the river. Spurs are the most widely used river training structures, and serve the following functions in river regulation :

i) Training the river along a desired course by attracting, deflecting or repelling the flow in a channel.
ii) Creating a slack flow with the object of silting up the area in the vicinity.
iii) Protecting the river bank by keeping the flow away from it.
iv) Contracting a wide river channel, usually for the improvement of depth for navigation.

Spurs can be used either singly or in series or in combination with other river training measures. Their design depends on

i) river discharge,
ii) angle of attack,
iii) sediment load,
iv) meander length,
v) curvature of river, and
vi) upstream and downstream river training measures.

Spur length is kept longer than 1.5 to 2 times the depth of flow, and is usually restricted to less than 20% of the river width. Spacing between adjacent spurs is generally kept 2 to 2.5 times the spur length. The top width of a spur should be between 3 and 6 m, and freeboard of 1 to 1.5 m above HFL (high flood level) should always be provided in case of non-submerged spurs.

It is always advisable to finalise the spur designs only after conducting model studies. Spurs can be classified based on

i) the method and material of construction – permeable and impermeable,
ii) the height of spur with respect to HFL – submerged or non-submerged,
iii) the functions – attracting, deflecting and repelling, and
iv) the plan shape of spur – T-headed type, hockey type etc.

Usually, permeable spurs are either tree spurs or pile spurs. Tree spurs (Fig. 9.2) are constructed by tying leafy trees with strong stem and branches to a rope which is firmly anchored to the bank at one of its ends and to a concrete block at the other end. Pile spurs are constructed by driving two to

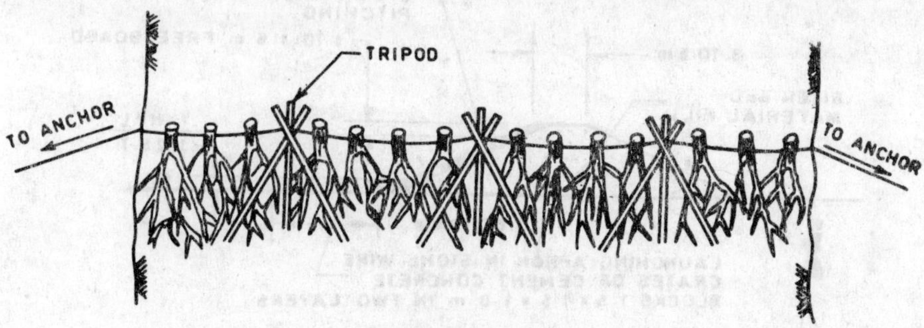

Fig. 9.2 Tree spur

three rows of inter-twined piles of timber or RCC or sheetpiles upto about 6 to 9 m inside the river bed. The space between the rows of piles is filled by alternate layers of 1.8 m thick brushwood weighted down by boulders or sand bags. Stone pitching, graded filter and a launching apron (to protect stone

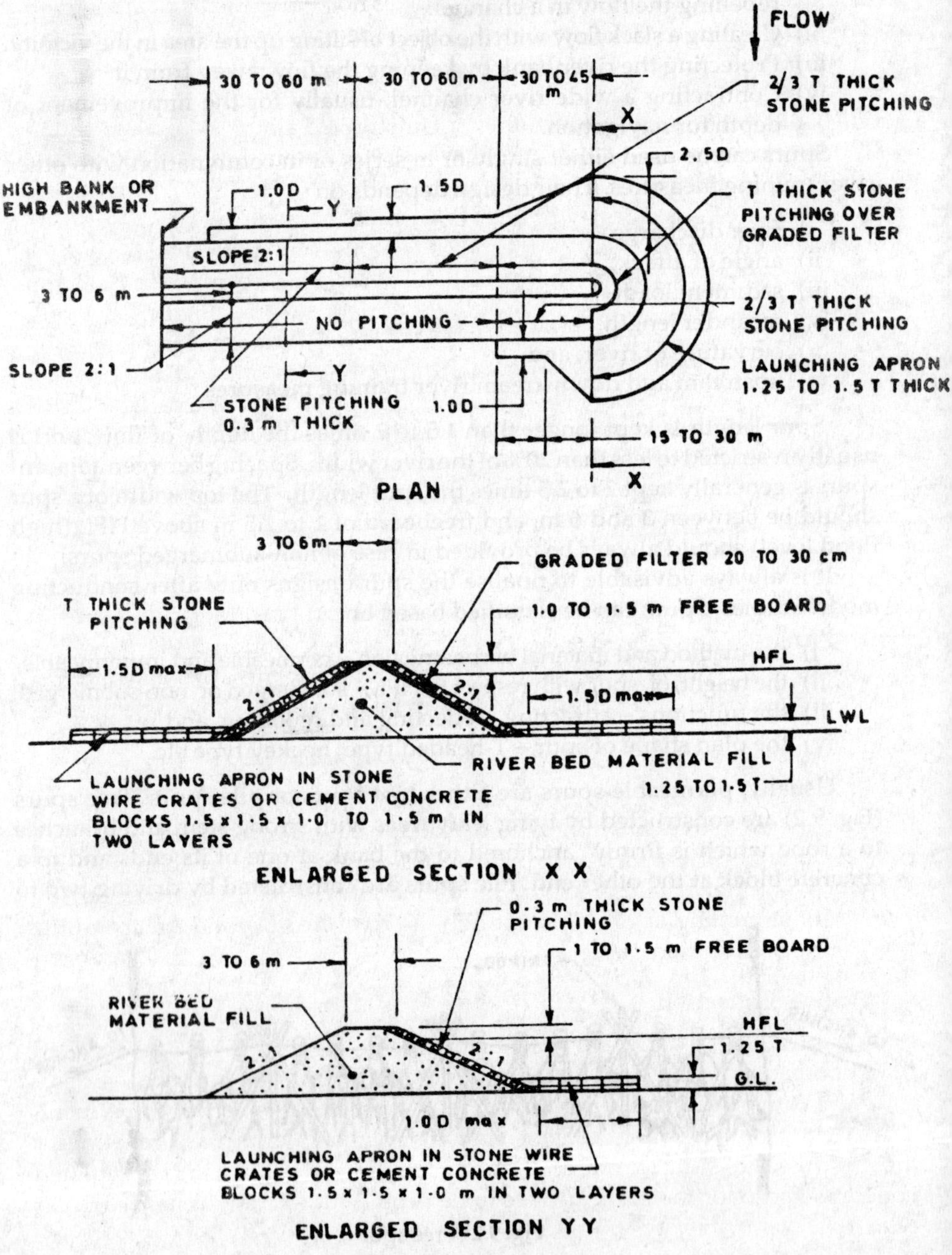

Fig. 9.3 Impermeable spur

pitching) are always provided in case of impermeable spurs constructed as an earthen embankment (Fig. 9.3). The side slopes vary between 1H : 1V to 5H : 1V with nose of the spur sloping at a flatter slope of about 5H : 1V. When spurs are oriented to point upstrem, they direct the flow away from the bank and are called repelling spurs. On the other hand, spurs pointing in the downstream direction attract the flow towards the bank and are known as attracting spurs. Spurs oriented with their axes normal to the bank are known as deflecting spurs which help in contracting the river channel.

9.3.3 Guide Banks

Guide banks are artificial embankments constructed along the flow direction both upstream and downstream of the abutment on one or both sides of the river for guiding the river flow past a bridge (or other hydraulic structures, such as weirs or barrages) without causing damage to the bridge and its approaches. Clear waterway between guide banks can be equated to Lacey's wetted perimeter [Eq. 5.6]. The overall waterway between guide banks is obtained by adding thickness of piers to the clear waterway. Figure 9.4 shows the plan and section of a typical guide bank. The elevation of the top of the guide banks is kept 1.5 to 2.5 m above the HFL of 100-year flood. The top width of guide banks is generally kept between 6 and 9 m. Locally available earth materials are used for constructing guide banks. To prevent erosion of the material from the river-side surface of guide bank, the surface is stone-pitched. This pitching is continued upto the rear side of the curved head. The size of stones used for pitching is given by

$$d = 0.046U^3$$

where d is equivalent diameter in meters and U is the average flow velocity in m/s. Angular and graded stones weighing between 450 and 1800 N (i.e., 45 and 180 kg) are generally used for this purpose. The thickness of stone pitching T in meters is related to river discharge Q (in m^3/s) by the following empirical relation:

$$T = 0.06Q^{1/3}$$

The thickness of stone pitching is increased for the curved head region.

Scour of the river bed may cause undermining of the stone pitching thereby resulting in failure of the guide banks. This can be prevented by providing launching apron of stones on the river bed beyond the toe of the guide banks, as shown in Fig. 9.4.

9.3.4 Bank Protection

Bank failures due to either wave action or erosive action of river flow can lead to river breach causing huge losses in terms of human lives, property, agriculture and other utilities. Measures of bank protection such as revetment, riprap, *etc.* provide a shield against erosion of bank material. Bank revetments are mattresses of suitable material, such as reinforced asphalt and articulated concrete, laid over the bank surface to be protected. Riprap of hard angular

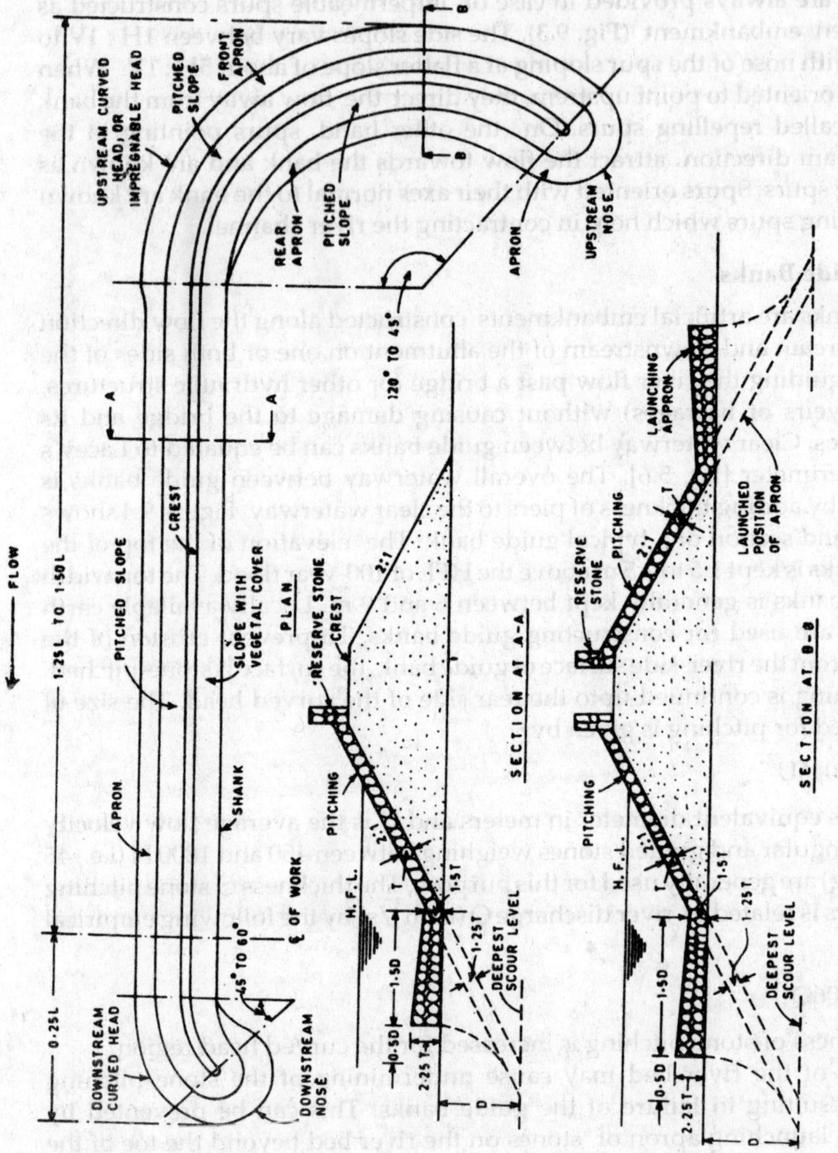

Fig. 9.4 Guide bank

rock fragments (or concrete blocks) laid on a thick layer of rubble or quarry chips is cheap and durable method of bank protection. Another way of providing bank protection is by means of flexible brick pitching (Fig. 9.5). For this purpose bricks having a pair of holes across their full width are laid on the bank slope and for some distance on the river bed at the toe of the bank. A G.I. wire passes through the brick holes. The wires are knotted at their ends and suitably anchored so that the bricks are held together and also small movement of bricks is possible.

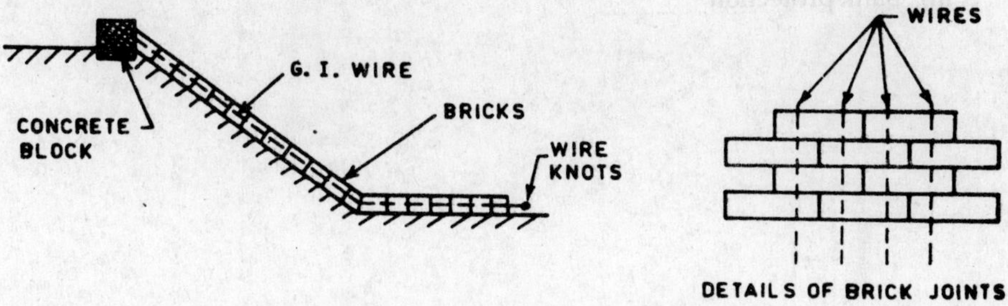

Fig. 9.5 Flexible brick pitching

9.3.5 Pitched Islands

An island created artificially on river bed with sand in its core and protected by stone pitching on all its sides is called pitched island. It can be used to correct an oblique approach upstream of weirs, barrages and bridges.

9.3.6 Marginal Bunds

Marginal bunds are embankments which are constructed along the river banks upstream of weir-like structures to protect low-lying areas from being flooded. These bunds extend to regions where the ground level is the same as that of top of the bund.

9.3.7 Cutoffs

Sometimes alluvial river flowing along curves or bends abandons a particular bend and establishes its main flow along a comparatively straight and short channel which is called cutoff. At times, it is advantageous to make an artificial cutoff by excavating a pilot channel of small cross-section and letting it develop by itself in due course of time so that the river in that region abandons the curved path and adopts the new course along the artificial cutoff. Artificial cutoff avoids the chaotic or non-equilibrium conditions which prevail during occurrence of natural cutoff. Artificial cutoffs shorten the travel distance, and increase ease of manoeuvring of a navigating vessel.

Artificial cutoff also diverts the river from a curved path which might be endangering important land area.

EXERCISES

1. Describe different types of rivers.
2. What are the objectives of river training ?
3. Describe the following river training methods :
   i) Spurs
   ii) Guide Banks
   iii) Bank protection

Chapter 10

Canal Headworks

10.1 GENERAL

An irrigation channel takes its supplies either from its source (a river or storage reservoir) in case of main canal, or from a channel in case of branch canal or a distributary. The structures constructed across a river source at the head (*i.e.*, the upstream end) of an offtaking main canal are termed *canal head works* or simply *headworks*. The headworks can be either diversion headworks or storage headworks.

Diversion headworks divert the required supply from the source to the offtaking channel and serve the following functions:

i) Diversion headworks regulate the supply of water into the canal.
ii) Diversion headworks raise water level in the river so that
   a) excavation in the head reach of the offtaking canal is reduced,
   b) command area is increased, and
   c) the command area can be easily served by flow irrigation.
iii) Diversion headworks control the entry of sediment into the offtaking canal.

Diversion headworks can be either (i) temporary, or (ii) permanent. For temporary diversion headworks, spurs or bunds are constructed across the source river. Since floods in the source river can damage such bunds, it may be necessary to repair such bunds rather frequently, and construct them after every flood that occurs in the source river. Permanent headworks have a permanent structure in the form of a weir (or a barrage) constructed across the river. Most of the headworks of important canal systems are of permanent type. Sometimes temporary headworks are constructed in the beginning and they are replaced by permanent headworks when the demand for irrigation has developed sufficiently.

10.2 LOCATION OF HEADWORKS

Most of the important rivers have four stages, *viz.*, the rocky, boulder, trough (or alluvial) and delta stages. Of these, the rocky and delta stages are generally unsuitable for siting headworks. Usually, the command area is away from the hilly stage, and it would, therefore, involve avoidable expenditure to construct a channel from headworks located in the hilly stage to its command area. In the delta stage, the irrigation requirements are generally less, and the nature of the river at this stage poses other problems.

The boulder and alluvial stages of a river are relatively more suitable sites for locating headworks. The choice between the boulder stage and the alluvial stage is mainly governed by the command area. If both stages are equally suitable for siting the headworks from command area consideration, the selection of the site should be made such that it results in the most economical alternative. The following features of the two stages should be considered while selecting the site for headworks:

i) The initial cost of headworks in the boulder stage is generally smaller than that in the alluvial stage because of: (a) local availability of stone, (b) smaller width of river (requiring smaller length of weir), (c) smaller scour depths which reduce the requirements of cutoffs and other protection works, and (d) close proximity of higher banks which means need for less extensive training works.

ii) The irrigation canal offtaking from a river in the boulder region will have a number of falls which may be utilised for generation of electricity. There is almost no scope for the generation of electricity in this manner in the alluvial reach of a river.

iii) If the existing irrigation demand is less but is likely to develop with the provision of irrigation facilities, it is possible to divert the river water into the irrigation channel by constructing a temporary boulder bund across the river. This bund will be washed away every year during the floods and will be reconstructed every year. This will, no doubt, delay the Rabi crop irrigation, but it is worthwhile to use temporary bunds for a certain period, and when the irrigation demand develops, permanent headworks may be constructed. In this manner, it would be possible to get returns proportional to expenditures incurred on the headworks. Construction of temporary bunds is generally not possible in the alluvial stage of the river.

iv) An irrigation channel offtaking in the boulder stage of the river will normally require a large number of cross-drainage structures.

v) Because of the nature of the boulder region, there is always a strong sub-soil flow in the river bed. This causes considerable loss of water and is of concern during the periods of short supply. Similarly, there will be considerable loss of water from the head reach of the offtaking channel. In alluvial reach of the river, this loss of water is much less.

vi) The regions close to the hills usually have a wet climate and grow good crops. The irrigation demand in the head reach of the channel offtaking in the boulder stage is, therefore, generally small. However, this demand would increase with the provision of irrigation facilities. In alluvial regions, the demand for irrigation is high right from the beginning.

Once the stage of a river has been chosen for locating the headworks, the site of the headworks is selected based on considerations of its suitability for the barrage (or weir), the undersluices and the canal head regulator.

For irrigation purposes, the site for headworks should result in a suitable canal alignment capable of serving its command area without much excavation. For siting the headworks, the river reach should, as far as possibe, be straight and narrow and have well-defined and non-erodible high banks. In the case of a meandering river, the headworks should be located at the nodal point.

From sediment considerations, the offtaking channel should be located at the downstream end of the outside of a river bend so that it has the advantage of drawing less sediment. However, a curved reach would need costly protection works against the adverse effects of cross currents. Moreover, if canals take off from both the banks, the canal taking off from the inner bank draws relatively more sediment.

In order to ensure adequate supply to the offtaking canal at all times, the undersluices should be sited in the deep channel. A river reach with deep channels on both banks and shallow channel at the centre is more suitable when canals offtake from both sides.

Besides, the site must be accessible and suitable for making the river diversion and other related arrangements at a reasonable cost.

10.3 LAY-OUT OF DIVERSION HEADWORKS

Diversion headworks (Fig. 10.1) mainly consist of a weir (or barrage) and a canal head regulator. A weir has a deep pocket of undersluice portion upstream of itself and in front of the canal head regulator on one or both sides. The undersluice bays are seperated from other weir bays by means of a divide wall. In addition, river training structures on the upstream and the downstream of weir and sediment excluding devices near the canal head regulator are provided. Detailed model investigations are desirable to decide the location and layout of headworks and its component units. A typical layout of diversion headworks is shown in Fig. 10.1.

10.3.1 Weir (or Barrage)

A weir is an ungated barrier across a river to raise the water level in the river, and diverts the water into the offtaking canal situated on one (or both) of the river banks just upstream of the weir. Weirs are usually aligned at right angles to the direction of flow in the river. Such weirs will have the minimum length and normal uniform flow through all the weir bays thereby minimising the channels of shoal formation and oblique flow.

To increase the water level, the weir crest is raised above the river bed. Part of the raising of the water level is obtained by shutters provided at the top of the weir crest. These shutters are dropped down during floods so that

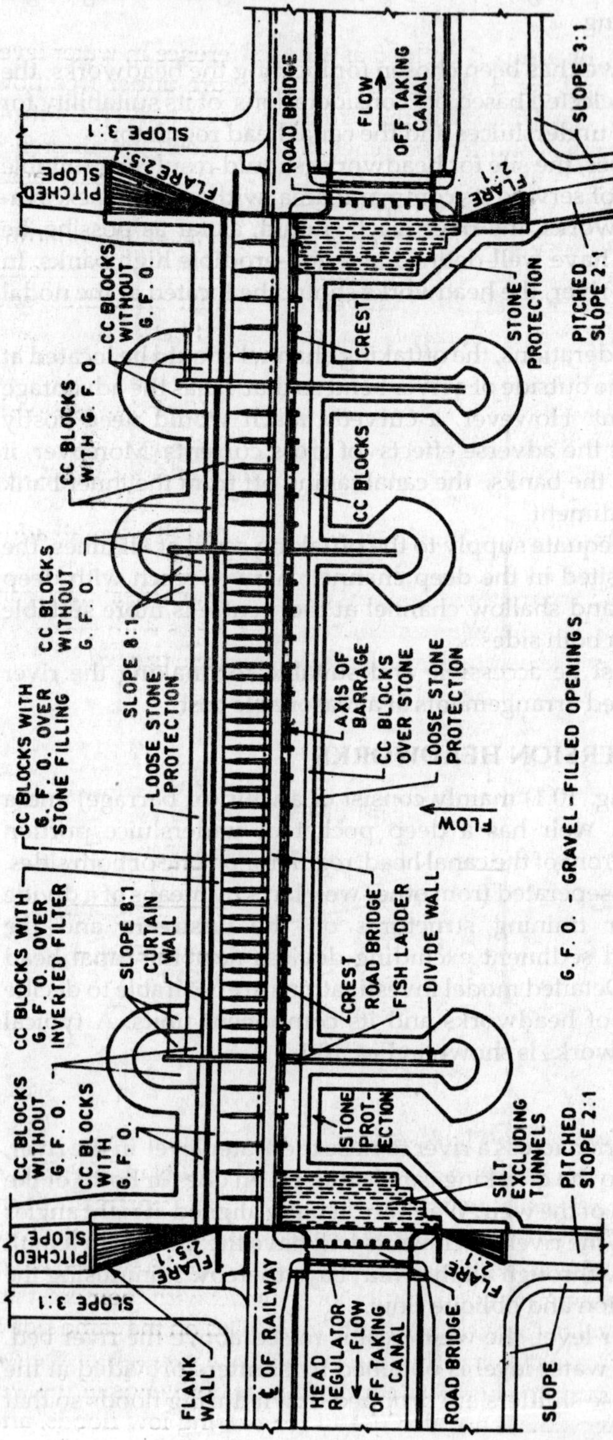

Fig. 10.1 Typical lay-out of diversion headworks

the afflux is minimum. The afflux is defined as the difference in water level between the upstream and the downstream of a structure under free flow conditions as a result of construction of the structure across a river. Controlling pond levels by means of shutters becomes difficult when the difference between the pond level and the crest level is higher than 2.0 m. In such cases, a gate-controlled weir, better known as barrage, is preferred.

Barrage is a gate-controlled weir with its crest at a lower level. The ponding up of river for diversion of water into the offtaking canal is achieved by means of gates (instead of shutters). Barrage and weir are similar structures, and differ only in a qualitative sense. Barrages are considered better than weirs due to the following reasons:

i) Because of the lower crest level of a barrage, the afflux during floods is small.
ii) Barrages offer better control on the river outflow and the canal discharge.
iii) A roadway across the river can be easily provided at a small additional cost.

Weirs (or barrages) can be either masonry weirs (with vertical upstream face) or rockfill weirs (with sloping apron) or concrete weirs with glacis. On pervious foundations only concrete weirs (Fig. 10.2) are constructed.

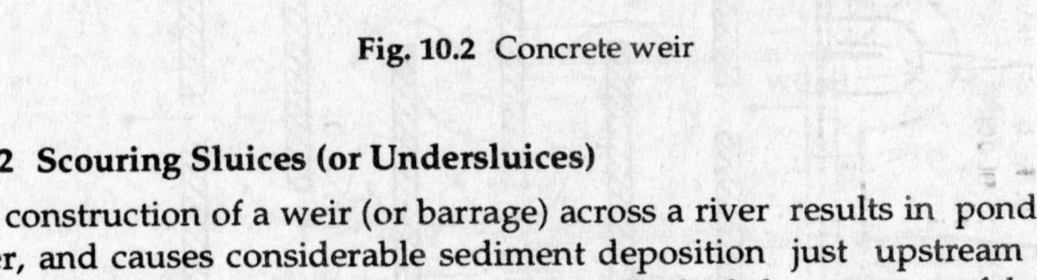

Fig. 10.2 Concrete weir

10.3.2 Scouring Sluices (or Undersluices)

The construction of a weir (or barrage) across a river results in ponding of water, and causes considerable sediment deposition just upstream of the canal head regulator. This sediment must be flushed downstream of the weir. This is done by means of scouring sluices (also known as undersluices) which are gate-controlled openings in continuation of the weir with their crest at a level lower than the level of the weir crest and are located on the same side as the offtaking canal. In case of two offtaking canals, one on each of the two banks of the river, scouring sluices are provided at both ends of the weir (Fig. 10.1). The scouring sluices are also useful for passing low floods, after meeting the requirements of the offtaking canal, without having to drop the weir shutters raising of which is a cumbersome task.

10.3.3 Divide Wall

The divide wall is constructed parallel (or nearly parallel) to the canal head regulator for separating the main weir base from the base of scouring sluice. As shown in Fig. 10.1, the wall extends on both sides of the weir. The divide wall separates the weir floor from the floor of the scouring sluices which is usually at a lower level than the weir floor. The divide wall also isolates the canal head regulator from the main river flow, and creates a still pond of water in front of the canal head regulator. This results in relatively sediment-free water entering into the offtaking canal. The divide wall also improves scouring of the deposited sediment in the undersluices by ensuring straight approach.

10.3.4 Fish Ladder

Different kinds of fish in a river migrate from upstream to downstream in the beginning of the winter in search of warmth, and return upstream before the monsoon for sediment-free clear water. While constructing a weir across a river, a narrow opening between the divide wall and the scouring sluices (where water is always present) is provided to allow for free movement of fish. This opening is called fish ladder or fish way or fish pass (Fig. 10.3) in which baffles or staggering devices are provided so as to keep flow velocity in fish ladder less than 3.0 m/s so that fish can easily travel upstream.

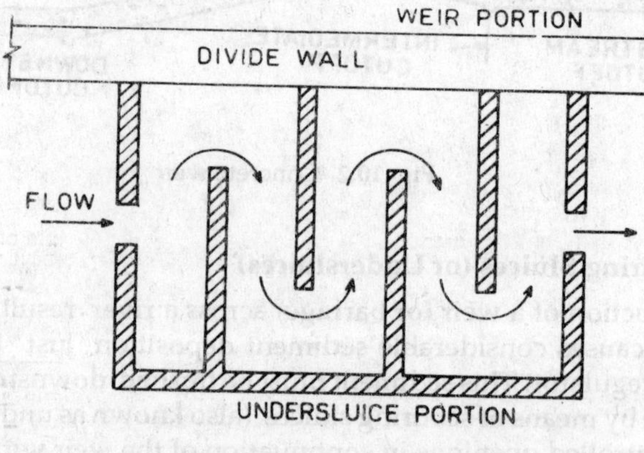

Fig. 10.3 Fish ladder

10.3.5 Canal Head Regulator

A canal head regulator (Fig. 10.4) regulates the discharge into the offtaking canal and also controls the entry of sediment into the canal. The head regulator

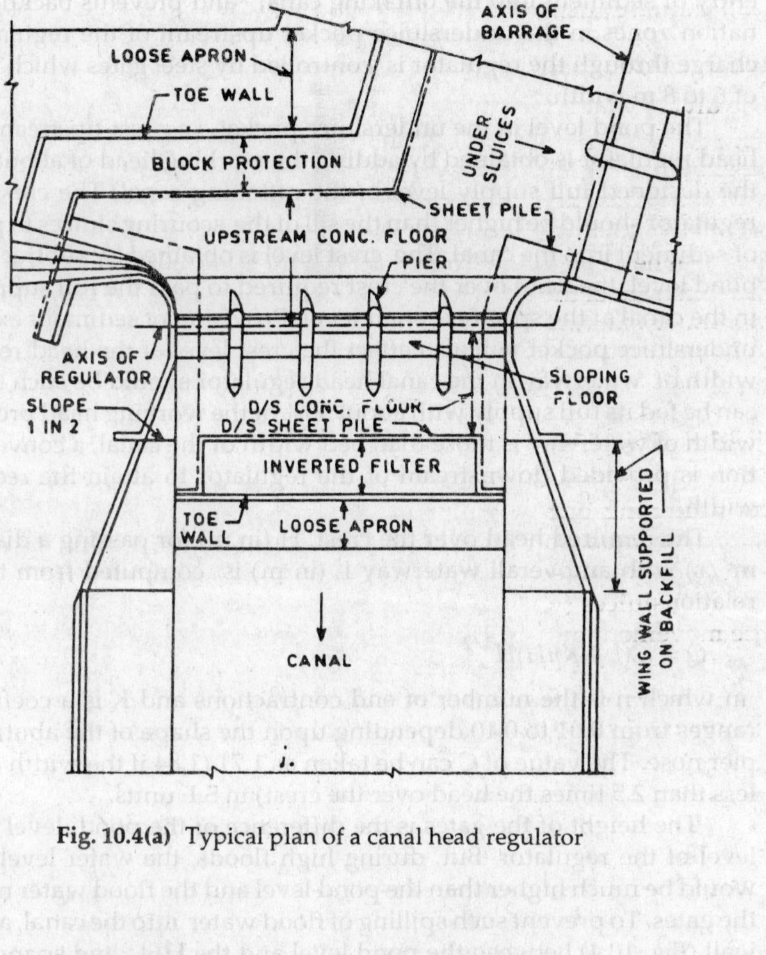

Fig. 10.4(a) Typical plan of a canal head regulator

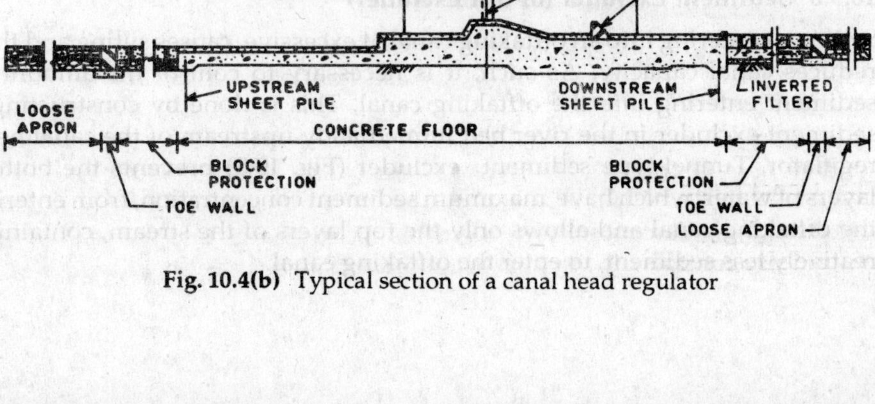

Fig. 10.4(b) Typical section of a canal head regulator

is usually aligned at an angle of 90° to 110° to the barrage axis to minimise entry of sediment into the offtaking canal, and prevents backflow and stagnation zones in the undersluice pocket upstream of the regulator. The discharge through the regulator is controlled by steel gates which are generally of 6 to 8 m width.

The pond level in the undersluice pocket, *i.e.*, just upstream of the canal head regulator is obtained by adding the working head of about 1 to 1.2 m to the designed full supply level of the offtaking canal. The crest of the head regulator should be higher than the sill of the scouring sluices to prevent entry of sediment into the canal. The crest level is obtained by subtracting from the pond level, the head over the crest required to pass the full supply discharge in the canal at the specified pond level. Provision of sediment excluder in the undersluice pocket will also affect the crest level of the head regulator. The width of waterway in the canal head regulator should be such that the canal can be fed its full supply with about 50% of the working head provided. If this width of waterway is more than bed width of the canal, a converging transition is provided downstream of the regulator to attain the required canal width.

The required head over the crest, H (in m) for passing a discharge Q (in m^3/s) with an overall waterway L (in m) is computed from the following relation :

$$Q = C(L - KnH)H^{3/2} \tag{10.1}$$

in which n is the number of end contractions and K is a coefficient which ranges from 0.01 to 0.10 depending upon the shape of the abutment and the pier nose. The value of C can be taken as 1.71 (1.84 if the width of the crest is less than 2.5 times the head over the crest) in S.I. units.

The height of the gates is the difference of the pond level and the crest level of the regulator. But, during high floods, the water level in the river would be much higher than the pond level and the flood water may spill over the gates. To prevent such spilling of flood water into the canal, an RCC breast wall (Fig. 10.4) between the pond level and the HFL, and spanning between adjacent piers is always provided.

A bridge and a working platform (for the operation of gates) are also constructed across the head regulator.

10.3.6 Sediment Excluder (or Silt Excluder)

Sediment entering into an offtaking canal, if excessive, causes silting and thus reduces canal capacity. As such, it is necessary to control the amount of sediment entering into the offtaking canal. This is done by constructing a sediment excluder in the river bed immediately upstream of the canal head regulator. Tunnel-type sediment excluder (Fig. 10.5) prevents the bottom layers of water, which have maximum sediment concentration, from entering the offtaking canal and allows only the top layers of the stream, containing reatively less sediment, to enter the offtaking canal.

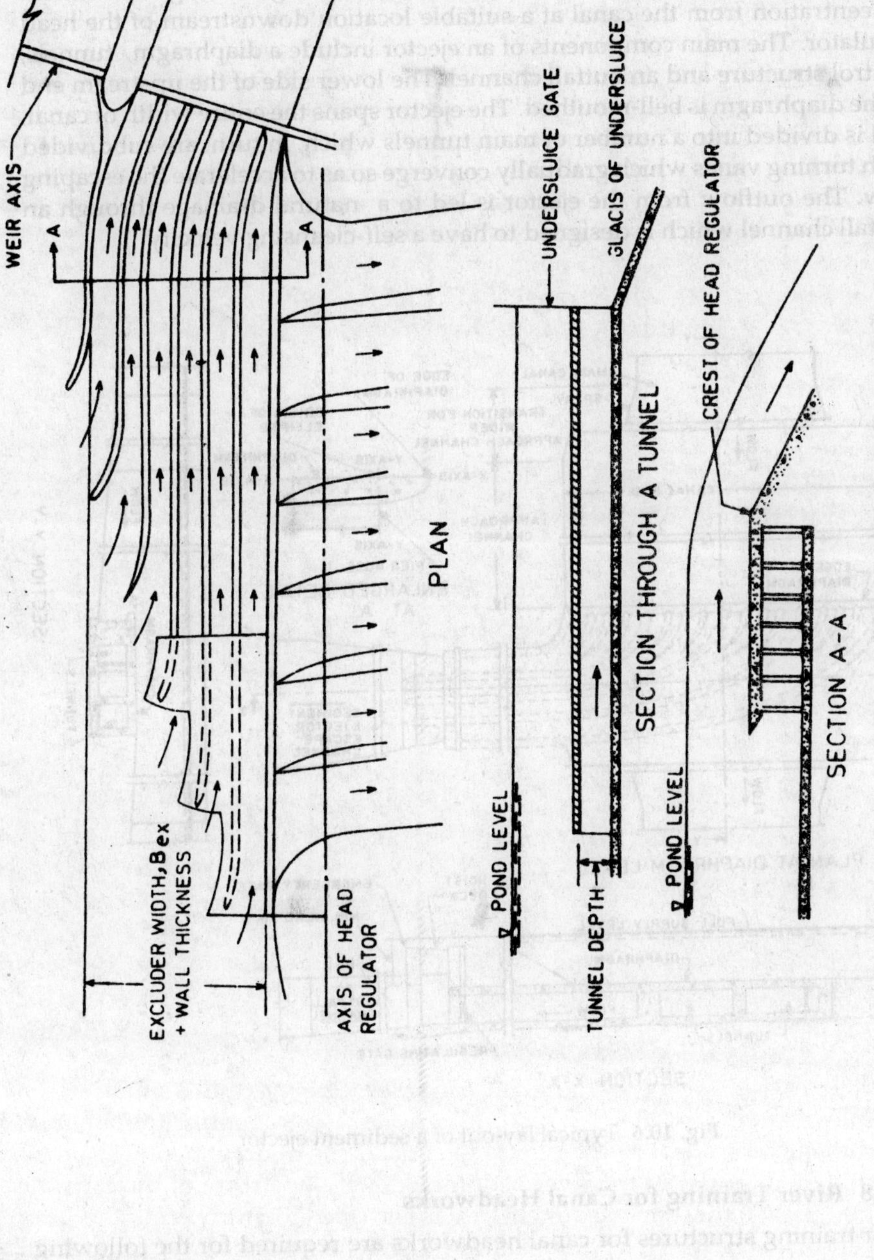

Fig. 10.5 Typical lay-out of a sediment excluder

10.3.7 Sediment Ejector (or Silt Ejector)

Sediment ejector, Fig. 10.6, is constructed in the offtaking canal (downstream of the head regulator) to eject the sediment that has entered the canal. Sediment ejectors eject the near-bed water layers having the largest sediment concentration from the canal at a suitable location downstream of the head regulator. The main components of an ejector include a diaphragm, tunnels, control structure and an outfall channel. The lower side of the upstream end of the diaphragm is bell-mouthed. The ejector spans the entire width of canal, and is divided into a number of main tunnels which, in turn, are subdivided with turning vanes which gradually converge so as to accelerate the escaping flow. The outflow from the ejector is led to a natural drainage through an outfall channel which is designed to have a self-cleansing velocity.

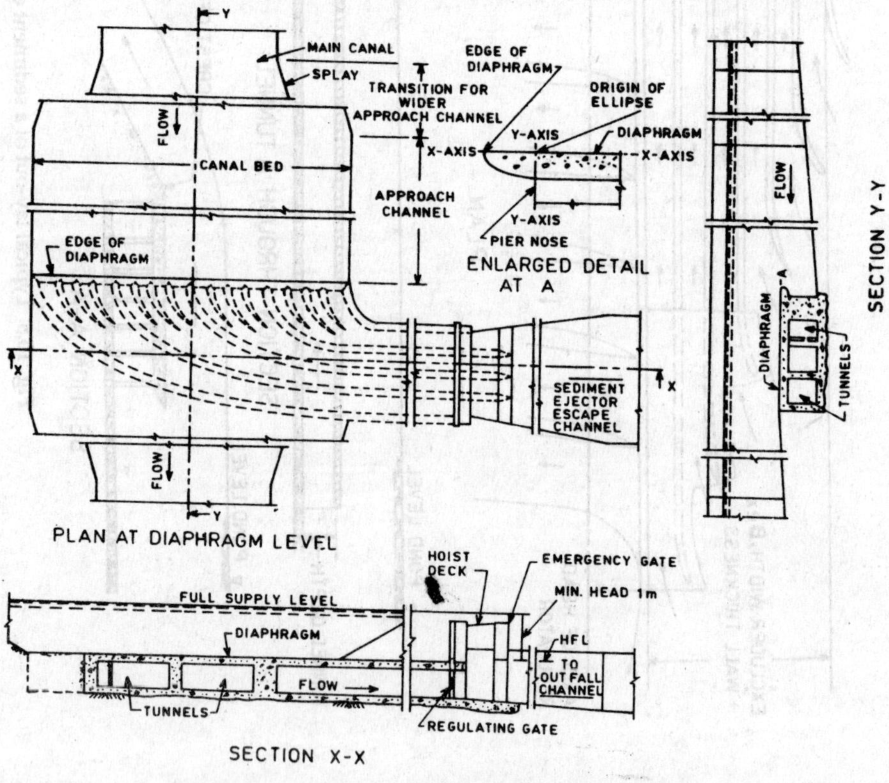

Fig. 10.6 Typical lay-out of a sediment ejector

10.3.8 River Training for Canal Headworks

River training structures for canal headworks are required for the following purposes:

i) To prevent outflanking of the structure.
ii) To minimise possible cross-flows through the weir (or barrage).
iii) To provide favourable curvature of flow at the head regulator from considerations of entry of sediment into the offtaking canal.

Following types of river training structures are generally provided at canal headworks.

i) Guide banks,
ii) Approach embankments,
iii) Afflux embankments, and
iv) Spurs.

A typical lay-out of river training structures for canal headworks is shown in Fig. 10.7. More details about river training methods have been discussed in the previous chapter.

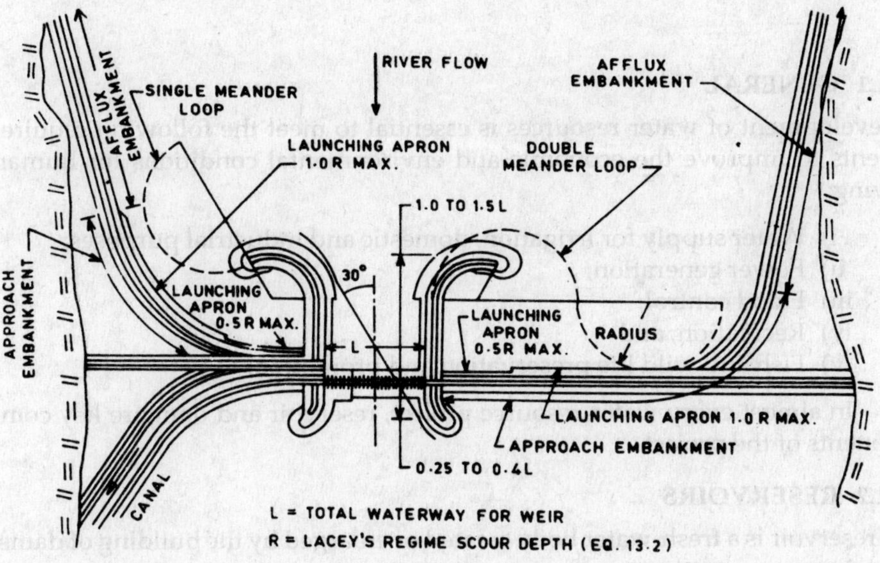

Fig. 10.7 Typical lay-out of river training structures for canal headworks

EXERCISES

1. What purposes do canal headworks serve?
2. Compare the features of locating canal headworks in different reaches of a river.
3. Differentiate between a weir and barrage.
4. Describe the functions of different parts of canal headworks.

Chapter 11

Reservoirs, Dams and Spillways

11.1 GENERAL

Development of water resources is essential to meet the following requirements to improve the economic and environmental conditions for human living:

i) Water supply for irrigation, domestic and industrial purposes;
ii) Power generation;
iii) Flood control;
iv) Recreation, and
v) Fish and wild life preservation and promotion.

In almost every water resource project, reservoir and dam are key components of the project.

11.2 RESERVOIRS

A reservoir is a fresh-water body created or enlarged by the building of dams, barriers or excavations.

11.2.1 Types of Reservoirs

A reservoir can be either (i) a storage or conservation reservoir, or (ii) a flood control reservoir. A storage reservoir stores excess water that flows in a river during the flood season for meeting different kinds of demand (water supply, power generation *etc.*) at a later date. Any storage reservoir also helps in moderating the floods and, therefore, provides protection against floods to some extent.

The purpose of constructing a flood control reservoir is to protect the area downstream of the reservoir from the damages due to floods. A flood control reservoir holds up flood waters when the river stage is rising and thus reduces the peak rate of flow and, therefore, the stage, *i.e.,* water level in the river downstream. The stored flood water is released when the flood is receding so that enough space is available in the reservoir for storing the excess water of the subsequent flood.

11.2.2 Planning of Reservoirs

The main factors to be considered in the planning of a reservoir are

i) Rim stability
ii) Water-holding capability
iii) Evaporation
iv) Storage zones
v) Seismicity
vi) Sedimentation

Rim stability and water-holding capability are interrelated. Rim failure can be caused due to either sliding or erosion of a segment of the reservoir rim. Seepage of water is mainly responsible for such failures. Major slides into a reservoir would, obviously, reduce the reservoir capacity considerably. Similarly, snow avalanches and masses of ice falling from hanging glaciers can cause serious problems. Besides reducing the capacity of the reservoir, a rapidly moving slide may also generate waves. A dam may be overtopped due to the resulting wave action or rise of the water surface on account of a major slide into the reservoir. If the reservoir site is likely to be affected by the slides and it cannot be abandoned, some restraining steps in reservoir operation should be taken to avoid serious failure. These steps could be in the form of limiting the filling and drawdown rates or imposing the maximum allowable water surface at a level lower than the maximum normal water surface. Alternatively, installation of drains to relieve water pressure along likely slip surfaces, some form of impervious lining and pinning the unstable mass to its parent formation by rock bolting can be resorted to for preventing slides. Stabilisation of the unstable mass can also be achieved by strengthening or replacing weak material. Grouting is the most common remedy for strengthening such weak masses. It may be desirable to plan the steps to be taken to mitigate the effects of a potential slide after it has occurred in spite of all preventive steps.

Reservoir water loss either to the air or to the ground can be a controlling factor in the selection of site for a conservation reservoir. For a flood control reservoir, water loss is of concern only if it relates to safety of the project. Lining of the surface through which seepage is expected is one of the preventive measures to reduce the reservoir water loss to the ground. At times, a blanket of impervious material extending from the heel of the dam is required. This too serves to control the seepage from the reservoir.

Loss of reservoir water to the air occurs due to direct evaporation from the reservoir surface. The evaporation losses are affected by the climate of the region, shape of the reservoir, wind conditions, humidity and temperature. From the considerations of evaporation, a reservoir site having a small surface area to volume ratio will be better than a saucer-shaped reservoir of equal capacity. Evaporation-retardent chemicals increase the surface tension of water by forming mono-molecular film and, thus, reduce evaporation.

The maximum elevation to which water level in a reservoir generally reaches during normal operating conditions is known as full (or maximum) reservoir level. This level usually coincides with the level of the spillway crest.

The minimum elevation to which water level in a reservior can be drawn under normal operating conditions is called minimum reservoir level (or dead storage level). This level is fixed by the level of the lowest outlet in the dam. The volume of water stored below this level is not available for use under normal conditions and, accordingly, this storage is termed as dead storage.

The storage volume between the minimum and maximum reservoir levels is called useful storage (or live storage).

During floods the reservoir level exceeds the full reservoir level and water starts flowing over the spillway. The storage volume between the maximum reservoir level and the reservoir level when the design flood passes over the spillway is called the surcharge storage.

Bank storage is the water which spreads out from a body of water, filling interstices of the surrounding earth and rock mass. This water is assumed to remain in the surrounding mass and does not continue to move to ultimately join the ground water or surface water as seepage water does. The storage zone is theoretically recoverable but, in a sense, is considered a loss. Storage zone is not mitigable. It must, however, be estimated for feasibility investigations and measured during reservoir operation for providing guidelines for reservoir regulation.

It appears that there is some effect of reservoir impoundment on the increased seismic activity of an area in which a large reservoir (having a storage capacity of more than 12×10^8 m^3 behind a dam higher than 90 m) has been constructed. However, there have been large reservoirs without increasing the seismic activity of the region. The increased seismic activity is attributed to the changes in the normal effective stresses in the underlying rock because of the increased pore pressure. The transmission of hydrostatic pressure through discontinuities in the underlying rock can have a triggering effect where a critical state of stress already exists. The relationship between the reservoir impoundment and the earthquake relationship is not fully understood. Hence, it is necessary that every large reservoir site is subjected to detailed geologic, geodetic and seismic studies for feasibility decision. These observations must be continued during the reservoir operation too in order to better understand the relationship between reservoir impoundment and seismic activity.

The streams bringing water to the reservoir bring sediments too. The sediment gets deposited in the reservoir due to the reduced stream velocity. The capacity of the reservoir is reduced on account of sediment deposition in the reservoir. Usually, a portion of the reservoir storage is reserved for the storage of the sediment. The life of a reservoir is predicted on the basis of the amount of sediment delivered to it, the reservoir size and its ability to retain the sediment. Sediment deposition at the initial stage may be beneficial in the sense that it may have the effect of a natural blanket resulting in reduced seepage loss. Measures to minimise sediment deposition in reservoirs include watershed protection through a vegetative management programme to prevent soil erosion, silt detention basins at inlets of smaller reservoirs and low level outlets in dams to provide flushing action for removal of sediment from the reservoir. Of the various measures, the watershed protection is the most effective as well as the costliest method.

Erosion in the catchment area can be reduced by soil conservation methods, such as afforestation, control of deforestation, control of grazing, checking gully formation by providing small embankments, *etc.*

11.2.3 Selection of Reservoir

Based on planning and other considerations, the guidelines for selection of site for a reservoir are as follows:

i) Availability of a suitable site for construction of dam.
ii) The hills surrounding the reservoir and the bed of the reservoir should be impervious.
iii) Availability of good storage capacity with minimum submergence of the adjacent land.
iv) A reservoir should not be sited downstream of such tributaries which bring-in excess sediment into the river.
v) Availability of deep gorge which results in larger capacity with lesser water surface area and, therefore, lesser evaporation loss.
vi) The cost of other associated works is less.
vii) The site with the possibility of land slides into the reservoir must be avoided.
viii) The site should not be, as far as possible, on valuable land being used for some other purposes, such as agriculture, forestry, communication and habitation by people.
ix) Sites with mineral deposits in and around the reservoir area should also be avoided.

11.3 DAMS

A *dam* is a barrier constructed across a river or stream to create a reservoir for impounding water or divert water from a stream or raise the water level and, in some cases, to impound water-borne sediments.

11.3.1 Classification of Dams

Dams can be classified as per their functions, material of construction, and structural design.

i) Classification based on function
   a) Storage (or impounding) dam is constructed across a river to create a reservoir for storing water during the period when the flow in the river is in excess. This stored water is then used for

irrigation, power generation and water supply when the demand exceeds the flow in the river.

b) Detention dam is primarily constructed to detain all or part of the flood waters of a river and released later in such a way that the region downstream of the dam is safe against flood damages. A dam can also serve both the functions of detention as well as storage.

c) Diversion dam is constructed for the purpose of diverting water into a canal. Such a dam is usually called diversion weir.

d) Coffer dam is a temporary dam constructed to keep water away from a specific area to keep it dry for some specific purpose, such as construction of the main dam. The coffer dam too acts like diversion dam.

e) Debris dam is constructed across a river to trap sediments of the river.

ii) Classification based on material of construction

a) Earth and rockfill dams are constructed of loose earth (ranging from fine material to big rock pieces) without any binding material. An earth dam having its major portion built of rocks is called rockfill dam. Such dams are also known as non-rigid dams.

b) Masonry dams are rigid dams constructed of either stone or brick masonry.

c) Concrete dams too are rigid dams constructed of concrete.

iii) Classification based on structural design

a) Earth and rockfill dams are non-rigid dams constructed of loose earth material. Shear strength of the soil used in the construction of these dams opposes the forces exerted on the dam by water. The difference between an earth and rockfill dam is that in case of rockfill dam major portion of the dam is primarily made of rock pieces, whereas in case of the earth dam it is the soil which is used for the construction of embankment. Conditions favouring selection of earth and rockfill dams are as follows:

i) Significant thickness of soil deposits overlying bedrock.
ii) Weak or soft bedrock which would not be able to resist high stresses from a concrete dam.
iii) Abutments of either deep soil deposits or weak rock.
iv) Availability of a suitable location for a spillway.
v) Availability of sufficient and suitable soils from required excavation or nearby borrow areas.

Earth dams are further divided into the following types:

i) Homogeneous earth dam
ii) Zoned earth dam

Homogeneous earth dams are constructed entirely or almost entirely of one type of earth material. A zoned earth dam, however, contains materials of different kinds in different parts of the embankment. Homogeneous earth dam is usually built when only one type of material is economically available, and/or the height of the dam is not very large. A homogeneous earth dam of height exceeding about 6 to 8 m should always have some type of drain [Fig. 11.1(a)] constructed of material more pervious than the embankment soil. Such drains reduce pore pressures in the downstream portion of the dam and, thus, increase the stability of the downstream slope. Besides, the drains control the outgoing seepage water in such a manner that it does not carry away embankment soil *i.e.*, piping does not develop. Such a dam is also categorised as homogeneous (sometimes 'modified homogeneous') dam [Fig. 11.1(a)].

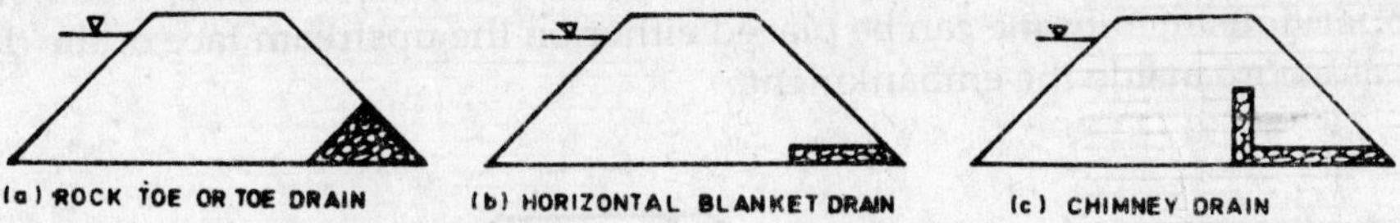

Fig. 11.1(a) Typical sections of homogeneous earth dam

The most common type of an earth dam usually adopted is the zoned earth dam as it leads to an economic and more stable design of the dam. In a zoned earth dam [Fig. 11.1(b)], there is a central impervious core which is flanked by zones of more pervious material. The pervious zones, also known as shells, enclose, support and protect the impervious core. The upstream shell provides stability against rapid drawdowns of reservoir, while the downstream shell acts as a drain to control the line of seepage and provides stability to the dam during construction and operation of the dam. The central core provides imperviousness to the embankment and reduces the seepage.

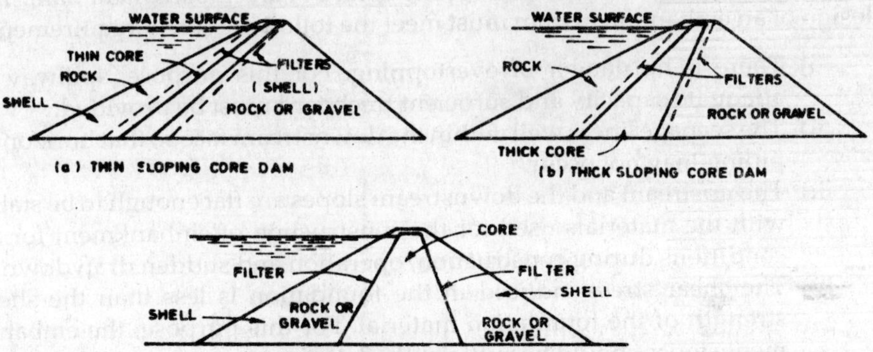

Fig. 11.1(b) Typical sections of core dam

The impervious core can be placed either as vertical core or upstream sloping core each of which has some advantages over the other. A vertical core results in higher pressure on the contact between the core and the foundation which, in turn, reduces the possibility of leakage along the contact. Besides, for a given quantity of impervious material, vertical core will have greater thickness. The main advantage of an upstream sloping core is that the main downstream shell can be constructed first, and the core placed later—an advantageous feature in areas having short spell of dry weather suitable for building a core of fine-grained soil. Also, foundation grouting can be carried out while the downstream embankment is being constructed.

A rock-fill dam (Fig. 11.2) is made of large-sized rock pieces to provide stability and an impervious membrane to provide watertightness. Materials used for the membrane are: earth, concrete, steel, asphalt and wood. The impervious membrane can be placed either on the upstream face of the dam or as a core inside the embankment.

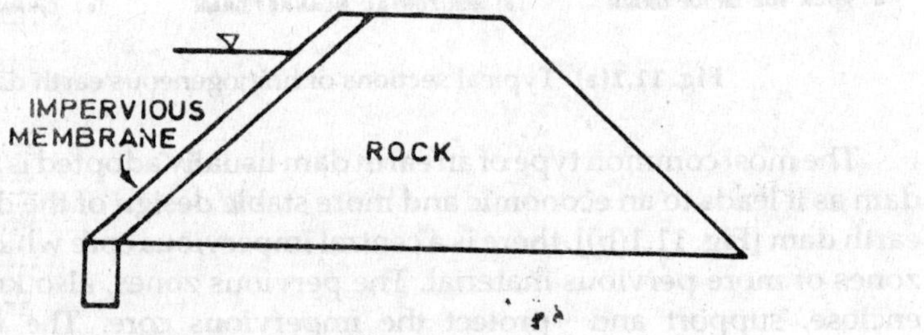

Fig. 11.2 Typical sections of a rock-fill dam

The major causes of failure of an earth dam are overtopping, piping, and earth slides in a portion of the embankment and its foundation (due to insufficient shear strength). Out of these three, overtopping is the most common cause of complete and catastrophic failure of an embankment dam. The design of an embankment dam must meet the following safety requirements:

i) There is no danger of overtopping. For this purpose, spillway of adequate capacity and sufficient freeboard must be provided.
ii) The seepage line is well within the downstream face so that horizontal piping may not occur.
iii) The upstream and the downstream slopes are flat enough to be stable with the materials used for the construction of embankment for all conditions during construction, operation and sudden drawdown.
iv) The shear stress induced in the foundation is less than the shear strength of the foundation material. For this purpose, the embankment slopes should be sufficiently flat.
v) The upstream and the downstream faces are properly protected against wave action and the action of rain water, respectively.

vi) There should not be any possibility of free passage of water through the embankment.

vii) Foundation seepage should not result in piping at the downstream toe of the dam.

viii) The top of the dam must be high enough to allow for the settlement of the dam and its foundation.

ix) The foundations, abutments and the embankment must be stable for all conditions of operation (steady seepage and sudden drawdown) and construction.

b) Gravity dam (Fig. 11.3) is a masonry or concrete dam which resists the forces exerted upon it due to all applied loads, and its own weight. The Bhakra dam in Punjab is a gravity dam. The downstream face of a gravity dam usually has a uniform slope which, if extended, would intersect the vertical upstream face at or near the maximum water level in the reservoir. The upper portion of the dam is made thick enough to accommodate the roadway or other required access as well as to resist the shock of floating objects. The upstream face of a gravity dam is usually kept vertical so that most of its weight is concentrated near the upstream face to resist effectively the tensile stresses due to reservoir water loading. The thickness of the dam provides resistance to sliding and may, therefore, dictate the slope of the downstream face which is usually in the range of 0.7 to 0.8 (H):1(V). The thickness in the lower part of the dam may also be increased by an upstream batter.

c) Arch dam (Fig. 11.4) is a curved masonry or concrete dam having its convex face upstream. Such a dam resists forces, exerted upon it due to water pressure, by arch action. The Idduki dam in Kerala is an arch dam.

d) Buttress dam (Fig. 11.5) has a sloping deck which retains water and is supported by a series of butteresses which are usually in the form of triangular reinforced concrete or masonry walls.

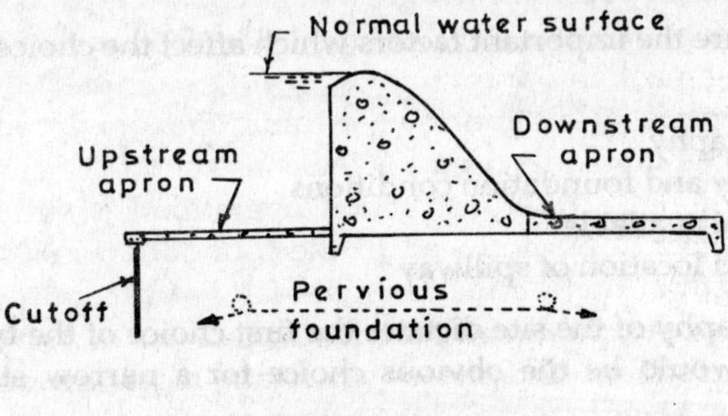

Fig. 11.3 Gravity dam

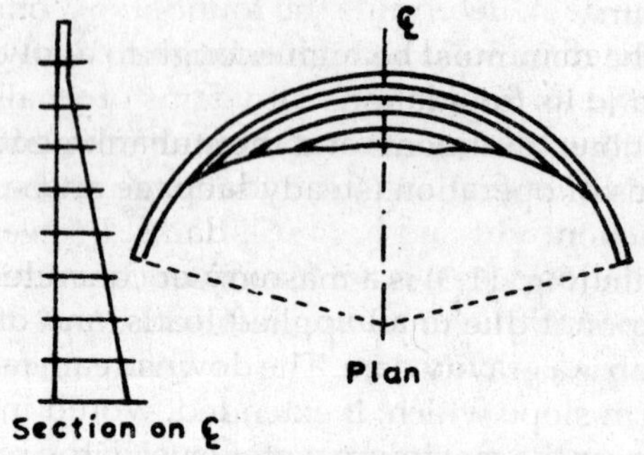

Fig. 11.4 The Constant-radius arch dam

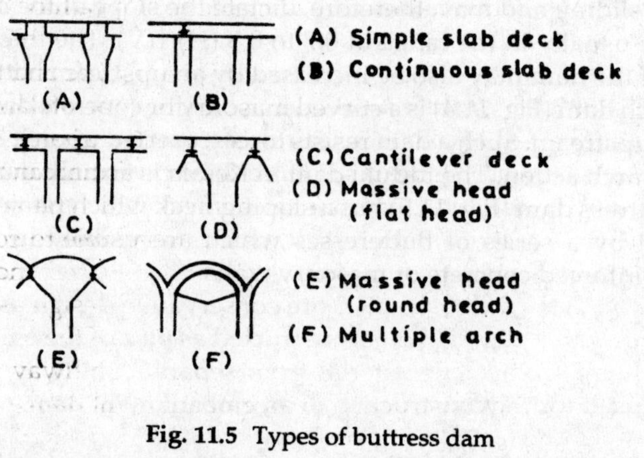

Fig. 11.5 Types of buttress dam

11.3.2 Choice of the Type of Dam

The following are the important factors which affect the choice of the type of dam.

i) Topography
ii) Geology and foundation conditions
iii) Material available
iv) Size and location of spillway

The topography of the site dictates the first choice of the type of dam. A concrete dam would be the obvious choice for a narrow stream flowing

between high and rocky abutments (*i.e.*, deep gorges). Broad valleys in plains would suggest an embankment dam with a separate spillway.

Geological and hydro-geological characteristics of the strata, which are to carry the weight of the dam, determine the foundation conditions. Any type of dam can be constructed on solid rock foundations. Well-compacted gravel foundations are suitable for concrete gravity dams of small height, earth-fill and rock-fill dams. However, effective water cutoffs are required to check the foundation seepage. Silt or fine sand foundations can be used to support concrete dams of small height and earth-fill dams. Problems of settlement, piping and the foundation seepage are associated with this type of foundation. Non-uniform foundations containing different types of strata will usually require special treatment before any type of dam is constructed on such foundation.

If the construction materials which are to be used in large quantity for the construction of dam are available in sufficient quantity within a reasonable distance from the site, the cost of the dam will be considerably reduced due to saving on transportation of the construction materials. If suitable soils for the construction of an earth-fill dam are locally available in nearby borrow pits, choice of an earth-fill dam would be the most economical. The availability of sand and gravel (for concrete) near the dam site would reduce the cost of a concrete dam.

Spillway is a major part of any dam and its size and type and the natural restrictions in its location will affect the selection of the type of dam. Spillway requirements are decided by the runoff and streamflow characteristics. As such, spillway on dams across streams of large flood potential can become the dominant part of the dam and put the selection of the type of dam to a secondary position. For large spillways, it may be desirable to combine the spillway and dam into one structure. This is possible only in concrete dams. Earth and rockfill dams are based on more conservative design assumptions and, hence, spillway is generally not constructed as part of the embankment. On the other hand, excavated material from separate spillway can be advantageously used for the construction of an embankment dam.

11.3.3 Selection of Site for a Dam

Site conditions and choice of type of dam are closely interrelated. Further, in case of embankment dams, site conditions considerably influence the design of the dam. Nevertheless, there are some guidelines which must be followed while selecting a suitable site for any type of dam.

i) Availability of suitable foundation: While an earth dam can be designed for and constructed on any type of foundation, concrete dams require relatively stronger foundation. Foundations can be improved to some extent by taking suitable steps for foundation treatment.
ii) Considerable economy will be achieved if the dam is sited at the narrowest section in the river valley subject to fulfilment of other requirements.

iii) Spillway is an important component of a dam. In case of a concrete dam, it may be accommodated in the main dam section. But, in case of earth dams, it has to be away from the main dam and, hence, suitable site should be available for the spillway too.

iv) From economic considerations, it would be advantageous if the bulk of the construction material is available close to the dam site. In case of earth dams, the design is so made as to use locally available material as much as possible.

v) The area upstream of the dam must be suitable for the requirements of a reservoir.

vi) The environmental considerations, including displacement of local people, require that there is minimum damage to the local environment, and minimum hardship to the local people. At times, these become governing factors in selecting the site of a dam.

vii) The selected site should be such that it results in overall economy in construction, maintenance and operation of the water resource project.

11.4 SPILLWAYS

A spillway is a structure which provides waterway for disposing of surplus flood waters from a reservoir after it has been filled to its maximum capacity so that the safety of the dam is not endangered because of overtopping of the dam. A spillway can be made as either an integral part of the dam (only if it is not an earth dam), or an independant structure. In any case, its spilling capacity (*i.e.*, discharge capacity) must be adequate to discharge surplus water downstream of the reservoir in a safe manner. The surplus water flowing over the spillway is finally discharged into the same river across which the dam was constructed. Since the flowing water will possess excessive kinetic energy at the foot of the spillway, energy dissipators are always provided at the foot of the spillway so that this surplus water does not cause erosion of the channel bed and endanger the foundation of spillway and other structures in the vicinity.

11.4.1 Components of Spillway

Main components of a spillway are: (i) control structure, (ii) conveyance structure, (iii) terminal structure, and (iv) entrance and exit channels.

i) Control Structure

The control structure of a spillway regulates and controls the outflows from the reservoir. It is usually located at the upstream end of the spillway, and consists of some form of overflow crest. In some cases, however, the control may be at the downstream end. For example, in a morning glory spillway, the downstream tunnel rather than the crest controls the flow at higher heads. In plan, the overflow crests can be straight, curved, U-shaped, semicircular or circular. The crest can be sharp, broad, ogee-shaped or of other cross-section.

ii) Conveyance Structure

The outflow released through the control structure is usually conveyed to the downstream river channel through a discharge channel or waterway. Free fall spillways, however, do not require any such conveyance structure. The conveyance structure can be the downstream face of the dam (if the spillway has been constructed in the main body of the dam), or an open channel excavated along the ground surface of one of the abutments, or an underground tunnel excavated through one of the abutments. The conveyance structure too can have a variety of cross-sections depending upon the geologic and topographic characteristics of the site and hydraulic requirements.

iii) Terminal Structure

When water flows from the reservoir level to the downstream river level, the static energy is converted into kinetic energy which, if not properly dissipated, may cause enough scour near the toe of the dam to damage the dam, spillway and other structures. Therefore, suitable stilling basins at the downstream end of the spillway are usually provided so that the excess kinetic energy is destroyed, and the discharge into the river does not result in objectionable scour. The excess kinetic energy can be dissipated by a hydraulic jump basin, a roller bucket or some other suitable energy dissipator or absorber. In some cases, however, the overflowing water may be delivered directly to the stream if the stream bed consists of erosion-resistant bed rock. The incoming jet should always be projected some distance downstream from the end of the structure by means of structures, such as flip buckets or cantilevered extensions.

Hydraulic jump is one of the best means to dissipate the excess energy of the falling water. Hence, wherever the tail water conditions are suitable for the formation of hydraulic jump, it is usual to provide hydraulic jump type stilling basins which have been comprehensively studied. Alternatively, bucket type energy dissipators are provided.

When the tail water depth is either too small or too large for the formation of hydraulic jump, the high amount of energy at the toe of spillway can be dissipated by the use of bucket type energy dissipators. These can be either (i) trajectory (or deflector) bucket, or (ii) roller (or submerged) bucket energy dissipators.

i) *Trajectory (or Deflector) Bucket:* When tail water depth is lower than the depth required for the jump formation and the bed of the river channel is composed of sound rock capable of withstanding the impact of trajectory jet, trajectory bucket (also known as deflector or ski-jump bucket) (Fig. 11.6) is generally used as energy dissipator. The incoming jet of water leaves the bucket as free-discharging upturned jet and falls into the stream channel some distance downstream from the end of the spillway. The upturned jet gets split into number of bubbles or smaller jets. The energy is dissipated on

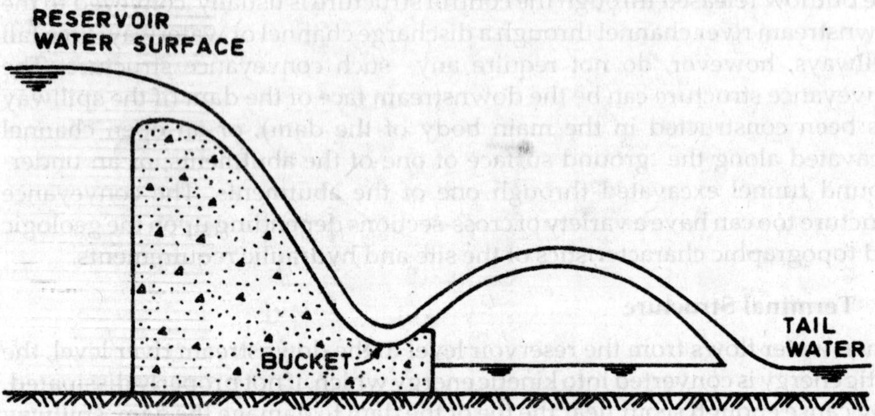

Fig. 11.6 Trajectory bucket

account of the increased air resistance because of splitting of the jet as well as the impact against water and the channel bed downstream.

ii) *Roller (or submerged) Bucket:* Roller bucket is used when tail water depth is greater than 1.1 times the required conjugate depth for the formation of the hydraulic jump and the river bed rock is good. Roller buckets can be either solid or slotted (Fig. 11.7). The general hydraulic action responsible for the dissipation of energy is shown in Fig. 11.8. The energy dissipates through the formation of two rollers; one is on the surface of the bucket and moves anticlockwise (considering that the flow is to the right), and the other is a ground roller moving in a clockwise direction and which forms immediately downstream of the bucket (Fig. 11.8). The intermingling of the incoming flow with the rollers as well as the movements of the rollers dissipate the energy of the water effectively and prevent excessive scouring downstream of the bucket.

iv) Entrance and Exit Channel

Entrance channel conveys water from the reservoir to the control structure, while the exit channel conveys the flow from the terminal structure to the stream channel downstream of the dam. Entrance and exit channels are, however, not required for such spillways which draw water directly from the reservoir, and discharge it directly into the stream channel as in the case of overflow spillway in a concrete dam. In spillways which are placed along the abutments or located near saddles or ridges, entrance and exit channels would be needed.

11.5 TYPES OF SPILLWAYS

Spillways are usually referred to as controlled or uncontrolled depending on whether spillway gates for controlling the flow have been provided or not.

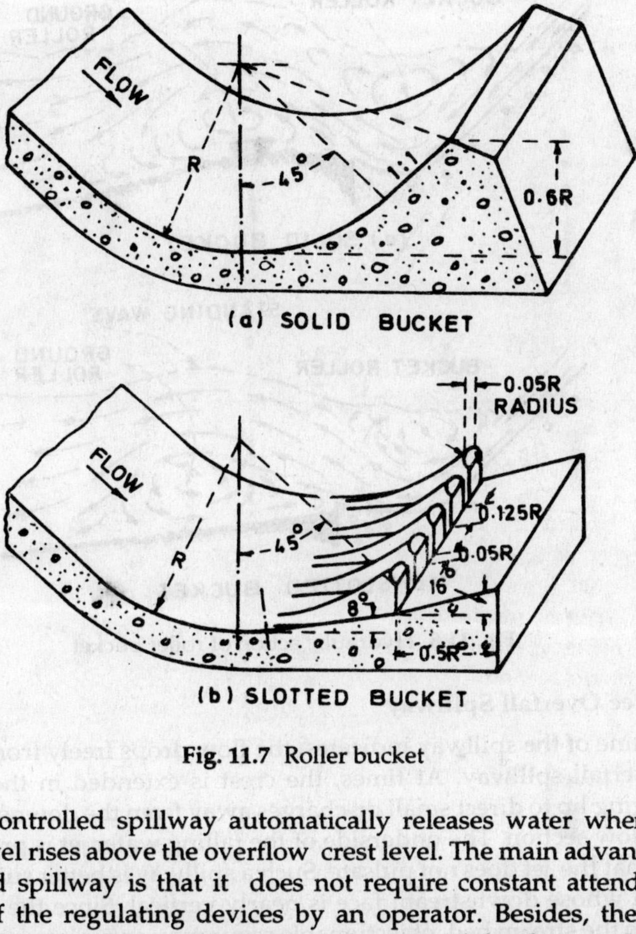

Fig. 11.7 Roller bucket

Free or uncontrolled spillway automatically releases water whenever the reservoir level rises above the overflow crest level. The main advantage of an uncontrolled spillway is that it does not require constant attendance and operation of the regulating devices by an operator. Besides, there are no problems related to the maintenance and repair of the devices. If it is not possible to provide sufficiently long uncontrolled spillway crest or obtain large enough head to meet the requirements of spillway capacity, one has to provide regulating gates. Such gates enable release of water, if required, even when the reservoir level is below the normal reservoir water surface level. Most common types of spillways are as follows:

i) Free overfall (straight drop) spillway
ii) Ogee (overflow) spillway
iii) Side channel spillway
iv) Chute (open channel or trough) spillway
v) Shaft (or morning glory) spillway
vi) Siphon spillway
vii) Cascade spillway
viii) Tunnel (conduit) spillway

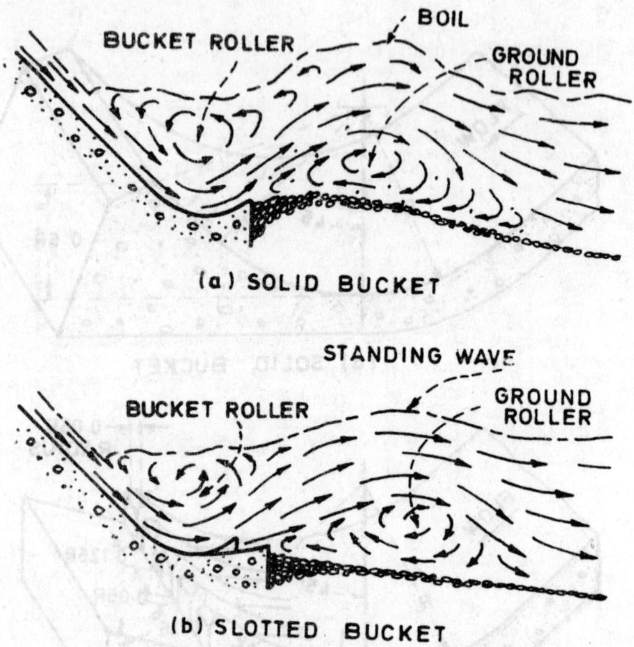

Fig. 11.8 Hydraulic action of roller bucket

11.5.1 Free Overfall Spillway

As the name of the spillway indicates, the flow drops freely from the crest of a free overfall spillway. At times, the crest is extended in the form of an overhanging lip to direct small discharges away from the downstream face of the overflow section. The underside of the falling water jet is properly ventilated so that the jet does not pulsate. Such a spillway is better suited for a thin arch dam whose downstream face is nearly vertical. Since the flow usually drops into the stream bed, objectionable scour may occur in some cases and a deep plunge pool may be formed. If erosion cannot be tolerated, a plunge pool is created by constructing an auxiliary dam downstream of the main dam. Alternatively, a basin is excavated and it is provided with a concrete apron. When tail water depth is sufficient, a hydraulic jump would form when the water jet falls upon a flat apron. Free overfall spillways are restricted only to situations where the hydraulic drop from reservoir level to tail water level is less than about six metres.

11.5.2 Ogee (Overflow) Spillway

An ogee spillway has a control weir whose profile is as shown in Fig. 11.9. The upper part of the spillway surface matches closely to the profile of the lower nappe of a ventilated sheet of water falling freely from a sharp-crested weir. The lower part of the spillway surface is tangential to the upper curve and

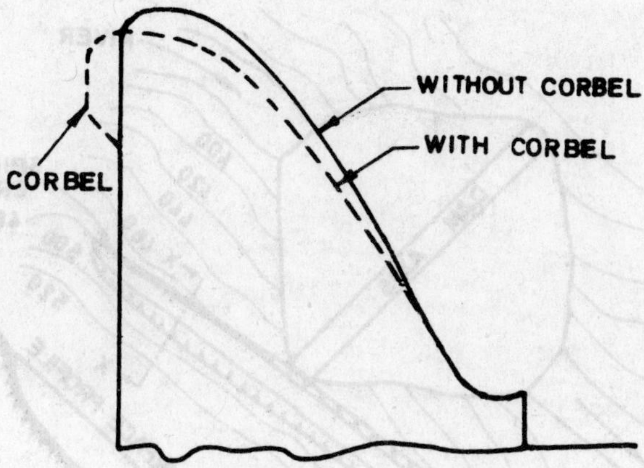

Fig. 11.9 Ogee spillway

supports the falling sheet of water. The downstream end of the spillway is in the form of a reverse curve, which turns the flow onto the apron of a stilling basin or into the spillway discharge channel. Ogee spillway is generally used for concrete and masonry dams. It is ideally suited to wider valleys where sufficient crest length may be provided.

The profile of an ogee spillway is designed for a given design discharge (or corresponding design surcharge head). When the flowing discharge equals the design discharge, the flow adheres to the spillway surface with minimum interference from the boundary surface and no access of air to the underside of the water sheet. The discharge efficiency is maximum under such condition and the pressure along the spillway surface is atmospheric. If the flowing discharge exceeds the design discharge, the water sheet tends to pull away from the spillway surface and, thus, produces subatmospheric pressure along the surface of the spillway. While negative pressure may cause cavitation and other problems, it increases the effective head as well as the discharge. On the other hand, positive hydrostatic pressure will occur on the spillway surface, if the flowing discharge is less than the design discharge.

An upstream overhang, known as corbel, is added to the upstream face of the spillway as shown in Fig. 11.9. The effect of the corbel is to shift the nappe (and, hence, the spillway profile) backward which results in saving of concrete. If the height of the vertical face of the corbel is kept more than 0.3 times the head over the crest, the discharge coefficient of the spillway will be practically the same as if the vertical face of the corbel extended for the full height of the spillway.

11.5.3 Side Channel Spillway

The control weir of a side channel spillway (Fig. 11.10) is located alongside and approximately parallel to the upstream portion of the spillway discharge

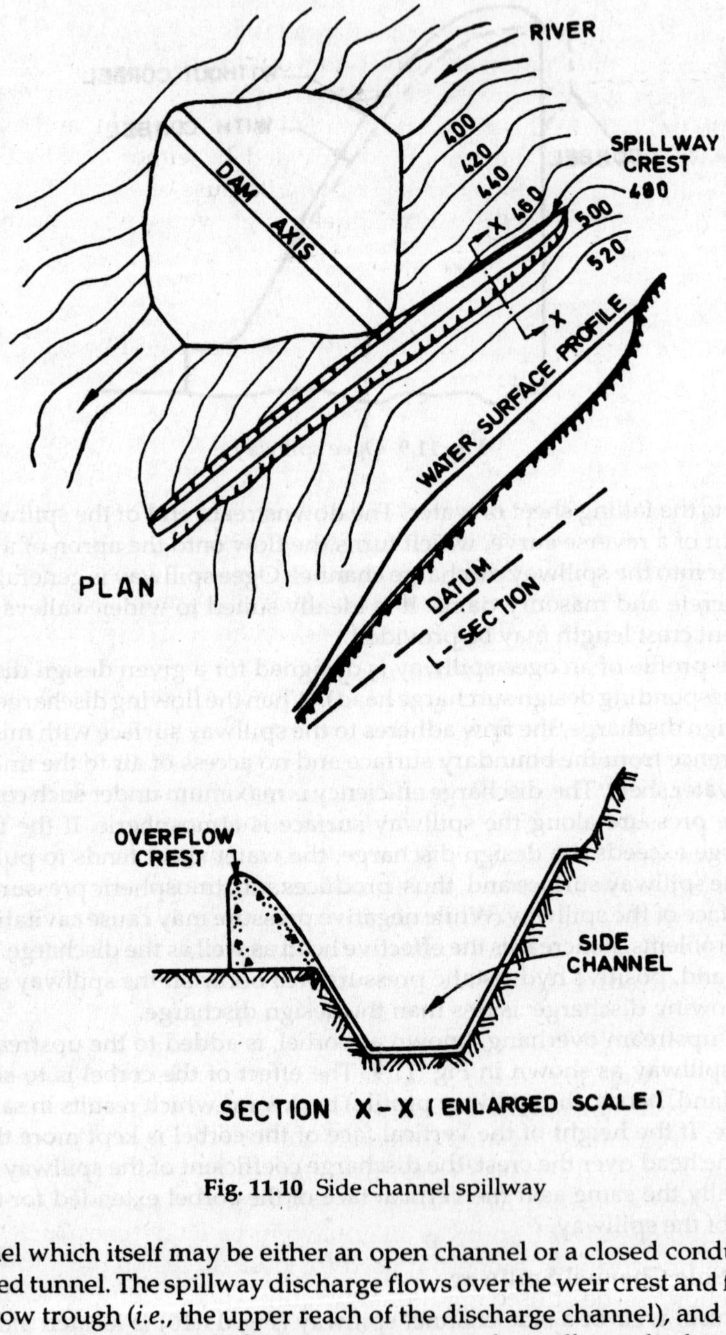

Fig. 11.10 Side channel spillway

channel which itself may be either an open channel or a closed conduit or an inclined tunnel. The spillway discharge flows over the weir crest and falls into a narrow trough (*i.e.*, the upper reach of the discharge channel), and takes an approximately 90°-turn before continuing into the spillway discharge channel. The control structure of a side channel spillway generally consists of an ogee crest which, in plan, may be straight, curved, semicircular or U-shaped. The overflow section may be broad-crested instead of ogee-shaped. Side channel trough is usually of trapezoidal cross-section with minimum width to depth ratio. Higher width to depth ratio would result in poor diffusion of the increasing incoming flow with the channel flow due to relatively shallow depth. Moreover, the amount of excavation would also increase for larger bed widths. While the flow in the side channel trough should preferably be subcritical, the flow in the discharge channel is supercritical, and a control section downstream of the trough is provided by either constricting the channel width or raising the channel bottom. Because of spatial flow conditions, the depth of flow in the side channel trough would never be the same at different sections.

11.5.4 Chute Spillway

In a chute (or trough) spillway, the spillway discharge flows in an open channel (named as 'chute' or 'trough') right from the reservoir to the downstream river. The open channel can be located either along the abutment of the dam or through a saddle (Fig. 11.11). The channel bed should always be kept in excavation and its side slopes must be designed to be stable with sufficient margin of safety. As far as possible, bends in the channel should be avoided. If it becomes necessary to provide a bend, it should be gentle. The spillway control structure can be an overflow crest, or a gated orifice or some other suitable control device. The control device is usually placed normal or nearly normal to the axis of the chute. The simplest form of a chute spillway is an open channel with straight centre line and constant width. However, very often the axis of either the entrance channel or the discharge channel is curved to suit the topography of the site. The flow condition varies from subcritical upstream of the controlling crest to critical at the crest and supercritical in the discharge channel. The chute spillway is ideally suited with earthfill dams because of: (i) the simplicity of their design and construction, (ii) their adaptability to all types of foundation ranging from solid rock to soft clay, and (iii) overall economy usually obtained by the use of large amounts of spillway excavation for the construction of embankment. The chute spillway is also suitable for concrete dams constructed in narrow valleys across a river whose bed is erodible for which ogee spillway becomes unsuitable.

11.5.5 Shaft Spillway

In a shaft spillway (Fig. 11.12), water enters a horizontal crest, drops through a vertical or sloping shaft and then flows to the downstream river channel through a horizontal or nearly horizontal conduit or tunnel. A rock outcrop projecting into the reservoir slightly upstream of the dam would be an ideal site for a shaft spillway. Depending upon the level of the rock outcrop and the required crest level, spillway may have to be either constructed or excavated. The diversion tunnels, if used for river diversion purposes during construction, can be utilised for discharge tunnels of the spillway. Radial piers

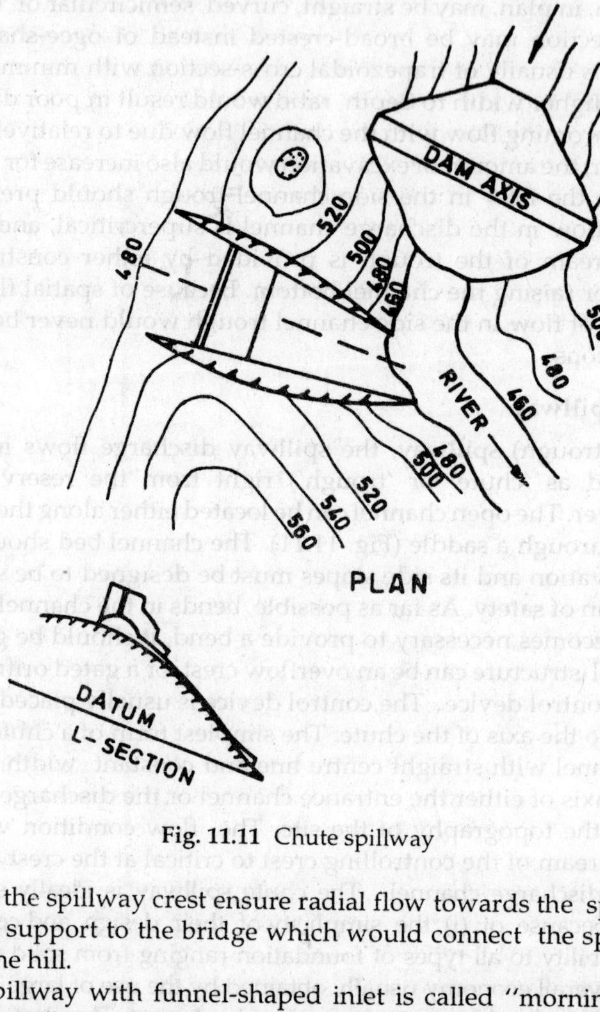

Fig. 11.11 Chute spillway

provided on the spillway crest ensure radial flow towards the spillway, and also provide support to the bridge which would connect the spillway with the dam or the hill.

Shaft spillway with funnel-shaped inlet is called "morning glory" or "glory hole" spillway. One of its distinguishing characteristics is that near-maximum capacity of the spillway is attained at relatively low heads. Therefore, shaft spillway is ideal when maximum spillway discharge is not likely to be exceeded. Because of this feature, however, the spillway becomes unsuitable when a flow larger than the selected inflow design flow occurs. This disadvantage can be got rid of by providing an auxiliary or emergency spillway and using shaft spillway as service spillway.

11.5.6 Siphon Spillway

A siphon spillway (Fig. 11.13) is essentially a closed conduit system which uses the principle of siphonic action. The conduit system is in the shape of an

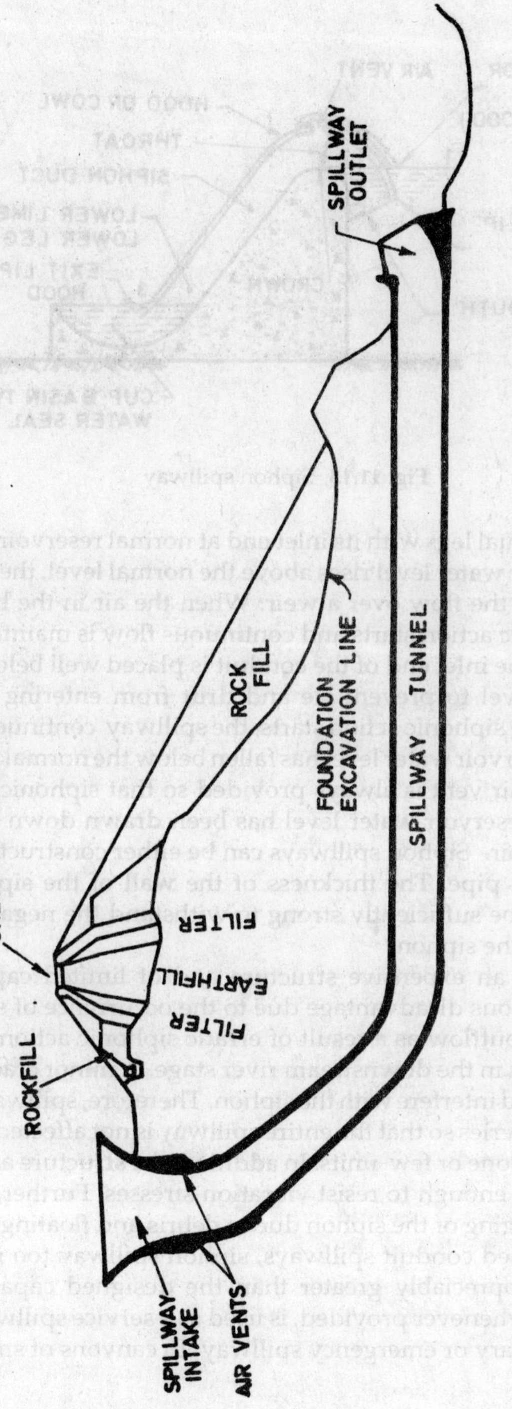

Fig. 11.12 Shaft spillway

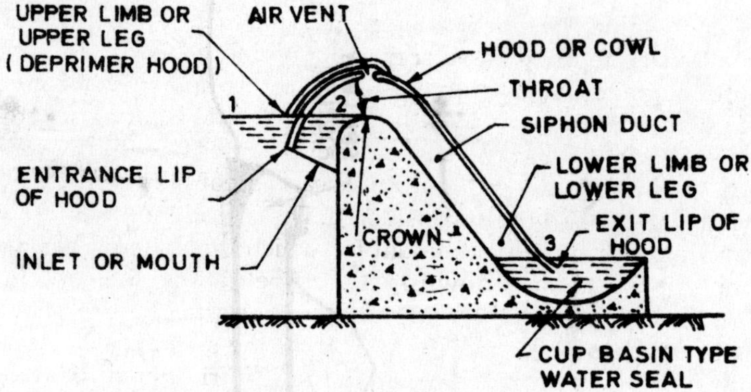

Fig. 11.13 Siphon spillway

inverted U of unequal legs with its inlet end at normal reservoir storage level. When the reservoir water level rises above the normal level, the initial flow of water is similar to the flow over a weir. When the air in the bend has been exhausted, siphonic action starts and continuous flow is maintained until air enters the bend. The inlet end of the conduit is placed well below the normal reservoir water level to prevent ice and drift from entering the conduit. Therefore, once the siphonic action starts, the spillway continues to discharge even when the reservoir water level has fallen below the normal level. As such, a siphon-breaker air vent is always provided so that siphonic action can be broken once the reservoir water level has been drawn down to the normal level in the reservoir. Siphon spillways can be either constructed of concrete or formed of steel pipe. The thickness of the wall of the siphon structure should, however, be sufficiently strong to withstand the negative pressures which develop in the siphon.

Besides being an expensive structure and of limited capacity, siphon spillway has a serious disadvantage due to the occurrence of sudden surges and stoppages of outflow as a result of erratic siphonic action, thus causing severe fluctuations in the downstream river stage. A minor crack in the cover of the siphon would interfere with the siphon. Therefore, spillways are usually constructed in batteries so that the entire spillway is not affected even if cracks have developed in one or few units. In addition, the structure and foundation have to be strong enough to resist vibration stresses. Further, there exists a possibility of clogging of the siphon due to debris and floating material. Like other types of closed conduit spillways, siphon spillway too is incapable of handling flows appreciably greater than the designed capacity. As such, siphon spillway, whenever provided, is used as a service spillway in conjunction with an auxiliary or emergency spillway. In canyons of small width and small flood discharge, the suitability of a siphon spillway should always be examined.

11.5.7 Cascade Spillway

In case of very high dams, the kinetic energy at the toe of the dam will be very high and the tail water depth in the river may not be adequate for a single-fall hydraulic jump or roller bucket stilling basin. Narrow and curved canyons consisting of fractured rock would not be suitable for trajectory buckets. In such situations, especially for high earth and rockfill dams for which spillway is a major structure, possibility of providing a cascade of falls with a stilling basin at each fall (Fig. 11.14) must be considered. The cascade spillway is likely to be an ideal choice for high rockfill dam for which the material has been obtained from a quarry located downstream of the dam so that the flood waters may be discharged over the quarry face. As the quarry would usually be excavated in benches, these may as well form the steps in the cascade. Cascade spillway is being provided at 218 m high Tehri dam on Bhagirathi river in the Ganga valley of the Central Himalayas. At Darmouth dam in Australia, the spillway to pass 2700 m^3/s of flood discharge would be an unlined cascade in granite. The benches of the cascade will be 5 m high and of varying widths to suit the topography of the site. Although a cascade spillway, during floods, would be an attraction, it may not be always acceptable for environmental reasons which demand that the quarries be always located upstream of the dam and below the normal water surface level of the reservoir so as to cause minimum disfigurement of the land.

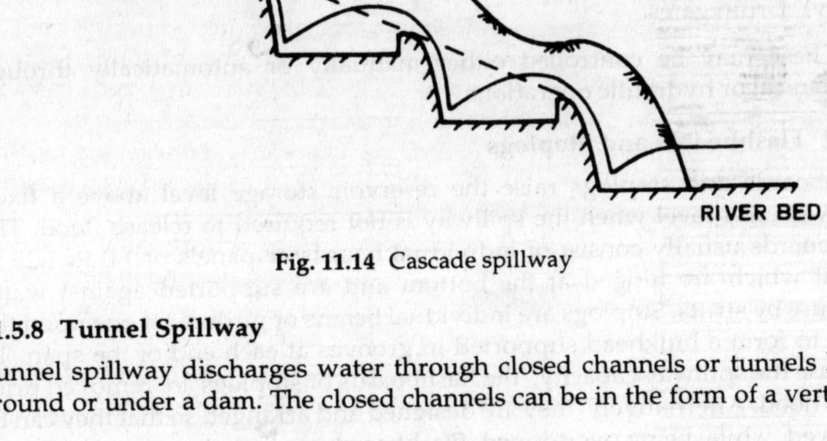

Fig. 11.14 Cascade spillway

11.5.8 Tunnel Spillway

Tunnel spillway discharges water through closed channels or tunnels laid around or under a dam. The closed channels can be in the form of a vertical or inclined shaft, a conduit constructed in an open cut and backfilled with earth materials, or a horizontal tunnel through earth or rock. In narrow canyons with steep abutments as well as in wide valleys with abutments far away from the stream channel, tunnel spillways may prove to be advantageous. In such situations, conduit of the spillway can be easily located under the dam near the stream bed.

11.6 GATES FOR SPILLWAY CRESTS

Free or uncontrolled overflow crest of a spillway is the simplest form of control as it automatically releases water whenever the reservoir water level rises above the crest level. For such crests, there is no need of constant attendance and regulation of the control devices by an operator. Besides, the problems of maintenance and repair of the controlling device also do not arise. However, when sufficiently long uncontrolled crest or large surcharge head for the required spillway capacity cannot be obtained, a regulating gate may be necessary. Such regulating devices enable the spillway to release storages even when water level in the reservoir is below the normal reservoir water surface. Gates can be provided on all types of spillways except the siphon spillway. The installation of gates involves additional expenditure on the initial cost, repair and maintenance of gates. The selection of type and size of the controlling device depends on several factors, such as: (i) discharge characteristics of the device, (ii) climate, (iii) frequency and nature of floods, (iv) winter storage requirements, (v) the need for handling ice and debris, and (vi) special operating requirements, such as presence of operator during periods of flood, the availability of electricity, operating mechanism, *etc.* In addition, economy, reliability, efficiency and adaptability of the regulating device must also be looked into.

The following types of regulating devices are generally used:

i) Flashboards and stoplogs
ii) Rectangular lift gates
iii) Radial gates
iv) Drum gates.

These may be controlled either manually or automatically through mechanical or hydraulic operations.

11.6.1 Flashboards and Stoplogs

Flashboards and stoplogs raise the reservoir storage level above a fixed spillway crest level when the spillway is not required to release flood. The flashboards usually consist of individual boards or panels of 1.0 to 1.25 m height which are hinged at the bottom and are supported against water pressure by struts. Stoplogs are individual beams or girders set one upon the other to form a bulkhead supported in grooves at each end of the span. To increase the spillway capacity, the flashboards or stoplogs are removed prior to the flood. Alternatively, they are designed and arranged so that they can be removed while being overtopped. Flashboards and stoplogs are simple and economical type of regulating device which provide an unobstructed crest when these are removed. However, they have several disadvantages:

i) they present a hazard, if not removed in time to pass floods, especially where the reservoir area is small and the stream is subject to flash floods,
ii) they require the attendance of an operator or crew to remove them, unless they are designed to fall automatically,
iii) ordinarily they cannot be restored to position while flow is passing over the crest,
iv) if they are designed to fail when the water reaches certain stage, their operation is uncertain, and when they fail they release sudden and undesirably large outflows, and
v) if the spillway functions frequently, the repeated replacement of flashboards may be costly.

11.6.2 Vertical Lift Gates

These are usually rectangular and made of steel which span horizontally between guide grooves in supporting piers and move vertically in their own plane. The gates are raised or lowered by an overhead hoist and water is released by undershot orifice flow for all gate openings. Sliding gates offer large sliding friction due to water pressure and, therefore, require large hoisting capacity. The use of wheels (along each side of the gate) would reduce the amount of sliding friction and thereby permit the use of a smaller hoist. Vertical lift gates have been used for spans and heights of the order of 20 and 15 m, respectively. At larger heights, however, the problem of raised operating platform becomes important.

11.6.3 Radial (or Tainter) Gates

These are made of steel plates which form a segment of a cylinder which itself is attached to supporting bearings by radial arms. The cylindrical plate is kept concentric to the supporting pins so that the entire thrust of the waterload passes through the pins and only a small amount of moment needs to be overcome in raising or lowering the gate. The hoisting loads then include only the weight of the gate, the sliding friction and the frictional resistance at the pins. The small hoisting effort required for the operation of the radial gates makes hand operation at small installations possible. Besides, they require less head rooms compared to that required by verticai lift gates. All these advantages make the radial gates more adaptable.

11.6.4 Drum Gates

Drum gates are hollow (and, therefore, buoyant), triangular in section and made of steel plates. The drum gate is hinged at the upstream lip of a hydraulic chamber in the weir structure in which the gate floats. Water introduced into or drawn from the hydraulic chamber causes the gate to swing upwards or downwards. The inflow or outflow of water to the chamber is governed by controls located in the piers adjacent to the chambers.

EXERCISES

1. What are the main factors which affect the selection of a dam?
2. Write a note on planning of reservoirs.
3. Explain the functions of different components of a spillway and suitability of different types of spillways for different site conditions and other requirements.
4. What types of gates are generally used for spillway crests?
5. Name different types of dams. What safety considerations one should keep in mind while designing an earth dam?

Bibliography

1. Asawa, G.L., *Irrigation Engineering*, 2nd ed., New Age International (P) Ltd., New Delhi, 1996.
2. Bharat Singh., Agriculture and Irrigation, National Seminar on New Perspectives in Water Management held at Indore, 1989.
3. Chambers, R., *Managing Canal Irrigation*, Oxford and IBH Publishing Co. Pvt. Ltd., New Delhi, 1988.
4. Driscoll, F.G., *Ground Water and Wells*, Johnson Division, Minnesota, USA, 1986.
5. Golze, A.R. (Ed.), *Handbook of Dam Engineering*, Van Nostrand Reinhold Company, New York, 1977.
6. Hansen, V.E., O.W. Israelsen and G.E. Stringham, *Irrigation Principles and Practices*, 4th ed., John Wiley & Sons, 1979.
7. Kennedy, R.G., The prevention of silting in Irrigation Canals, Paper No. 2826, Proc. ICE (London), Vol. 119, 1895.
8. Lacey, G., *Regime flow in incoherent alluvium*, C.B.I.P. Publication No. 20, 1939.
9. Malhotra, S.P., *The Warabandi System and its Infrastructure*, CBIP Publication No. 157, April, 1982.
10. Mitra, A.C., *Irrigation Manual No. 9*, CBIP, New Delhi, 1940.
11. Sherard, J.L., Woodward, R.J., Gizienski, S.F. and W.A. Clevenger, *Earth and Earth-Rock Dams*, John Wiley & Sons, Inc. U.S.A., 1963.
12. Swaminathan, M.S., Irrigation and Our Agricultural Future, First A.N. Khosla Lecture delivered at the University of Roorkee, 1981.
13. Todd, D.K., *Ground Water Hydrology*, John Wiley & Sons, 1959.
14. ___________, *Report of the Irrigation Commission*, Vol. I, Ministry of Irrigation, Govt. of India,1972.
15. ___________, *Drip Irrigation in India*, INCID, New Delhi, 1994.
16. ___________, *Handbook of Agriculture*, Indian Council of Agricultural Research, New Delhi, 1980.
17. ___________, I.S. 3873-1978, "Code of Practice for Laying in-situ Cement Concrete Lining on Canals."
18. ___________, I.S. 5331-1969, "Guide for Selection of Type of Linings for Canals."
19. ___________, I.S. 7873-1975, "Code of Practice for Lime Concrete Lining for Canals."
20. ___________, I.S. 4515-1967, "Code of Practice for Boulder Lining for Canals."
21. ___________, I.S. 7113-1973, "Code of Practice for Soil-Cement Lining for Canals."
22. ___________, *Irrigation Canal Falls*, C.B.I.P. Publication No. 10, New Delhi, 1935.
23. IS 7114-1973 — "I.S. Code for criteria for hydraulic design of cross regulators for canals."
24. IS 6522-1972 — "I.S. Code for criteria for design of silt vanes for sediment control in offtaking canals."
25. IS 7871-1975 — "I.S. Code for criteria for hydraulic design of groyne walls (curved wing) for sediment distribution at offtake points in a canal."

26. IS 7880-1975 — "I.S. Code for criteria for hydraulic design of skimming platform for sediment control in offtaking canal."
27. IS 6936-1973 — "I.S. guide for location, selection and hydraulic design of canal escapes."
28. __________ "IS Codes of Practice for Design of Cross-Drainage Works," IS 7784 (Pt. 1) — 1975 and IS 7784 (Pt. 2/Sec 1-5) — 1980-83.
29. IS: 7720-1975, "I.S. Code for Criteria for Investigation, Planning and Layout for Barrages and Weirs."
30. IS: 6966-1973, "I.S. Code for Criteria for Hydraulic Design of Barrages and Weirs."
31. IS: 6531-1972, "I.S. Code for Criteria for Design of Canal Head Regulators."
32. __________, *Design of Small Dams*, USBR., 1960.
33. __________, *Register of Large Dams in India*, C.B.I.P. Publication, 1979.

Index